THE MISHNAH IN CONTEMPORARY PERSPECTIVE

HANDBOOK OF ORIENTAL STUDIES
HANDBUCH DER ORIENTALISTIK

SECTION ONE
THE NEAR AND MIDDLE EAST

Editors

H. Altenmüller
B. Hrouda
B. A. Levine
R. S. O'Fahey
K. R. Veenhof
C. H. M. Versteegh

Number 87

THE MISHNAH IN CONTEMPORARY PERSPECTIVE

Volume 2

Edited by

Alan J. Avery-Peck and Jacob Neusner

Atlanta

Copyright © 2006 by Koninklijke Brill NV, Leiden, The Netherlands

This edition is published under license from Koninklijke Brill NV, Leiden, The Netherlands, by SBL Press.

All rights reserved. No part of this work may be reproduced or transmitted in any form or by any means, electronic or mechanical, including photocopying and recording, or by means of any information storage or retrieval system, except as may be expressly permitted by the 1976 Copyright Act or in writing from the publisher. Requests for permission should be addressed in writing to the Rights and Permissions Office, SBL Press, 825 Houston Mill Road, Atlanta, GA 30329 USA.

Library of Congress Control Number: 2016932778

Printed on acid-free paper.

CONTENTS

Preface vii

Anecdotal Evidence: The Yavneh Conundrum, *Birkat Hamminim*,
and the Problem of Talmudic Historiography 1
Daniel Boyarin
  University of California, Berkeley

On the Quality of the Rabbinic Text: The Opening of the
Mishnah 36
Dalia Hoshen
  University of Manchester

The Construction of Households in the Mishnah 55
Hayim Lapin
  University of Maryland

The Mishnah in Historical and Religious Context 81
Jacob Neusner
  Bard College

The Structure and Implicit Message of Mishnah
Tractate Nazir 110
Simcha Fishbane
  Touro College

Archaeology and the Mishnah's Halakhic Tradition:
The Case of Stone Vessels and Ritual Baths 136
Eyal Regev
  Bar-Ilan University

The Poetics of the Mishnah 153
Avraham Walfish
  Herzog Teachers Academy

Why We Cannot Assume the Historical Reliability of Attributions: The Case of the Houses in Mishnah-Tosefta Makhshirin 190
Jacob Neusner
  Bard College

Subject Index 213

PREFACE

In this second of our two-part project on the Mishnah in contemporary study, the editors place on display a broad selection of approaches to the study of the Mishnah in the contemporary academy. The work derives from Israel, North America, and Europe and shows the intellectual vitality of scholarship in all three centers of learning. What we prove in diverse ways is that the Mishnah forms a critical focus of the study of Judaism.

Why from the beginning has Mishnah-study formed the center of the curriculum of Judaism? The reason is that the document has earned its place. In the entire history of civilization, only a few traditions of learning set forth in singular documents have for more than a brief time sustained the life of a society. But the Mishnah has defined the life of Israel, the Jewish people throughout the world, from the time it was promulgated, at the end of the second century, to the present day. To find parallels to the astonishing power of that book to define the meaning of the life of the society to which it speaks, we should have to point, in India, to the Vedas, in Iran and India, to the Zoroastrian Scriptures, in Islam, to the Quran, and, in the Christian West, to the Bible, that is, the Old and New Testaments as Christianity put them together. The Quran, the Vedas, the Zoroastrian Avesta, above all, the Bible—these few writings still enjoy a paramount place. But among all the many other writings that have told entire societies what it meant to live in community, we cannot count very many that still deliver the same message, with the same authority, to the same world that they originally addressed. And among the enduring, world-defining documents that humanity has known, the Mishnah is surely the one of which fewest people have heard.

The Vedas, Quran, and Bible form part of common culture. So too, everyone knows the Hebrew Scriptures, the Old Testament of Christianity. They are easy to enter. But, even if it is known as the first document of the Oral part of the Torah of Sinai, the Mishnah is hardly accessible. Falling into the hands of someone who has never seen it before, the Mishnah must cause puzzlement. It provides naked information—contents out of context. It presents disputes about facts scarcely explained, facts hardly urgent outside of a circle of faceless disputants. The opening lines (famous among the students of the document) suffice to make the point (M. Ber. 1:1):

A. From what time do they recite the Shema in the evening?
B. From the hour that the priests [who had immersed after uncleanness and awaited sunset to complete the process of purification] enter [a state of cleanness, the sun having set, so as] to eat their heave offering—
C. "until the end of the first watch," the words of R. Eliezer.
D. And sages say, "Until midnight."
E. Rabban Gamaliel says, "Until the rise of dawn."

It would require many paragraphs to explain the meaning of these seventy-five words, and it would take many more to place the whole into its theological and religious context. Here is a fine example of the Mishnah's opacity, how its radical assumption that its audience brings to the document a vast corpus of learning shapes its discourse. On its own, out of all context, that well-known passage is simply incomprehensible, taking for granted, as it does, a considerable body of information. The issues and the argument presuppose modes of thought and analysis in no way articulated; nor is what is at stake self-evident. Consequently, we start with the impression that we join a conversation already long under way about topics we can never grasp anyhow.

No one can take for granted that what is before us makes sense in any context but the Mishnah's own, inaccessible world. The Mishnah in many tractates does not discuss topics of common interest. For before us is a remarkable statement of concerns for matters not only wholly remote from our own world, but, in the main, alien to the world of the people who made the Mishnah itself. It is as if people set out to write letters about things they had never seen, to people they did not know—letters from an unknown city to an undefined and unimagined world: the Mishnah is a letter, written on blank paper, from no one special, located in utopia, to whom it may concern, at an indeterminate time and no where in particular. Perhaps its very power to speak from deep to deep is its lack of locative specificity. But internal evidence within the Mishnah certainly proves mute about all questions of authorship: where, when, why, for what purpose, to which audience? We have no answers to such basic questions as these.

Equally surprising, the Mishnah is a book without an author. No where in its pages does it identify its authorities or sponsorship.

It permits only slight variations, if any, in its authorities' patterns of language and speech, so there is no place for individual characteristics of expression. It nowhere tells us when it speaks. It does not address a particular place or time and rarely speaks of events in its own day. It never identifies its prospective audience. In the entire mass of sayings and rules, there is scarcely an "I" or a "you." The Mishnah begins nowhere. It ends abruptly. There is no predicting where it will commence or explaining why it is done. Where, when, why the document is laid out and set forth are questions not deemed urgent and not answered.

While the Mishnah clearly addresses Israel, the Jewish people, it is remarkably indifferent to the Hebrew Scriptures. It makes no effort at imitating the Hebrew of the Hebrew Bible, as do the writers of the Dead Sea Scrolls. It does not attribute its sayings to biblical heroes, prophets, or holy men, as do the writings of the pseudepigraphs of the Hebrew Scriptures. It does not claim to emerge from a fresh encounter with God through revelation, as is not uncommon in Israelite writings of the preceding four hundred years; the Holy Spirit is not alleged to speak here. So all the devices by which other Israelite writers gain credence for their messages are ignored. Perhaps the authority of the Mishnah was self-evident to its authors. But, self-evident or not, they in no way take the trouble to explain to their audience why people should conform to the descriptive statements contained in their holy book.

If we turn to the contents of the document, we are helped not at all in determining the place of the Mishnah's origination, the purpose of its formation, the reasons for its anonymous and collective plane of discourse and monotonous tone of voice. For the Mishnah covers a carefully defined program of topics. But it never tells us why one topic is introduced and another is omitted or what the agglutination of these particular topics is meant to accomplish in the formation of a system or imaginative construction. Discourse on a theme begins and ends as if all things are self-evident—including, as we said, the reason for beginning at one point and ending at some other.

One might imagine upon first glance that the Mishnah is a simple rulebook. It appears on the surface to lack all traces of eloquence and style, revealing no evidence of system and reflection. First glance indicates that in hand is yet another shard from remote antiquity—no different from king-lists inscribed on ancient shards, the random catalogue of (to us) useless, meaningless facts: a cook-book, a placard of posted tariffs, detritus of random information, accidentally thrown up on the currents of historical time. Who would want to have made such a thing? Who would now want to refer to it?

The answer to that question is deceptively straight-forward. The Mishnah is important because it is a principal component of the canon of Judaism. Yet that answer begs the question: Why should some of the ancient Jews of the Holy Land have brought together these particular facts and rules into a book and set them forth for the Israelite people? Why should the Mishnah have been received, as much later on it certainly was received, as a half of the "whole Torah of Moses at Sinai" if it is already entirely obvious that little in the actual contents of the document evoked the character or the moral authority of the written Torah of Moses? This being the case, how can the Mishnah be deemed a book of religion, a program for consecration, a mode of sanctification? Why should Jews from the end of the second century to our own day have deemed the study of the Mishnah to be a holy act, a deed of service to God through the study of an important constituent of God's Torah, God's will for Israel, the Jewish people?

In fact, the Mishnah is precisely that, a principal holy book of Judaism. The Mishnah has been and now is memorized in the circle of all those who participate in the religion, Judaism. Of still greater weight, the three great documents formed around the Mishnah and so shaped as to serve, in part, as commentaries to the Mishnah, namely, the Tosefta (ca. 300 C.E.), the Talmud of the Land of Israel (ca. 400 C.E.) and, particularly, the Talmud of Babylonia (ca. 600 C.E.), mark the center of the curriculum of Judaism as a living religion. And all of this is present tense: the Mishnah, together with the Talmud and related writings, is studied and guides the life of Jews throughout the world.

When was the Mishnah made up, and who did the work? The world addressed by the Mishnah is hardly congruent to the world-view presented within the Mishnah. Let us now consider the time and context in which the document took shape. The Mishnah is made up of sayings bearing the names of authorities who lived, as we just said, in the later first and second centuries. (The book contains very little in the names of people who lived before the destruction of the Temple of Jerusalem in 70.) These authorities generally fall into two groups, namely, two distinct sets of names, each set of names randomly appearing together, but rarely, if ever, with names of the other set. The former set of names is generally supposed to represent authorities who lived between the destruction of the Temple in 70 and the advent of the second war against Rome, led by Simeon Bar Kokhba, in 132. The latter set of names belongs to authorities who flourished between the end of that war, ca. 135, and the end of the second century.

The Mishnah itself is generally supposed to have come to closure at the end of the second century, and its date, for conventional purposes only, is ca. 200. Now, of these two groups—sages from 70–130, and from 135–200—the latter is represented far more abundantly than the former. Approximately two thirds of the named sayings belong to mid-second century authorities. This is not surprising, since these are the named authorities whose (mainly unnamed) students collected, organized, and laid out the document as we now have it. So, in all, the Mishnah represents the thinking of Jewish sages who flourished in the middle of the second century. It is that group which took over whatever they had in hand from the preceding century—and from the whole legacy of Israelite literature even before that time—and revised and reshaped the whole into the Mishnah. Let us briefly consider their world, because the urgent question presented by that world precipitated the answer that, from then to now, Jews have found compelling as the reference-point of their lives as a holy people.

In the aftermath of the war against Rome in 132–135, the Temple was declared permanently prohibited to Jews, and Jerusalem was closed off to them as well. So there was no cult, no Temple, no holy city, to which, at this time, the description of the Mishnaic laws applied. We observe at the very outset, therefore, that a sizable proportion of the Mishnah deals with matters to which the sages had no material access or practical knowledge at the time of their work. For the Mishnah contains a division on the conduct of the cult, namely, the fifth, as well as one on the conduct of matters so as to preserve the cultic purity of the sacrificial system along the lines laid out in the book of Leviticus, the sixth division. In fact, a fair part of the second division, on appointed times, takes up the conduct of the cult on special days, e.g., the sacrifices offered on the Day of Atonement, Passover, and the like. Indeed, what the Mishnah wants to know about appointed seasons concerns the cult far more than it does the synagogue. The fourth division, on civil law, for its part, presents an elaborate account of a political structure and system of Israelite self-government, in tractates Sanhedrin and Makkot, not to mention Shebuot and Horayot. This system speaks of king, priest, Temple, and court. But it was not the Jews, their kings, priests, and judges, but the Romans, who conducted the government of

Israel in the land of Israel in the time in which the second century authorities did their work.

So it would appear that well over half of the document before us speaks of cult, Temple, government, priesthood. The Mishnah takes up a profoundly priestly and Levitical conception of sanctification. When we consider that, in the very time in which the authorities before us did their work, the Temple lay in ruins, the city of Jerusalem was prohibited to all Israelites, and the Jewish government and administration that had centered on the Temple and based its authority on the holy life lived there were in ruins, the fantastic character of the Mishnah's address to its own catastrophic day becomes clear. Much of the Mishnah speaks of matters not in being in the time in which the Mishnah was created, because the Mishnah wishes to make its statement on what really matters.

If we now ask ourselves why people of general culture in our own age should take an interest in that long-ago time, the answer is not difficult to find. And it is not a claim for mere antiquarianism. The sages of the Mishnah addressed Israel at the very end of its thousand-year life of sanctification through God's service in the Temple, of anointed kings and holy priests organizing (at least in theory) time and space in accord with the model of the sacred Temple and along lines of structure emanating therefrom. The Mishnah is the work of men who survived the second war against Rome. When we realize that that war was fought roughly three generations after the destruction of the Temple, we notice yet another point of importance. When the Temple had been destroyed earlier, in 586 B.C., the prophetic promises of divine forgiveness had been kept. So the Temple was restored: Israel regained its homeland. Now, half a millennium later, the Temple had lain in ruins for another three generations. A great and noble war had been fought to regain Jerusalem, rebuild the Temple, and restore the cult. But what had happened was incomprehensible. The pattern established in the first destruction and restoration now proved no longer to hold. Indeed, nothing stood firm. This time around, not only was the Temple not rebuilt, the cult not restored. Jerusalem itself was declared off-limits to Israelites. The very center was made inaccessible.

In this context, it is not difficult to look for points of commonalty between one age of uncertainty and another, also cut loose from ancient moorings. What the second-century sages of the Mishnah have to teach the generations of the last decades of the twentieth century and the first of the twenty-first, is how to make use of imagination and fantasy to confront, defy, and overcome chaos and disorder. Behind the Mishnah lay the ruins of half a millennium of continuous, orderly, and systematic Israelite life, which had been centered on the regular and reliable offering of the produce of the field and flock upon the altar of the Temple in Jerusalem, the ordering of society around that Temple, the rhythmic division of time in response to that cult, and the placing of people and things into their proper station in relationship to that center. One disastrous war had ended in the destruction of the Temple. The second, three generations later, had made certain it would not be rebuilt in the foreseeable future—nor, as it now appears, ever. In the aftermath of these two terrible wars the Israelite nation entered upon an existence far more precarious in mind than in material reality. Within a century the social and agricultural effects of the wars had worn off. Galilean synagogues of the third and fourth century testify to an age of material surplus and good comfort. But it would be a very long time before the psychological effects of dislocation and disorientation would pass. In some ways, for the Jewish people, they never have. Our age, which looks back upon the destruction of enduring political and social arrangements in the aftermath of two terrible wars (with numerous skirmishes in-between and since), has the power to confront the second century's world of ancient Judaism, because, it seems, there is a measure of existential congruence between the two ages and their common problems. For both are the kind that challenge the imagination and the will.

So the Mishnah is a book deliberately formed for the very group, Israel, and purpose that, for nearly two millennia, it indeed has served. What can we say about the Judaism that the Mishnah founded, that is to say, about the meaning and purpose of the whole. The "Judaism" expressed by the Mishnah is concrete and not abstract; we are the ones who have to translate its details into a message we can make our own, and that enormous task for the mature student accounts for the power of the Mishnah to speak to age succeeding age.

The Mishnah's mode of speech—the way it speaks, not only what it says—is testimony to its highest and most enduring, distinctive value. Now let us take note. This language does not speak of sacred symbols but of pots and pans, of menstruation and dead creeping things, of ordinary water that, because of the circumstance of its collection and location, possesses extraordinary power; of the commonplace corpse and ubiquitous diseased person; of genitalia and excrement, toilet seats and the flux of penises, of stems of pomegranates and stalks of leeks;

of rain and earth and wood, metal, glass, and hide. This language is filled with words for neutral things of humble existence. It does not speak of holy things and is not symbolic in its substance. This language speaks of ordinary things, of things that everyone must have known. But because of the peculiar and particular way in which it is formed and formalized, this same language not only adheres to an aesthetic theory but expresses a deeply-embedded ontology and methodology of the sacred, specifically of the sacred within the secular, and of the capacity for regulation, therefore for sanctification, within the ordinary: All things in order, all things then hallowed by God who orders all things, so said the priests' creation-tale. The Mishnah is the other side of creation: a picture of that well-ordered, stable world that God called good, blessed, and sanctified. And, in its odd and strange portrait of a utopian, never-never-land, the Mishnah told Israel, the Jewish people, about that basic structure of life in society that, wherever they made their home, the holy people of God would comprise. And that accounts for the amazing power of the Mishnah to speak from age to age, and even to our own.

In the context of the study of the formation of Judaism, none need apologize for devoting sustained and systematic study to the Mishnah, which, along with Scripture, is the foundation-document of Rabbinic Judaism. The authors of the studies on the Mishnah collected in the present volumes represent the best of contemporary scholarship on that document. The editors invited a wide range of schools and viewpoints to participate, and we are proud of the quality and representative character of the studies at hand. We do not believe a more representative selection of contemporary Mishnah-study is available in any other collection.

To place the present studies in context, we call attention to a comparable exercise in defining the state of the question of the Mishnah, brought to press thirty years ago. That was one of two companion-works, produced to afford perspective on the condition of scholarship devoted to the Mishnah and the Talmuds. This the senior editor did to inform himself, as his own enterprise was getting under way, of the state of critical questions pertaining to the Rabbinic corpus of late antiquity. These titles, now reprinted, which he edited in 1970 and 1973 in the context of his doctoral seminar at Brown University (1968–1989), are as follows:

The Formation of the Babylonian Talmud. Studies on the Achievements of Late Nineteenth and Twentieth Century Historical and Literary-Critical Research. Leiden, 1970: Brill. Reprint: Binghamton, 2002: Global Publications Classics in Judaic Studies Series.

The Modern Study of the Mishnah. Leiden, 1973: Brill. Reprint: Binghamton, 2002: Global Publications Classics in Judaic Studies Series.

In addition, ten years later he returned to the state of scholarship in the following work, which remains in print today:

The Study of Ancient Judaism. N.Y., 1981: Ktav. Second printing: Atlanta, 1992: Scholars Press for South Florida Studies in the History of Judaism. Now: Lanham, 2001: University Press of America.
  I. *The Study of Ancient Judaism: Mishnah, Midrash, Siddur.*
  II. *The Study of Ancient Judaism: The Palestinian and Babylonian Talmuds.*

Those state-of-the-question-volumes helped delineate where scholarship then situated itself, identifying the problems that people found urgent and the methods used in solving those problems. Since that time much has changed. Many, both older and younger, both Americans, Europeans, and Israelis, both Jews and gentiles, including all those who have contributed to these pages, have brought about or participated in the contemporary revolution in the description, analysis, and interpretation of the Mishnah. In the contrast between the results portrayed thirty years ago and those set forth in these pages, we see what has happened in the present generation of learning. Nearly all the active, publishing scholars of the academy (as distinct from the yeshiva) who are now at work are represented here.

We note also that the project begun as *A History of the Mishnaic Law* is now fully in print, with the republication of the dissertations produced in the seminar on Rabbinic Judaism conducted at Brown University from 1968 through 1990 by the senior editor. These appear as follows:

Jacob Neusner, editor: *The Law of Agriculture in the Mishnah and the Tosefta.* Leiden, 2005: Brill.
  I. *A History of the Mishnaic Law of Agriculture. Berakhot, Peah.*
  II. *Demai, Kilayim., Shebiit*
  III. *Terumot, Maaserot, Maaser Sheni, Hallah, Orlah, Bikkurim*

A History of the Mishnaic Law of Purities. Leiden, 1974–1977: Brill. I–XXII.
  I. *Kelim. Chapters One through Eleven.* 1974.
  II. *Kelim. Chapters Twelve through Thirty.* 1974.
  III. *Kelim. Literary and Historical Problems.* 1974.
  IV. *Ohalot. Commentary.* 1975.
  V. *Ohalot. Literary and Historical Problems.* 1975.
  VI. *Negaim. Mishnah-Tosefta.* 1975.
  VII. *Negaim. Sifra.* 1975.
  VIII. *Negaim. Literary and Historical Problems.* 1975.

IX. *Parah. Commentary.* 1976.
X. *Parah. Literary and Historical Problems.* 1976.
XI. *Tohorot. Commentary,* 1976.
XII. *Tohorot. Literary and Historical Problems.* 1976.
XIII. *Miqvaot. Commentary.* 1976.
XIV. *Miqvaot. Literary and Historical Problems.* 1976.
XV. *Niddah. Commentary.* 1976.
XVI. *Niddah. Literary and Historical Problems.* 1976.
XVII. *Makhshirin.* 1977.
XVIII. *Zabim.* 1977.
XIX. *Tebul Yom. Yadayim.* 1977.
XX. *Uqsin. Cumulative Index, Parts I–XX.* 1977.
XXI. *The Redaction and Formulation of the Order of Purities in the Mishnah and Tosefta.*
XXII. *The Mishnaic System of Uncleanness. Its Context and History.*

The Judaic Law of Baptism. Tractate Miqvaot in the Mishnah and the Tosefta. A Form-Analytical Translation and Commentary, and a Legal and Religious History. Atlanta, 1995: Scholars Press for South Florida Studies in the History of Judaism. Second Printing of *A History of the Mishnaic Law of Purities.* Volumes XIII and XIV.

A History of the Mishnaic Law of Holy Things. Leiden, Brill: 1979. I–VI.
I. *Zebahim. Translation and Explanation.*
II. *Menahot. Translation and Explanation.*
III. *Hullin, Bekhorot. Translation and Explanation.*
IV. *Arakhin, Temurah. Translation and Explanation.*
V. *Keritot, Meilah, Tamid, Middot, Qinnim. Translation and Explanation.*
VI. *The Mishnaic System of Sacrifice and Sanctuary.*

Form Analysis and Exegesis: A Fresh Approach to the Interpretation of Mishnah. Minneapolis, 1980: University of Minnesota Press.

A History of the Mishnaic Law of Women. Leiden, Brill: 1979–1980. I–V.
I. *Yebamot. Translation and Explanation.*
II. *Ketubot. Translation and Explanation.*
III. *Nedarim, Nazir. Translation and Explanation.*
IV. *Sotah, Gittin, Qiddushin. Translation and Explanation.*
V. *The Mishnaic System of Women.*

A History of the Mishnaic Law of Appointed Times. Leiden, Brill: 1981–1983. I–V.
  I. *Shabbat. Translation and Explanation.*
  II. *Erubin, Pesahim. Translation and Explanation.*
  III. *Sheqalim, Yoma, Sukkah. Translation and Explanation.*
  IV. *Besah, Rosh Hashanah, Taanit, Megillah, Moed Qatan, Hagigah. Translation and Explanation.*
  V. *The Mishnaic System of Appointed Times.*

A History of the Mishnaic Law of Damages. Leiden, Brill: 1983–1985. I–V.
  I. *Baba Qamma. Translation and Explanation.*
  II. *Baba Mesia. Translation and Explanation.*
  III. *Baba Batra, Sanhedrin, Makkot. Translation and Explanation.*
  IV. *Shebuot, Eduyyot, Abodah Zarah, Abot, Horayyot. Translation and Explanation.*
  V. *The Mishnaic System of Damages.*

Plans are presently underway to reprint the forty-three volumes of the *History of the Mishnaic Law*.

Jacob Neusner
Research Professor of Theology
Bard College

Alan J. Avery-Peck
Kraft-Hiatt Professor of Judaic Studies
College of the Holy Cross

ANECDOTAL EVIDENCE: THE YAVNEH CONUNDRUM, *BIRKAT HAMMINIM*, AND THE PROBLEM OF TALMUDIC HISTORIOGRAPHY

Daniel Boyarin
University of California, Berkeley

> What could have served in the past as solid foundations had become, through Foucault's archaeological retrospective, an open site: the clearing away of a new space for investigation and the opening of new questions.
>
> Donald F. Bouchard

To commence the archaeological excavation of the relationship between Judaism and Christianity in late antiquity, it is necessary first to clear away at least some of the debris of the strata of previous mythologies, narratives, and interpretations that have accumulated over and around the subject. Then we can attempt new restorations of the buildings of history from the same fragments that have been interpreted before us.

We begin with a conundrum. Like the first humans in both Platonic and Rabbinic mythology, the icon of the Council of Yavneh, which allegedly founded Rabbinic Judaism in the closing decades of the first century C.E., has two directly opposing (and mutually exclusive) visages. One face is said to have welcomed difference and included it, the other to have shunned difference and excluded it. Shaye Cohen has written in a now near-classic essay:

> A year or two before the church council of Nicea Constantine wrote to Alexander and Arius, the leaders of the contending parties, and asked them to realize that they were united by their shared beliefs more than they were separated by their debate on the nature of the second person of the Trinity. Let them behave like members of a philosophical school who debate in civil fashion the doctrines of the school (Eusebius, *Life of Constantine* 2.71). The council of Nicea ignored the emperor's advice and expelled the Arians. The sages of Yavneh anticipated Constantine's suggestion. They created a society based on the doctrine that conflicting disputants may each be advancing the words of the living God.[1]

---

[1] Shaye J. D. Cohen, "The Significance of Yavneh: Pharisees, Rabbis, and the End of Jewish Sectarianism," in *Hebrew Union College Annual* LV (1984), p. 51. For a less

Much of Christian and Jewish scholarship before Cohen had portrayed Yavneh (Jamnia, supposed date circa 90 C.E.) very differently. As Cohen himself described the "usual view" (in order to dispute it):

> Sectarianism ceased when the Pharisees, gathered at Yavneh, ejected all those who were not members of their own party. Christians were excommunicated, the biblical canon was purged of works written in Greek and apocalyptic in style, and the gates were closed on the outside world, both Jewish and non-Jewish. Functioning in a "crisis" atmosphere, the rabbis of Yavneh were motivated by an exclusivistic ethic; their goal was to define orthodoxy and to rid Judaism of all those who would not conform to it. In this interpretation, the "synod" of Yavneh becomes a prefiguration of the church council of Nicea (325 C.E.): one party triumphs and ousts its competitors.[2]

Cohen's claim that Yavneh was not a council in which an orthodoxy was established and heretics and Christians expelled, but rather a pluralistic one in which there was "created a society based on the doctrine that conflicting disputants may each be advancing the words of the living God," has been largely adopted by scholars who have further unsettled the narrative of what supposedly took place at Yavneh, including especially the closing of the canon of the Hebrew Bible and the alleged expulsion of the Jewish Christians, and it has become near dogma by now in many quarters. As one major historian has written: "[T]here is virtually unanimous agreement that in the aftermath of the destruction of the Temple, in the generations between 70 C.E. and the publication of the Mishnah, Jews learned how to live together without paying the price of sectarian divisiveness."[3] Martin Goodman, however, has departed from this unanimity, reviving and revising the account that Cohen's work overthrew, arguing that there was, in fact, after Yavneh, less "tolerance" of difference rather than more. Josephus serves

---

idealized account of the intentions of Constantine in convening the council, see Athanasius, *Athanasius Werke*, H. G. Opitz, ed. (Berlin, 1934), vol. III, pp. 41–42, as well as discussion and literature cited in Richard Lim, *Public Disputation, Power, and Social Order in Late Antiquity* (Berkeley and Los Angeles, 1994), p. 184. The role of Constantine would seem to have been as much the prevention of free discussion as the promotion of it (Lim, *Disputation*, p. 215). The actual Constantinian document can now conveniently be consulted in Eusebius, *Life of Constantine*, introduction, translation and commentary by Averil Cameron and Stuart G. Hall (Oxford and New York, 1999), pp. 116–120.

[2] Cohen, "Yavneh," p. 28.
[3] Albert I. Baumgarten, *The Flourishing of Jewish Sects in the Maccabean Era: An Interpretation* (Leiden, 1997), p. 134.

as one of Goodman's major sources.⁴ Goodman proposes that while the "sects" of the Second-Temple period constituted a Judaism which suffered (if not irenically) internal differences, the Judaism of the rabbis in the post-Yavneh period was exclusivistic and allowed for no other forms of Judaism at all. It is very well known that Josephus is our primary ancient source for Jewish sectarianism in the pre-Rabbinic period. Much of the early part of Book XVIII of the *Jewish Antiquities* consists of an elaborate excursus on Jewish sectarianism in the first century (as we find in *Wars* 2, as well), including the famous and controversial discussions of Jesus, James the brother of Jesus, and John the Baptist and his followers. It is remarkable, therefore, that in his *Contra Apionem*, Josephus describes the Jews the following terms:

> To this cause above all we owe our remarkable harmony. Unity and identity of religious belief, perfect uniformity in habits and customs, produce a very beautiful concord in human character. Among us alone will be heard no contradictory statements about God, such as are common among other nations, not only on the lips of ordinary individuals under the impulse of some passing mood, but even boldly propounded by philosophers; some putting forward crushing arguments against the very existence of God, others depriving Him of His providential care for mankind. Among us alone will be seen no difference in the conduct of our lives. With us all act alike, all profess the same doctrine about God, one which is in harmony with our Law and affirms that all things are under His eye. (C. Ap. 2. 179–81)

This statement stands in seemingly obvious contradiction to Josephus's careful accounts of Judaism as divided into three "philosophiai" as we find in the *Antiquities* passage (XVIII, 11),⁵ as well as to his reference to them as "haireseis," the etymological origin of our term "heresies," in other passages, such as *Antiquities* (13.171, 293 and passim). Unless we assume that in the *Contra Apionem* Josephus is simply obfuscating for the purposes of apologetic, we must conclude that he did not perceive the "haireseis" of his time as in any way disturbing the essential religious and communal unity of the Jewish People,⁶ even less than the

---

⁴ Martin Goodman, "The Function of Minim in Early Rabbinic Judaism," in H. Cancik, H. Lichtenberger, and P. Schäfer, eds., *Geschichte—Tradition—Reflexion: Festschrift für Martin Hengel zum 70 Geburtstag* (Tübingen, 1996), vol. 1, pp. 501–510.
⁵ Flavius Josephus, *Jewish Antiquities, Books XVIII–XX*, translated by L. H. Feldman, Loeb Classical Library (Cambridge, 1965), p. 9 and passim.
⁶ Goodman makes the point that if Josephus were willfully obfuscating, then he would hardly have included explicit cross-references within the text to both the Wars and the Antiquities where his extensive discussion of the Jewish "haireseis" occur.

divisions among the Greeks, which from his point of view were more extreme.[7]

Historian Seth Schwartz has made a similar point to that of Goodman: "Differences should not be allowed to obscure the fact of the elite's basic, though not absolute, social cohesion to which Josephus testifies (the tensions he describes *demonstrate* rather than refute this point)."[8] It is generally accepted that even allowing for exaggeration of the irenic nature of the situation on the part of Josephus, for Josephus and presumably at his time, the term "haireseis" in Jewish Greek did not in any way conform to the later meaning of "heresy" or of *minut*,[9] its virtual Hebrew equivalent, in later Christian and Rabbinic usage

---

Obviously, he did not expect his readers to see here a contradiction, Goodman, "Minim," p. 502. See also Marcel Simon, "From Greek Hairesis to Christian Heresy," in Mélanges R. M. Grant, *Early Christian Literature and the Classical Intellectual Tradition* (Paris, 1979), pp. 101–116.

[7] Philo also, in his Legatio ad Gaium, presupposes strong shared Jewish religious identity, both of Semitic and of Greek speakers, throughout the Empire. Surely, as Josephus indicates, there was more fundamental difference between Cynics and Epicureans and Pythagoreans than even between Pharisees, Sadducees, and Essenes, who for all their divisions, were all committed to observance of God's Torah in accord with their understanding therefore, such that the Sabbath, kashruth, circumcision, confession of the Shema were all common to the three groups. The Temple, moreover, was a divisive element, insofar as much sectarian difference had to do with practice and control there, but it was also a unifying factor; all Israelites in some fashion revered the same Temple, except, of course, for the Samaritans. For lucid and concise description of the "common core of second Temple Judaism," see James D. G. Dunn, *The Partings of the Ways between Christianity and Judaism and Their Significance for the Character of Christianity* (London and Philadelphia, 1991), pp. 18–36. Also E. P. Sanders, *Jewish Law from Jesus to the Mishnah: Five Studies* (London, 1990). See the insightful remarks of Stephen Motyer, *Your Father the Devil? A New Approach to John and "the Jews"* (Carlisle, 1997), p. 77.

[8] Seth Schwartz, *Imperialism and Jewish Society from 200 B.C.E. to 640 C.E.* (Princeton, 2001).

[9] Simon, "Hairesis," pp. 104–105. Simon emphasizes that Marcus Aurelius was to found in Athens four chairs of philosophy, one for each of the great "haireseis," Platonists, Aristotelians, Epicureans, and Stoics. One could imagine Josephus founding such an academy as well, with a chair of Pharisaism, one of Sadducaism, and one of Essenism. The case of Acts is interesting. When Paul says in Acts 24:14: "I am a follower of the new way (the 'hairesis' they speak of), and it is in that manner that I worship the God of our fathers," this can be interpreted in two ways, as Simon points out. Either Paul is claiming the true way, while the Jews say it is just another school of Judaism, or Jews are already referring to Christianity as a hairesis in the later sense of heresy. I see no reason to adopt the second choice and citing Justin (pace Simon) begs the question. Acts 26:5 demonstrates beyond a shadow of a doubt that for Luke, hairesis still means religious choice and not heresy! See also Allen Brent, "Diogenes Laertius and the Apostolic Succession," in *Journal of Ecclesiastical History* 44, no. 3 (July 1993), p. 368, who writes that "the Church of Rome of the mid- to late second century resembled a collection of philosophical schools."

respectively.¹⁰ In other words, the "sectarianism" of the pre-Yavneh period did not preclude inclusiveness or a sense of a "pluralistic" Israel. On the other hand, in the Mishnah, it is absolutely clear that the Sadducees were not tolerated by the rabbis as simply another "philosophy" but were considered heretics. The "significance of Yavneh," as represented in the Mishnah, hardly constitutes "a society based on the doctrine that conflicting disputants may each be advancing the words of the living God."¹¹

Goodman has, therefore, compellingly shown there was, in many ways, after Yavneh, less "tolerance" of difference rather than more. It was, after all, during that time—after Yavneh—that the category of *minim* and *minut* (heretics and heresy) first appears on the Jewish scene.¹² Following Goodman, it would seem, then, that although we can accept Cohen's argument that the focal point for sectarian division over the Temple with the concomitant production of a particular kind of sectarianism (separatism from the "corrupted" Jerusalem center or conflict over hegemony there) had vanished with the destruction of the Temple, nevertheless the epistemic shift marked by the invention of Rabbinic Judaism included the production of a category of Jewish "outsiders" defined by doctrinal difference. Jewish sectarianism had been replaced, on Goodman's reading, by Jewish orthodoxy and Jewish heresy, a modified version of the pre-Cohen view. It is not, then, that sectarianism had disappeared but that one group was beginning to achieve hegemony and could now plausibly portray itself as Judaism tout court, and thus performing an act more like Nicaea than Cohen had proposed, an act of radical exclusion and not one of inclusion and pluralism.

It can hardly be denied, nevertheless, that, a la Cohen, talmudic tradition fashions itself as a collective that avoids schism through pluralism, declaring: "these and these are the words of the Living God" (B. Erub. 13b and B. Git. 6b; see below); it displays tolerance, even appetite, for paradox and disagreement on issues even of fundamental importance for practice and belief. These are traits that contemporaneous

---

¹⁰ Throughout this work, I shall be referring to Christian and Rabbinic as the relevant binary opposition and not Christian and Jew, for obvious reasons.

¹¹ Robert Daum's comprehensive work on Yavneh materials supports this conclusion; Robert Daum, "Describing Yavneh: The Founding Myths of Rabbinic Judaism," Ph. D. Diss. (Berkeley: University of California, 2001). Note especially his conclusion, pp. 4–8, that in the Mishnah virtually all of the explicit Yavneh materials are about authority and power conflicts.

¹² Goodman, "Minim."

late ancient ecclesial Christianity, with its history of constant schism and anathema, seems unwilling to foster. Gerald Bruns was, therefore, surely on to something when he wrote, "From a transcendental standpoint, this [Rabbinic] theory of authority is paradoxical because it is seen to hang on the heteroglossia of dialogue, on speaking with many voices, rather than on the logical principle of univocity, or speaking with one mind. Instead, the idea of speaking with one mind ... is explicitly rejected; single-mindedness produces factionalism."[13] There is a certain elasticity to the rabbis' form of orthodoxy that Cohen has compellingly identified.

We seem, ourselves, then, to have arrived at an aporia. We have two opposite accounts of the role of the Council of Yavneh in the history of Judaism and Christianity and in the origins of the "parting of the ways."

The basic historiographical premise underlying the work of both Cohen and Goodman is what leads to the impasse we have been examining. Both accounts of the inclusive or exclusive nature of Yavneh assume, more or less, that Rabbinic literature, when read critically, can provide us with useful information about the events that took place there. The historiography of Judaism in the Rabbinic period, together with its implications for history of Christianity, had been, until quite recently, founded on the assumption that the kind of historical information that Rabbinic legends could yield was somehow directly related to the narrative contents that they displayed, which were understood as more or less reliable, depending on the critical sensibility of the scholar.[14] This scholarship was not, of course, generally naive or pious in its aims or methods, merely very old fashioned. It asked the critical questions that Marc Bloch ascribed to an earlier generation of historians: "The documents most frequently dealt with by the early scholars

---

[13] Gerald Bruns, "The Hermeneutics of Midrash," in Regina Schwartz, ed., *The Book and the Text: The Bible and Literary Theory* (Oxford, 1990), p. 199.

[14] For a somewhat egregious but not otherwise particularly exceptional example of this, see Joan E. Taylor, *Christians and the Holy Places the Myth of Jewish-Christian Origins* (Oxford and New York, 1993), pp. 28–29. She seems to assume that the narrative of Aqiba and Eliezer's (not Eleazar, another name, another rabbi, pace Taylor) arrest for apostasy as preserved in the Talmud is a reliable historical source, only questioning some of its details. She has, moreover, misunderstood the story itself; what is cited is not an "apocryphal saying" but a midrash in the name of Jesus, and this makes all the difference. For my interpretation of this story, see Daniel Boyarin, *Dying for God: Martyrdom and the Making of Christianity and Judaism*, The Lancaster/Yarnton Lectures in Judaism and Other Religions for 1998 (Stanford, 1999).

either represented themselves or were traditionally represented as belonging to a given author or a given period, and deliberately narrated such and such events. Did they speak the truth?"[15] As Bloch shows, such historians did not take the narrations of such documents as the "truth," and the same goes for the historicans of the Rabbinic period who have followed them.[16] More often than not, in fact, they concluded that the Rabbinic narratives did not speak the truth. Nevertheless, with respect to Yavneh, the results of such critical research have been paradoxical, to say the least. Goodman and Cohen, both reading critically,[17] have produced seemingly compelling accounts of the nature of the Rabbinic Judaism founded at Yavneh and the activity of that council, but since we don't usually imagine that "these and these are the words of the Living God," they can't both be right, of course, hence the conundrum of Yavneh. As long as historians like Cohen and Goodman (not to mention the earlier consensus) claim to be describing the same object, "the historical Yavneh,"[18] then we seem to arrive at the aporia. A similar aporia has been identified for ancient Greek history by Jonathan Hall: "The apparent impasse between the proponents and opponents of an archaelogical visible Dorian invasion arises from the fact that both camps subscribe to the same fallacy—namely, that an ethnic group must necessarily be identifiable in the archaeological record."[19] Although the "fallacy," of course, is a different one, the structure of the problem

---

[15] Marc Bloch, *The Historian's Craft: Reflections on the Nature and Uses of History and the Techniques and Methods of Those Who Write It* (New York, 1953), p. 89.

[16] I thus somewhat disagree with Neusner's characterization of the field, as in his *Reading and Believing: Ancient Judaism and Contemporary Gullibility* (Atlanta, 1986), p. 19, and throughout that book. Nevertheless, while the precise contours of our critiques are different, the results are similar both in terms of the methods that we reject and (to a great extent) in terms of those that we propose, though I would add that I find Neusner's unfavorable comparison of Jewish studies to New Testament Studies somewhat unfortunate. He writes that, "One question which to New Testament scholars is deemed unavoidable is how to tell what, if anything, Jesus really said among the sayings attributed to him, and what Jesus really did among the deeds assigned to him," *Believing*, p. 33, and this is meant to produce an unfavorable judgment of talmudic studies, which allegedly does not ask such questions. From where I sit (and perhaps Neusner after fifteen years has changed his perspective as well), those questions, which indeed do characterize much New Testament research are equally as gullible as the very similar questions that are, to my mind, being asked in talmudic studies. I would argue that access to the historical Jesus is as unavailable to us as access to the historical Aqiba, or, for that matter, the historical Moses.

[17] On Cohen's essay, see also Neusner, *Believing*, pp. 82–89.

[18] As they, I think, take themselves.

[19] Jonathan M. Hall, *Ethnic Identity in Greek Antiquity* (Cambridge, 1997), p. 129.

is (I suppose) the same: the impasse between those who see Yavneh as the production of a pluralistic community and those who see it as the production of an exclusivistic orthodoxy arises from the fact that both camps are still trying to discover the "historical Yavneh," are still reading the texts as about that "real" Yavneh. However, if we abandon the quest for the historical Yavneh and search instead for the different Yavnehs portrayed by the different Rabbinic texts, in order to understand the different uses to which Yavneh has been put at different moments of Rabbinic history, then the contradiction may disappear.

A recurring question within the quest of the historical Yavneh had to do with the question of the credibility of a given text or passage of Rabbinic literature or the recovery of its "historical kernel." Even when such recovery is successful and convincing, however, this leaves us with very slim and thin bits of historical knowledge.[20] As long as we are engaged in the process of extracting the fact from the fiction in Rabbinic legend, we shall learn precious little about the history of the Rabbinic group and even less about the histories of those other Jewish groups which it is seeking to control and suppress. If, however, the object of research is the motives for the construction of a narrative that is taken to attest to the political context of its telling or retelling, rather than the "historical kernel" or truth contained in the narrative of the narrative,[21] then all texts are by definition equally credible (which is not to say, of course, that they are all equally intelligible.) This point—hardly "postmodern"—can also be seconded via reference to Marc Bloch. Bloch distinguishes between two kinds of documents that a historian may use. On the one hand there are what he calls "intentional" texts, citing as his example the History of Herodotus; on the other hand, there are, the texts that are not intentional, and, in Bloch's view are, precisely therefore, all the more valuable for the historian:

> Now, the narrative sources—to use a rather baroque but hallowed phrase—that is, the accounts which are consciously intended to inform their readers, still continue to provide valuable assistance to the schola.... Nevertheless, there can be no doubt that, in the course of its development, historical research has gradually been led to place more and more confidence in

---

[20] Here I am in complete agreement with Neusner that the formulation of our questions should be: "What do we know if we do not know that Rabbi X really said what is attributed to him? What sort of historical work can we do if we cannot do what Frankel, Graetz, and Krochmal thought we could do?," Neusner, *Believing*, p. 33.

[21] Cf. also Alon Goshen-Gottstein, *The Sinner and the Amnesiac: The Rabbinic Invention of Elisha Ben Abuya and Eleazar Ben Arach* (Stanford, 2000), p. 9.

the second category of evidence, in the evidence of witnesses in spite of themselves.[22]

However, as Bloch states clearly, even the most intentional of texts, and the Rabbinic narratives of Yavneh are nothing if not intentional in his sense, also teach us that which they did not want us to know; they "permit us to overhear what was never intended to be said."[23] In this sense, we can have equal "confidence" in all texts.[24] The question of the "narrative source" versus the "witnesses in spite of themselves" can be seen, now, as a distinction between protocols of reading texts and not as an essential difference between the texts themselves. As Bloch concludes: "Everything that a man says or writes, everything that he makes, everything he touches can and ought to teach us about him."[25] Whatever else Rabbinic narratives might be, they are certainly something that someone has said and written, and even when we don't know who said or wrote them "originally," we can frequently determine who (that is, at what historical period), someone has "touched them." I seek to learn, then, about those who have touched the stories, those who have passed on and inscribed the anecdotes within the Rabbinic documents they have produced, teaching us, perhaps, what they never intended to say: "Because history has tended to make more and more frequent use of unintentional evidence [history] can no longer confine itself to weighing the explicit assertions of the documents. It has been necessary to wring from them further confessions which they had never intended to give."[26]

All texts inscribe willy-nilly the social practices within which they originate, and many also seek to locate the genealogy of those social practices in a narrative of origins, producing a reversal of cause and effect. This reversal is a mode of narration that is particularly germane to the project of replacing traditional patterns of belief and behavior ("We have always done it this way") with new ones that wish, nevertheless, to claim the authority of hoary antiquity. In short, narratives of origin are particularly useful in the invention of orthodoxies, and thus are particularly useful texts in which to study their invention.

---

[22] Bloch, *Craft*, pp. 60–61.
[23] Ibid., p. 63.
[24] I heard this point made thirty years ago by my teacher, Professor Saul Liberman.
[25] Bloch, *Craft*, p. 66.
[26] Ibid., p. 89.

Although all of the institutions of Rabbinic Judaism are projected in Rabbinic narrative to an origin called "Yavneh," "Yavneh," seen in this way, is the effect, not the cause, of the institutions and discursive practices that it is said to "originate" in the myth: Rabbinic Judaism and its primary institutions and discursive practices, "Torah," the Study House, and orthodoxy.[27] Demystifying the Rabbinic narrative of the origins of these practices and of their hegemony allows us to inquire into their "causes" somewhere else, namely, in the complex interactions and negotiations that produced Rabbinic Judaism itself as one of the two successfully competing forms of postbiblical religion to emerge from late antiquity, the other being, of course, orthodox Christianity. Thus, although traditional scholarly historiography refers to Yavneh as a founding council that "restored" Judaism and established the Rabbinic form as hegemonic following the disaster of the destruction of the Temple, if we want to study how people conceived of themselves as belonging to a group, it is more useful to approach Yavneh as an effect of a narrative whose purpose is to shore up the attempt at predominance on the part of the rabbis (and especially the Patriarchate) in the wake of the greater debacle following the Fall of Betar in 135.[28] That which the rabbis wished to enshrine as authoritative, they ascribed to events and utterances that took place at Yavneh, and sometimes even to divine voices that proclaimed themselves at that hallowed site.

As opposed to the early third-century Mishnah, the Talmud (especially the Babylonian Talmud) indeed frequently thematizes and valorizes sanctified and unresolved controversy precisely through narratives about Yavneh. The watchword quoted by Cohen, "These and these are the words of the Living God," was, according to talmudic legend,

---

[27] Cf. Neusner, *Believing*, p. 37.

[28] See Jacob Neusner, who makes a closely related point in "Judaism after the Destruction of the Temple: An Overview," in his *Formative Judaism: Religious, Historical, and Literary Studies, Third Series: Torah, Pharisees, and Rabbis* (Chico, 1983), pp. 83–98. For the impact that this revisionist work has already had on New Testament studies, see, e.g. Motyer, *Your Father*, p. 75. Motyer, however, seems too readily to assume that Neusner's conclusions have been generally accepted, not noticing that the very example he gives of work done under the "old paradigm" was published quite a bit after Neusner's. Moreover, at least in his "The Formation of Rabbinic Judaism: Yavneh (Jamnia) from A.D. 70 to 100," in Wolfgang Haase, ed., *Aufstieg und Niedergang der Römischen Welt Principat: Religion Judentum: Pälastinisches Judentum* (Berlin, 1979), pp. 3–42, Neusner seemed prepared to ascribe a much greater role to a real, historical Yavneh than I would. See on this point, discussion in Isaiah M. Gafni, *Land, Center and Diaspora Jewish Constructs in Late Antiquity* (Sheffield, 1997), p. 64.

pronounced by a divine voice at Yavneh (B. Erub. 13b and B. Git. 6b). Rabbinic textuality, far more than other Jewish or Christian textualities, is marked, almost defined, by its rhetoric of openness to dissenting opinions, by its endless deferral of final decisions on hermeneutical, theological, halakhic, and historical questions, by heteroglossia, by the non-logocentric modes of interpretation known as midrash. This characteristic of Rabbinic textuality is well thematized within talmudic texts themselves, that is, it is a self-conscious trait of Rabbinic religion, much as doctrinal rigor is of fourth-century Christianity. Just as the notion of orthodoxy grew within Christianity from the second to the fourth century, however, so also (I suggest) the notion of heteroglossia grew within Rabbinic circles during these same centuries. The two descriptions, one of an exclusivistic and one of a pluralistic Yavneh, are best emplotted diachronically as two stages in the development of Rabbinic ecclesiology itself: Heteroglossia is the endpoint of a historical process and not an essential or timeless description of the Rabbinic formation. Just as Christian orthodoxy received its definitive formation in the fourth century, post-dating the anti-gnostic formulation of pre-Nicene apologists and heresiologists, so too the social form, that is, the heteroglossic regime of power/knowledge of Rabbinic orthodox Judaism, was formulated much later than the Mishnah. The codified "dissensus," the agreement to disagree that we identify in these latter assemblages,[29] was as efficient a mode of power for the achievement of "consensual orthodoxy" for Rabbinic Judaism and the exclusion of its rivals as were the creeds and councils of orthodox Christianity.

Anecdotal Evidence

This focus on the historical and diachronic development of the institutions and discursive practices of Rabbinic Judaism raises some serious historiographical problems. Rabbinic literature presents us with no

---

[29] I substitute this for "documents" both to maintain the archaeological metaphor and to indicate a less intentional or authorial character to the texts than Neusner would have them display. Thus while I accept his general approach that what we learn best from the Mishnah is about the late second and early third centuries and what we learn best from the Babylonian Talmud is about the late fourth through the sixth centuries, I would argue that what is learned is less coherent, formed, and controlled than his documentary history of ideas would suggest. The notion of a stratum or assemblage of verbal artifacts seems to me to work better.

historical documents and virtually no extended historical narratives. It would not be unfair to say that classical Rabbinic literature (by which I mean the texts produced between the third and sixth centuries) has no historical writing at all. What we do have are myriad anecdotes, most of them in several widely varying versions, about the important founding "events" of the Rabbinic school tradition and its primary actors, the rabbis. In addition, this literature contains extensive discussions of points of ritual and civil law based to greater or lesser extent (depending on genre) on a particular method of interpretation of the Bible—midrash.

How, then, can we "learn Torah" to speak history? In my previous projects on this literature, and especially in *Carnal Israel*, I "finessed" this problem by working in an essentially synchronic version of cultural poetics, treating the whole of Rabbinic literature as one ideologically differentiated and contested cultural territory. This method essentially permitted me to avoid the problem of historical referentiality and analyze the texts as sites of struggle and cultural problematic without reference to a "real" outside. The present project does not allow for such an approach, since I am trying to tell a story here of diachronic development, both of and within Rabbinic Judaism, as but one particular institution and set of religious ideas among Jews in late antiquity. A referential "outside" to the text has to be invoked, therefore. Accordingly, great attention needs to be paid to the procedures by which such hypotheses can be generated and justified without falling into the traps of either naive positivism or "postmodern" nihilist constructivism—"It's all made up anyway, so I can make it up too." Hans Kellner has "redescribed [history] as a discourse that is fundamentally rhetorical," and, moreover, the same author continues, "representing the past takes place through the creation of powerful, persuasive images which can be best understood as created objects, models, metaphors or proposals about reality."[30]

Even, however, the most trenchant versions of a "postmodern" historiography, such as that of Hayden White, presuppose some access to knowledge of "facts" or "events:"

---

[30] Hans Kellner, "Introduction: Describing Redescriptions," in Frank Ankersmit and Hans Kellner, eds., *A New Philosophy of History* (Chicago, 1995), p. 2. I find comfort in learning from Kellner that at least some of the confusion that I feel between desire to say something at least tentatively real about the past and conviction that this is probably impossible (or at any rate that I ought to think so) is shared by "real" historians too; Kellner, "Introduction," pp. 10–11.

> The events are made into a story by the suppression or subordination of certain of them and the highlighting of others, by characterization, motific repetition, variation of tone and point of view, alternative descriptive strategies, and the like—in short, all of the techniques that we would normally expect to find in the emplotment of a novel or a play.... The same set of events can serve as components of a story that is tragic or comic, as the case may be, depending on the historian's choice of the plot structure.[31]

White's characterization of historical narratives explicitly assumes that some knowledge of the "events" is granted, common among historians as different in their interpretations of the French Revolution as Michelet, Toqueville, and Taine.[32] However, because of the extraordinary problems of evidence in regard to Rabbinic history, it is not only historical interpretation that is at issue but the very events themselves that are put into question, according to different theoretical protocols for reading Rabbinic literature.[33]

Interestingly the questions about evidence in and from Rabbinical texts seem strikingly alike for "modernist" and "postmodernist" historians. Rabbinic literature provides particular problems of evidence, owing to its complexly generated, redacted, anecdotal literary character, rendering the question of context itself—in its most brutally literal a form—a matter of selection, interpretation, and analysis. Moreover, Rabbinic literature does not come associated with "authors" to whom intentions could, even problematically, be ascribed. If post-structuralism has declared the death of the author,[34] the rabbis produce their literature in a world in which the author has not yet been born, as it were. It follows that even when a general theoretical stance towards historiography has been

---

[31] Hayden White, "The Historical Text as Literary Artifact," in Brian Fay, Philip Pomper, and Richard T. Vann, eds., *History and Theory: Contemporary Readings* (Malden, 1998), p. 18.

[32] "The different kinds of historical interpretations that we have of the same set of events such as the French revolution as interpreted by Michelet, Tocqueville, Taine, and others;" White, "Historical Text," p. 28.

[33] In a sense, then, we need to go beyond White and assert that at least for Rabbinic history, the very description or articulation of the events is always already implied by the plot structure assumed by the historian. What might substitute for White's "events" in this instance, again at least in this instance, are the texts themselves, and then we could rewrite the above-quoted (previous note) sentence as "The different kinds of historical interpretations that we have of the same set of texts such as the Talmuds as interpreted by Graetz, Lieberman, Alon, and others."

[34] Michel Foucault, "What is an Author?" in Donald F. Bouchard, ed., *Language, Counter-Memory, Practice: Selected Essays and Interviews* (Ithaca, 1977), pp. 124–127.

adopted, questions of method specific to the task of a talmudic history yet remain, since much if not nearly all of our evidence for this historiography consists of already emplotted narratives, either themselves historiographical or history-like in their rhetoric. Whether or not we accept Hayden White's notion of historiography as being fiction-like, the materials upon which Rabbinic history must be based, are for the most part, fictions indeed. With Rabbinic narratives we have neither an author about whom we can know anything nor even a sure historical or social context (as we frequently do when studying the texts of other cultures including contemporaneous Christian texts), only a roughly established time of redaction to go on.[35]

On the other hand, one could say that it is this very characteristic of Rabbinic textuality that provides the materia for the work of historiography; not a problem, then, but the very object of our investigations. A formulation of Hall's will serve me well: "The present objective is to attempt an identification of the social groups who thought themselves through these genealogies. Because, however, the field of myth is relatively autonomous, it is necessary to treat mythical episodes as phenomena rather than as epiphenomena, and this dictates that any approach should initially be conducted independently 'from within.'"[36] We are not writing, then, the biography of an individual, or even the history of an institution, so much as the history of a text, including its ostensible motivations and effects (and these perhaps implicate some kind of history of institutions, competing groups, or at any rate sites of power/knowledge).

The problem of dating of developments within Rabbinic Judaism remains fraught with difficulty. First occurrence in the literature, even when we can reasonably project a date for that first occurrence constitutes, of course, only a terminus ante quem (latest possible date) for the ideologeme at issue; the question is, of course, to what extent the silence of prior sources where one might expect the term or concept to appear constitutes a terminus post quem (earliest possible date). Any given

---

[35] For a helpful articulation of these special problems of writing history with Rabbinic texts, see Jacob Neusner, *The Documentary Foundation of Rabbinic Culture: Mopping up after Debates with Gerald L. Bruns, S. J. D. Cohen, Arnold Maria Goldberg, Susan Handelman, Christine Hayes, James Kugel, Peter Schaefer, Eliezer Segal, E. P. Sanders, and Lawrence H. Schiffman* (Atlanta, 1995), pp. 8–13. While I do not entirely associate myself with Neusner's characterization of the state of scholarship in our field, for all its exaggeration, it is not entirely inapposite, nonetheless.

[36] Hall, *Ethnic*, p. 86.

statement in the Mishnah might very well reflect any earlier tradition. However, in spite of the advances of recent research strategies, we cannot ever be certain that a given text existed in the precise form in which we find in the Mishnah prior (or much prior) to the redaction of that text. On the other hand, we can be certain, of course, that the passage was current and deemed relevant at the time of the editing of the Mishnah.[37] In any case, what should be clear is that we can hardly credit the semimythical narratives of Yavneh that we find in the Mishnah (even less so in the later texts) with bearing any positivistic probative weight. We are searching for the historicist background of a narrative now, not for the historical reality that it is deemed to convey in its content. I would not dare to write a "canonical history of ideas" based on this method,[38] but I would hold, with Jacob Neusner, that the burden of proof, at least, is on those who wish to assert the utility of late legends and texts in the reconstruction of much earlier events. Rather, assuming that which we can know, namely that the traditions in question were in existence at the presumed time of the redaction of the Rabbinic texts and that they were presumably significant at that time, we can hypothesize connections and nexuses. A good-sense approach to dating of traditions within Rabbinic texts in the postneusnerian era is that of Alan Segal: "Since we are dealing with a culture which distinguished various levels of antiquity of traditions in order to formulate legal precedents and valued older traditions more highly, we must rule out the earlier dating by methodological premise unless and until other evidence warrants it."[39]

That most scholars in past generations took the narratives that are incorporated into the Talmud about the history of the Rabbinic movement

---

[37] "Materials designated 'traditional' are always a selection from those that could be so designated. The ones selected are those that figure centrally in the organization of Christian materials favored by the party that puts them forward: therefore, what is labeled 'tradition' always has links to a preferred course of Christian behaviors now;" Kathryn Tanner, *Theories of Culture: A New Agenda for Theology, Guides to Theological Inquiry* (Minneapolis, 1997), p. 163. This does not necessarily mean, with respect to the Mishnah, for instance, that every statement included or story told represented literally the halakhic practice of the redactors, but it does mean that these statements and their meanings were deemed a significant part of the discursive practice of their time and place and thus are relevant for the description of the religious discourse thereof.

[38] Pace Jacob Neusner, *The Canonical History of Ideas: The Place of the So-Called Tannaite Midrashim* (Atlanta, 1990).

[39] Alan F. Segal, *Two Powers in Heaven: Early Rabbinic Reports about Christianity and Gnosticism* (Leiden, 1977), p. 27. See too Neusner, *Believing*, p. 78, on where the burden of proof ought to lie.

"at face value" does not mean, of course, that scholars have naively and simply received the stories as representation of historical events—although that has also been done in certain quarters. Various modes of critical analysis have been employed to extract the so-called "kernel of truth" from the narratives.[40] My assumption is simply that the stories told in third, fourth, and fifth-century texts have virtually no probative value for the first century; that is, their contents do not point to any first-century reality outside of the third-century (or later) texts. This does not mean, of course, that they never contain information about the first century, just that we cannot know when they do and when they don't. Observing the different forms that a given tradition takes, even when cited as tannaitic in origin, from, say the Palestinian to the Babylonian Talmud, when we can observe the differences, hardly provides confidence that detail and particularly verbal detail survives extended transmission, and it is usually precisely that detail that we need for traditional historiography.[41]

Nuancing this point somewhat, perhaps one might rather say that the "kernels" of so-called (positivistic) historical truth that one might extract from these contradictory narratives makes for mighty slim pickings. The point is not, then, that, Gedaliah Alon, for instance, is wrong in his conclusion that Yavneh was some sort of Roman internment camp—his conclusion makes sense—but that there is so much more to be said about it when we shift the questions that we ask. Those same variations in the traditions, once an obstacle to be removed, now become the very stuff of history, especially when they contradict each other.

---

[40] See also Shamma Friedman, "Literary Development and Historicity in the Aggadic Narrative of the Babylonian Talmud: A Study Based upon B.M. 83b–86a," in Nahum W. Waldman, ed., *Community and Culture: Essays in Jewish Studies in Honor of the 90th Anniversary of Gratz College* (Philadelphia, 1985), pp. 67–80.

[41] There is nothing startling, I think, about this claim. In his recent work on Paulinus of Nola, Dennis Trout has remarked the difficulty of determining the events and motivations of his subject's life, because even the writings of contemporaries, such as Ambrose and Augustine, about him are so overlayered with rhetorical purpose and biblical types; Dennis E. Trout, *Paulinus of Nola: Life, Letters, and Poems* (Berkeley and Los Angeles, 1999), pp. 4–9. As Trout remarks, p. 5, "biographical modeling for polemical ends was practically endemic to late-ancient culture;" nor is this, in itself, a novum of Trout's work (although very well formulated there). Attending to the rhetoric of the ancient "biographical" text, then, even to the point of near-total skepticism vis-à-vis its value for biographical research, hardly constitutes, then, a "post-modern" gesture. For a similar critical approach with respect to a problem in the historiography of modern Judaism, see Moshe Rosman, *Founder of Hasidism: A Quest for the Historical Baal Shem Tov* (Berkeley and Los Angeles, 1996).

Accordingly, I make no attempts whatsoever to reconstruct from them events of that century but rather attempt to read them in the context of the time of their production, as evidence for the ideological work that they are doing within the cultural and social context in which they have been produced. This involves a shift from the utterance and its referent to the act of uttering as the focus of inquiry.[42] The modes of interpretation employed are, accordingly, seemingly more similar to the modes of interpretation of fictions[43] than of historical documents, still less of historical facts.[44]

The mode of interpretation that is formative for me is that called the "New Historicism." Although this is not the place to rehearse the assumptions and practices of this mode of reading, suffice it to say for the moment that it issues from the postulate that literature is not produced out of the free-will act of an "author" but rather that language/discourse

---

[42] Jacob Neusner, "Beyond Historicism, after Structuralism: Story as History in Ancient Judaism," in his *Method and Meaning in Ancient Judaism* 3rd series (1981), p. 238, and for recent comment, Goshen-Gottstein, *Sinner*, pp. 4–5. In contrast, however, to Goshen-Gottstein's notion that we have only access to "the religious ideals of the sages," via this approach, I would argue (and frequently will) that the fractures and ruptures within the narratives as well as their other intertextual dimensions provide access (at least in theory) to realities that are not only ideal. I share Goshen-Gottstein's sense that the best way to read Rabbinic texts, by and large, is with the methods of the analysis of fiction; we disagree, somewhat however, in our assessments of what those methods might be and what they might promise us. Goshen-Gottstein's insight that it is the very form of the Rabbinic non-biography that teaches us much about Rabbinic culture is very well taken. The collective personality projected, imagined, invented by the Rabbinic texts (The Torah) bespeaks a very different sort of subjectivity than the one comprehended by our modern biographies, and that, as much as anything, is the payoff of the research; Goshen-Gottstein, *Sinner*, pp. 16–18. Where we sharply part company, however, is in his assumption that if the Rabbinic texts are not "true narrations of historical events," then they can only teach us the "issues, concerns, and values" of the rabbis themselves. I believe that by searching hard for what the Rabbinic texts are not telling us, indeed what they are telling us not, what they seek to conceal from us, we can find intimations of a social and cultural world beyond the confines of the Beth Midrash itself. One of the biggest inspirations for my specific historicist method, then, is the work of Pierre Macherey, *A Theory of Literary Production* (London, 1978). And see perhaps closer to home Galit Hasan-Rokem, *The Web of Life—Folklore in Rabbinic Literature: The Palestinian Aggadic Midrash Eikha Rabba* (Stanford, 2000).

[43] Keith Hopkins, "Novel Evidence for Roman Slavery," in *Past and Present* 138 (1993), pp. 3–27.

[44] This proposed paradigm shift is much wider than late-ancient Jewish history of course. As Dominick LaCapra has recently written, "A relatively self-sufficient research paradigm was in certain ways important for the professionalization of history as a discipline, and attacks on tendencies that question it may be taken as one indication of the extent to which it is still understood (perhaps misleadingly) as essential to the discipline even today. This paradigm enjoins gathering and analyzing (preferably archival)

speaks through authors and their texts. The literary text is, then, no less historically concrete and accessible than is the document:

> Nor is it unusual for literary theorists, when they are speaking about the "context" of a literary work, to suppose that this context—the "historical milieu"—has a concreteness and an accessibility that the work itself can never have, as it were easier to perceive the reality of a past world put together from a thousand historical documents than it is to probe the depths of a single literary work that is present to the critic studying it. But the presumed concreteness and accessibility of historical milieu, these contexts of the texts that literary scholars study, are themselves products of the fictive capability of the historians who have studied those contexts. The historical documents are not less opaque than the texts studied by literary critics.[45]

The historian's task is, then, to reconstruct a discourse, a regime of power/knowledge through contextualized examination of some of the products of that discourse read as symptoms. In other words, the dominant cognitive strategy of this work is that of synecdoche.[46] And frequently enough, "probing the depths" of a single text before us may well prove more illuminating than the concatenation of a thousand texts treated as documents—that is, at any rate, the belief upon which this work of historical writing is predicated.

My claim is that contextualizing the fragments of narrative within Rabbinica in the time of their narration (and not the time of their narrative contents) is the stronger, more intuitive, and even methodologically more conservative position.[47] In reading Rabbinic anecdotal narrative,

---

information about an object of study in contrast to reading and interpreting texts or textualized phenomena. (In this exclusionary sense, reading a text, especially a published text, is not doing research);" Dominick LaCapra, "History, Language, and Reading: Waiting for Crillon," in Brian Fay, Philip Pomper, and Richard T. Vann, eds., *History and Theory: Contemporary Readings* (Malden, 1998), p. 94. LaCapra's essay makes many of the points that I am making here.

[45] White, "Historical Text," p. 23.
[46] Cf. Ibid., p. 27.
[47] This approach, by itself, is not uniquely mine, of course. A whole generation of younger scholars of Rabbinic Judaism, either trained by Jacob Neusner or under his tutelage in more metaphorical senses, have been pursuing this method for the last three decades. For an excellent example, see David Goodblatt, "From History to Story to History: The Rimmon Valley Seven," in Peter Schäfer, ed., *The Talmud Yerusalmi and Graeco-Roman Culture* (Tübingen, 1998), vol. I, pp. 173–199. The results of Goodblatt's excellent critical analysis are curiously thin, however. I think that the addition of a discourse analysis perspective would have served him well in achieving more positive results. This does not, by itself, however provide as much methodological stability as one would wish, for while we can assume, with Neusner, that the presence of a textual element within a document of, say, the fifth century attests to its significance, in

I attempt to construe the anecdote in a field of other anecdotes, reading it both closely and contextually in the fashion pioneered by the practitioners of the "New Historicism."[48] This method of interpreting anecdotal evidence has seemed to me a highly productive mode of reading the stories of the past, enabling the description/redescription/construction of the complex ideological texture of the moment: "The historian's task is not so much to collect facts as to relate signifiers."[49] Relating sign to sign synchronically, I thus attempt to build a description of a semiotic (and therefore discursive) state of the cultural system. I am describing, then, signs, interpreting texts. There is an implicit claim that these texts and systems of texts amount to something real "out there" but no claim that we can predict or even ever know how they do: "A linguistic characteristic, a point of law embodied in a text, a rite as defined by a book of ceremonial or represented on a stele, are realities just as much as the flint, hewn of yore by the artisan of the stone age—realities which we ourselves apprehend and elaborate by a strictly personal effort of the intelligence."[50] Rabbinic texts, for all their anecdotal form are, then, flint-like realities, requiring no more, but no less, interpretative effort than any other artifacts. This is the point most richly elaborated in my experience in the writings of the New Historicists.

---

some shape or form, at that time, we cannot, pace Neusner, presume that this moment marks the appearance of the emergence of that significance within Rabbinic culture. At best this would be an argument e silentio; at worst an argument against the very palpable fact that Rabbinic texts do have historical depth; they are anthological, and many of the pieces can be shown to be older than the contexts in which they first appear to us; Richard Kalmin, *Sages, Stories, Authors, and Editors in Rabbinic Babylonia* (Atlanta, 1994). We cannot, in short, in my opinion write a "documentary" or "canonical" history of Rabbinic ideas; Neusner, *Canonical History*; Daniel Boyarin, "On the Status of the Tannaitic Midrashim," in *Journal of the American Oriental Society* 113 (1993), pp. 455–465. What we can do, I think, modifying somewhat Neusner's original and productive insight, is attempt a supple diachronic study of the growth, development, shift within discursive elements by observing their appearance within the overall contextual structure of different Rabbinic texts historically (that is in both time and space) contextualized. Thus the function of a signifier such as "Yavneh" or "Beruriah" (David Goodblatt, "The Beruriah Traditions," in *Journal of Jewish Studies* 26 [1975], pp. 68–86) can be studied within the context of the third-century Palestinian Mishnah and the fifth-century Babylonian Talmud and the results usefully compared to yield historical data upon which the historian may construct her narratives.

[48] Catherine Gallagher and Stephen Greenblatt, *Practicing New Historicism* (Chicago, 2000).
[49] Richard T. Vann, "Turning Linguistic: History and Theory and History and Theory, 1960–1975," in Frank Ankersmit and Hans Kellner, eds., *A New Philosophy of History* (Chicago, 1995), p. 57, paraphrasing Barthes.
[50] Bloch, *Craft*, p. 55.

However, I seek to extend the "New Historicist" synchronic construction of discursive moments by plotting two such synchronic states on a timeline, by contextually reading narrative (aggadic) and legal (halakhic) texts from a given document or documentary group together,[51] attempting to describe certain differences between these synchronic moments, then providing some hypotheses having to do with the multiple overdeterminations of those differences. I'm interested in the ways that certain shifts seem to cohere with each other in a manner that makes sense of them. I am thus not only describing synchronic systems of signs, but also attempting to narrate the shift from one such system to a later one and thus to write some kind of a history. The next step (or sometimes a heuristically prior step) involves an attempt to site the suggested historicized interpretation in a still broader textual/contextual field, including primarily patristic and other Christian textual materials, in order to develop a broader understanding of socio-cultural processes producing and being produced by the Rabbinic texts. To mobilize the archaeological metaphor once more, I am trying to identity various textual artifacts as belonging to a single stratum of the remains of Rabbinic religious culture, to reconstruct and interpret the assemblage, and then to relate the different assemblages so reconstructed one to another.

Before Foucault, another French historian (indeed one of Foucault's mentors at least in a derived sense), Marc Bloch had already mobilized the language of archaeology, to be sure in a somewhat different sense from Foucault's, in thinking about the historiographical project. In his now-classic *The Historian's Craft*,[52] Bloch begins his remarkable chapter on historical observation by explicitly invoking archaeological evidence against the notion that all historical evidence is "indirect," that is, filtered through another's intentions before reaching the historian. His example regards the bones of children immured in very ancient Syrian fortresses and the inference that these are the remains of human sacrifice.[53] Bloch argues that the inferences from these data, fully "historical" in nature, are at least as reliable as the up-to-the-minute reports

---

[51] Daniel Boyarin, *Carnal Israel: Reading Sex in Talmudic Culture*, The New Historicism (Berkeley and Los Angeles, 1993), Introduction, and see Neusner, *Canonical History and anidmadversions in Boyarin*, "Status." Despite our striking differences of opinion, there are striking convergences in method between Neusner's work and mine.

[52] Bloch, *Craft*. This is, not incidentally, a book that has brought me much comfort for its explicit permission to the "non-historian" to write history, p. 21.

[53] Ibid., p. 52.

of lieutenants that Napoleon had to deal with in making his strategical adjustments during the Battle of Austerlitz. Had Bloch remained, however, at that level of argument, he would not be helping me very much here, for, truth to tell, I make little enough use, not knowing quite how, of archaeological evidence in the strict sense. Bloch, however, takes us a vital step further, writing:

> Now, a great many vestiges of the past are equally as accessible [as those Syrian bones]. Such is the case not only with almost all the vast bulk of the unwritten evidence, but also with a good part of that which is written. If the best-known theorists of our methods had not shown such an astonishing and arrogant indifference toward the techniques of archaeology, if they had not been as obsessed with narrative in the category of documents as they were with incident in the category of actions, they would doubtless have been less ready to throw us back upon an eternally dependent method of observation.[54]

Immediately below I shall explore further Bloch's contribution to my approach. For the moment, let me mobilize but one aspect of "the techniques of archaeology:" stratification. Archaeologists, it is well known, infer much from the ways that artifacts are found in particular strata of their excavations, building up more complete pictures of the world of those artifacts by coordinating the remains from a particular stratum. Similarly, by piecing together the different relics of discourse that we find within a given stratum of Rabbinic literature, we can begin to reconstruct richer pictures of that stratum.

Comparison with a roughly analogous (but also interestingly different) historiographical situation may be helpful. Jonathan M. Hall has undertaken a detailed study of the traditions relating to the origins and movements of the various "ethnic" groups that made up the Greek people in early antiquity. These narratives which have reached us in written texts produced sometimes a millennium or more later than the events have been taken by many scholars to be the records of memories of the historical movements and divisions of original ethnic groupings, notably the Dorians in archaic Greece. In a character sketch of these "historically positivist" approaches which could be applied as well, mutatis mutandis, to the procedures of most historians of Rabbinic Judaism as well, Hall writes:

> The series of somewhat contradictory variants in which such myths exist are then understood as pathological aberrations from a 'real' historical

---

[54] Ibid., p. 53.

memory—a collective amnesia, or even polymnesia, resulting from the passage of time. The task of the historical positivist is to reconcile these contradictory variants within a single, rationalising work of synthesis in order to reveal 'what actually happened.... The problem with the historically positivist approach is that it views myths of ethnic origins as the passive trace-elements of groups whose 'objective' existence is deemed to stand independently of those same myths.[55]

Indeed, this could be understood as the very essence of positivist historiography, namely its twin assumptions that there is a real objective historical past that is external to the documents within which that past has been "represented" and that the discovery of that objective past is external to the subjectivity of the researcher and her own assumptions and historical conditionings (or can be made so).[56] In contrast, Hall suggests that if we do not accept ethnicity as a "primordial given" but rather as an ongoing project of construction of identity "that is repeatedly and actively structured through discursive strategies," then these very narratives, these myths of origins can be understood as elements in these discursive strategies, as at least some of the "media through which such strategies operate ... as cognitive artifacts which both circumscribe and actively structure corporate identity, so that whenever the relationships between groups change, then so do the accompanying genealogies." According to Hall, the mythical variants, instead of being the problem for historiography in which guise they appear in traditional positivist historiographies, become now instead a resource for history writing, as these very variants indicate "specific stages in the discursive construction of ethnicity."[57]

The analogy to my project should be apparent. Similarly abandoning positivist historiography that considers the aggadot (legends) of Yavneh as more or less corrupted memories and traces of the actual events that took place there with the concomitant necessity to extract the historical kernel out of the variants and corruptions of the legendary texts, I too am investigating how the shifting and varying legends themselves indicate specific stages in the discursive construction of religious identity as seen by the rabbis. This enables the work to take up a position between the positivist historiography most excellently represented by Gedaliah Alon and an opposite extreme that would see absolutely no historical value in the legends of the rabbis. The work is not, however,

---

[55] Hall, *Ethnic*, p. 41.
[56] See also Ibid., pp. 6–7.
[57] Ibid., pp. 42–43.

positivist in that it recognizes the inevitable textuality of this very historical record. Not an attestation to something outside of themselves which we can discover (or reconstruct, or even construct) in order to hypothesize things "as they really were," these literary artifacts are the very stuff of the history themselves and their interpretation as historical objects can be no more "objective" than could any interpretation of any literary text as such. It is just that in this case the interpretation itself takes as part of is interpretative goal the interpretation of the "outside" reality to which the text can be explained as alluding by indirection.

I have further modified the synchronic approach by supposing that the Rabbinic narratives do not only give us insight into the static or synchronic moment of their own production but also record some form of historical memory of broad shifts and conflicts that have taken place and are taking place.[58] For example, I would now read a biographical narrative that tells the story of the death of a rabbi after a particularly bitter dialectical contest and the regret of his opponent at having "caused his death" and lost his intellectual partner as possibly teaching us something about the abandonment of certain types of dialectic within the Rabbinic movement in fourth/fifth-century Babylonia (where the story was told), while teaching us next to nothing, of course, about the lives of those individual rabbis (Palestinians of the third century).[59] I do, moreover, believe that there is some (limited) historical depth to be afforded by the gap between the sources and redactional level of the major Rabbinic texts (not equal to the gap between time of redaction and the ostensible time of the "speakers" of the sources, however). These are, after all, texts composed out of the found objects of earlier texts and traditions, suggesting that a gap between the redactional deployment of these objects in his narrative and some earlier partly reconstructable deployments can be discerned.[60] Once again, in Hall's words:

> Faced with both the totality, or system, of the genealogies and the individual genealogemes, one is able to discern how the latter are hierarchically clustered to constitute the former. Yet within the overall system one

---

[58] Another way of saying this would be to suggest that the use of these narratives is analogous to the use of "oral traditions" in historiography, on which see William A. Graham, *Beyond the Written Word: Oral Aspects of Scripture in the History of Religion* (Cambridge, 1987), p. 14.

[59] This example was suggested by my friend, Dr. Dina Stein.

[60] This is, I concede a methodologically somewhat risky departure from the principles articulated by Arnold Maria Goldberg to the effect that once edited, the text is exclusively synchronic. See his Arnold Maria Goldberg, "Der Diskurs Im Babylonischen Talmud. Anregugengen Für eine Diskursanalyse," in *Frankfurter Judaistische Beiträge* 11

will also be able to recognise "fracture points"—that is, nodes which contradict or challenge the internal logic. Sometimes these fracture points will occur between variant versions and reflect both authorial and sociopolitical intention, but sometimes they will arise within individual accounts which may betray originally diverse social applications.[61]

This also gives us some possibility of discerning a dynamism, a diachrony within the documents, a kind of internal variation within the document, particularly when we can grasp tension between the "redactor" and the "source" or when we can perceive a diachronic shift between them analogous in kind to the variations taken to indicate diachronic shifts and tensions between the different documents as well.[62]

The Quest of the Historical Yavneh Versus the Search for the Yavneh(s) of Faith

Following this approach, and reading Yavneh as the effect of discursive and social practices and not the cause of them, we can see how different sets of such practices occurring in diverse Rabbinic times and places produced (and still produce) different "Yavnehs," different legends of origin for those practices. The form of textuality to which Cohen's description answers and which is almost definitional for what we think of as Rabbinic Jewish textuality then appears as a product of the latest strata in the development of classical Rabbinic Judaism and its texts, while earlier strata suggest an ecclesiology (if not quite a set of textual practices) more like that which we think of as belonging to Christian orthodoxy from Irenaeus on.

Viewing the shifts in the narrative conceptions of Yavneh as a series of diachronically linked synchronic moments, not as conflicting accounts

---

(1983), pp. 1–45. To this Schaeffer has added the following paraphrase: "The text as it stands is exclusively synchronic and since we cannot go back beyond this state, there remains only the classifying description of that which is there. A historical differentiation is deliberately, excluded because in effect the texts do not permit it;" Peter Schäfer, "Research Into Rabbinic Literature: The State of the Question," in *Journal of Jewish Studies* 37 (1986), p. 145. I confess to being somewhat mystified at Neusner's objection to this point of Goldberg's, since it would seem on one reading to be most congenial to the documentary approach; Neusner, *Foundation*, p. 38.

[61] Hall, *Ethnic*, p. 87.

[62] This is, hopefully, a way of reconciling the powerful insights of Neusner's documentary hypothesis with the equally compelling insights of such scholars as Kalmin, who have focused on the manifest indications of historical depth within the documents.

of the "real" council of Yavneh, has profound effects on our understanding of the chronology of the "parting of the ways," because conceptions of Yavneh and its Pharisaic ecclesiology are at the very heart of the stories that we tell of how Christianity and Judaism became separate religions. This modern scholarly moment is no different. Just as for the "classic" approach disputed by Cohen (and in other ways by many other scholars), Yavneh marked the point at which Judaism socially drove the Christians out of the synagogue, for Cohen himself, Yavneh was the moment at which a Rabbinic ecclesiology was founded that would forever mark Jewish orthodoxy as structurally different in highly significant ways from that of orthodox Christianity.

The problem is not unlike, I suggest, the problem of the very different portrayals of Jesus in the different Gospels.[63] Just as each Gospel presents us with a different Jesus, so the different Rabbinic texts present us with different Yavnehs, each in accord with the Rabbinic ecclesiology being promoted by the community within which the given Rabbinic text was produced.

In addition to an essential agreement in historiographical method between Cohen and Goodman, there is a common substantive thrust to their work as well. In both accounts, Christianity gets separated off from Judaism very early, in Goodman (and in the traditional view) via the exclusiveness of the Yavneh project, in Cohen precisely owing to its inclusiveness, which produces a structural differentiation of the two religions. In one fashion or its opposite, then, both of these scholars (and most of their fellows—I use them here as synecdoche of very widespread trends within Rabbinic-period historiography) accept the mutually orthodox narrative of both Christianity and Judaism to have been separate and bounded entities quite early on in their histories.

Viewed as what produced the narrative of Yavneh, not as what is contained or reflected within it, the processes of social and structural differentiation of Rabbinic Judaism from Christianity of which both Goodman and Cohen speak were centuries-long, multiply determined, and ramified. "Yavneh" was the work of four centuries. We have very little access to what really happened at Yavneh, the historical Yavneh, and the different Yavnehs projected by different Rabbinic texts are as specific and as differentiated in their religious ideologies as the different

---

[63] See also William Scott Green, "What's in a Name? The Problematic of Rabbinic Biography," in his *Approaches to Ancient Judaism: Theory and Practice* (Missoula, 1978), vol. I, pp. 77–96.

Jesuses projected by the different Gospels. Studying these different Yavnehs of faith gives us, therefore, access to a diachronic developmental pattern within Rabbinic ecclesiology.

A perhaps more precisely homologous comparison than the Gospels is provided by the literary construction of the Council of Nicaea itself within Christian textual practice. As historians of Christianity have observed for some time now, "Nicaea" is largely the retrospective textual and then legendary construction of a primal scene of the triumph of orthodoxy.[64] A solution to the seeming aporia in descriptions of Rabbinic Judaism as rigid and exclusivistic or as inclusive and elastic is to realize that Yavneh itself, like Nicaea, is a foundation legend, or rather, a series of changing legends.[65] Just as the authority of the Council of Nicaea took time to produce, the portrayal of Yavneh in the Rabbinic literature of the early third century underwent a reinterpretation in the second half of the fourth century to receive a normative status. In any case, that retold and ultimately definitive Yavneh legend finally fits Cohen's description of the "creation of a society based on the doctrine that conflicting disputants may each be advancing the words of the living God."[66] As already remarked, the very phrase that Cohen refers to here is never found in early sources, but only in the two Talmuds of late antiquity. In the Palestinian Talmud we find it:

> It is taught, a heavenly voice went out and said, "These and these are the words of the Living God, but the Law is like the School of Hillel." Where did the voice go out? R. Bibbi said in the name of R. Yohanan, "In Yavneh the voice went out" (Y. Yabmut [sic] 1:6, 3b).

---

[64] See Michel René Barnes, "The Fourth Century as Trinitarian Canon," in Lewis Ayres and Gareth Jones, ed., Christian Origins: Theology, Rhetoric, and Community (London, 1998), pp. 47–67, testifying compellingly to this consensus. See also Lim, *Disputation*, pp. 182–216, and Virginia Burrus, *Begotten, not Made: Conceiving Manhood in Late Antiquity* (Stanford, 2000), pp. 57–59.

[65] It must, however, be made clear that, even though it is a foundation myth, the idea of a Synod at Yavneh is hardly a "myth of Christian scholarship," pace David Aune, "On the Origins of the 'Council of Yavneh' Myth," in *Journal of Biblical Literature* 110, no. 3 (Fall, 1991), pp. 491–493. Both the early third-century Mishnah and the later Talmud are full of material that suggests that Yavneh was imagined as a council by Jewish texts much before Spinoza. Both the exclusivist and the pluralist version of Yavneh are encoded, then, within Rabbinic literature itself. Both the early one of conflict and exclusion and the later one of "agreement to disagree" are versions of Yavneh. This will emerge when we read the different "myths" of the Council of Yavneh in the third century tannaitic or fourth-fifth century amoraic contexts of their literary production, and not in the first-century context of their ostensible subject-matter, as the nineteenth-century (and later) positivist historians had done.

[66] Cohen, "Yavneh," p. 51.

Cohen is right, I think, but for Cohen's prospective "creation," substitute a retrospective, nostalgic, and utopian "imagination of a society." The Yavneh that he describes is a product of the late myth-making discourse of the Talmud.

The Myth of Yavneh and the "Curse of the Christians"

Considering the Council of Yavneh as a real historical, religious, political event, New Testament scholars have accredited to reaction against the activities of this conciliar body everything from the ire against Jews in the Gospel of John to Jesus's Sermon on the Mount in Matthew.[67] Our efforts in Jewish historiography to account for Yavneh will have, therefore, in addition to their obvious consequences for understanding the history of Rabbinic Judaism, some necessary and immediate consequences for Christian interpretation and church history. A vitally important case in point for the current inquiry is the so-called *birkath hamminim*, or "curse of the heretics," sometimes even referred to as the "curse of the Christians," which, allegedly instituted at the real Yavneh toward the end of the first century, is frequently taken as the cause of the "final break" between Judaism and Christianity. Until quite recently in many scholarly quarters (and to this day in most popular ones) this liturgical curse was taken as a project for driving the Jewish-Christians out of the Synagogue and the precipitating factor of the final break between Christianity and Judaism, the so-called "parting of the ways." This reconstruction of the history has been thoroughly called into question in recent years by both Jewish and Christian scholars, beginning with Peter Schäfer, Günther Stemberger, and Reuven Kimelman.[68] In the United States by 1985, Wayne Meeks

---

[67] William David Davies, *The Setting of the Sermon on the Mount* (Cambridge, 1976), pp. 256–315. "The majority opinion is that the First Gospel was composed in the final quarter of the first century A.D."; W. D. Davies and Dale C. Allison Jr, Matthew, *International Critical Commentary* (Edinburgh, 1988), vol. I, p. 128. The chronology, accordingly, works only if we assume the Council of Yavneh to have been a real event as recorded in Rabbinic literature.

[68] Peter Schäfer, "Die Sogenannte Synode von Jabne. Zur Trennung von Juden und Christen Im Ersten/zweiten Jahrhundert n. Chr," in *Judaica* 31 (1975), pp. 54–64; 116–24; Günther Stemberger, "Die sogennante 'Synode von Jabne' und das frühe Christentum," in *Kairos* 19 (1977), pp. 14–21; Reuven Kimelman, "Birkat Ha-Minim and the Lack of Evidence for an Anti-Christian Jewish Prayer in Late Antiquity," in E. P. Sanders, A. I. Baumgarten, eds., *Aspects of Judaism in the Greco-Roman Period*, and Alan Mendelson, *Jewish and Christian Self-Definition* (Philadelphia, 1981), vol. 2, pp. 226–244; 391–403.

would recognize that "the Birkat ha-minim has been a red herring in Johannine research."[69] In 1992, the leading Israeli scholar of early Christianity, David Flusser, would write: "[i]t has been proven conclusively that the Blessing of the Heretics was not established at Yavne in order to remove the Christians from the community of Israel,"[70] and, by 1995, Stephen G. Wilson would remark in turn, "it is equally true that the Johannine evidence has been a red herring in trying to understand the Birkat ha-minim."[71]

There is every reason to doubt that the so-called curse of the heretics was formulated under Gamaliel II at Yavneh or that it existed at all before the end of the second century. The only source we have for this "Yavnean" institution is a Babylonian talmudic story from the fourth or fifth century of Rabban Gamaliel's asking Samuel the Small to formulate such a blessing, the latter forgetting it a year later and meditating for two or three hours in order to remember it (B. Ber. 28b–29a). This hardly constitutes reliable evidence, or indeed evidence at all.[72] The aroma of legend hovers over this entire account.[73] In the Palestinian Talmud Berakhot 4:3, 8a, apologetic reasons for retroactively ascribing this "blessing" to Yavneh are indicated explicitly. One might as well attempt to write the history of early Britain on the basis of *King Lear* or of colonial America using James Fenimore Cooper as one's only source.

---

[69] Wayne A. Meeks, "Breaking Away: Three New Testament Pictures of Christianity's Separation from the Jewish Communities," in Jacob Neusner and Ernest S. Frerichs, eds., *"To See Ourselves as Others See Us:" Christians, Jews, "Others" in Late Antiquity* (Chico, 1985), pp. 102–03. In earlier work, Meeks had completely "bought" the Martyn hypothesis; Wayne A. Meeks, "The Man from Heaven in Johannine Sectarianism," in *Journal of Biblical Literature* 91 (1972), p. 69.

[70] See, for instance David Flusser, "Some of the Precepts of the Torah from Qumran (4QMMT) and the Benediction against the Heretics," in *Tarbis* LXI, no. 3–4 (April–September 1992), p. 371 (Hebrew with English summary). In 1993, P. W. van der Horst published a critical survey of the entire question: "The Birkat Ha-Minim in Recent Research," in *Hellenism-Judaism-Christianity: Essays on Their Interaction, Contributions to Biblical Exegesis and Theology* (Leuven, 1998), pp. 113–124.

[71] Stephen G. Wilson, *Related Strangers: Jews and Christians 70–170 C.E.* (Minneapolis, 1995), p. 180. Jack T. Sanders, *Schismatics, Sectarians, Dissidents, Deviants the First One Hundred Years of Jewish-Christian Relations* (Valley Forge, 1993), pp. 58–61, still reflects, however, the older views, as does Dunn, *Partings*, p. 222. I am also in obvious disagreement with Birger Pearson, "1 Thessalonians 2:13–16: A Deutero-Pauline Interpolation," in *The Emergence of the Christian Religion: Essays on Early Christianity* (Harrisburg, 1997), pp. 72–73, n. 74, although only on this point.

[72] Pace Stemberger, "Synode," p. 16.

[73] And yet, on the basis of these data, Skarsaune is prepared to conclude that, "The prayer was introduced between 70 and 100 A.D., and had for its purpose to prevent Jewish Christians and other heretics from staying within the synagogue community;" Oskar Skarsaune, *The Proof from Prophecy—A Study in Justin Martyr's Proof-Text Tradition:*

Stephen G. Wilson has clearly made the point:

> The influence of the Yavnean sages on Jewish thought and practice between 70 and 135 C.E. and beyond should not be overestimated. Their decisions were not imposed overnight, nor were they felt uniformly across all Jewish communities. The Rabbinic account of the introduction of the Birkat ha-minim [curse against the heretics] is thus a retrospective, punctiliar summary of what was in reality a lengthy process. The spread of their influence was gradual and almost certainly did not encompass all Jewish communities until well beyond the second century.[74]

Not only should we not overestimate "the influence of the Yavnean sages," we should also not overestimate our knowledge of the activity of those sages between 70 and 135, since the earliest information we have about them is from the Mishnah redacted at the end of the second century. Moreover, *birkath hamminim* is not mentioned in that document at all. Our very first attestation of this institution, in a rhetorical form indicating that it is a novum, in fact is found in the Tosefta, generally regarded as having been edited some time around the middle of the third century. Finally, we should not, indeed cannot, assume Rabbinic power over or even influence on virtually any Jewish community other than perhaps their own sub-group of Palestinian (and later Babylonian) Jews until we can document it very late in the period. The Rabbinic account of the introduction of the *birkath hamminim* is thus not only a summary at a single point in time of what had been a lengthy process, as Wilson has seen clearly, but also one for which the earliest evidence is from the mid-third century, one which tells us, even for then, very little about Jewish practice at all.

Text-Type, Provenance, Theological Profile (Leiden, 1987), p. 290. Skarsaune insists that "the patristic evidence cannot easily be dismissed," but, as I shall argue immediately, there simply is no patristic witness that counts as evidence for the proposition that a formal liturgical curse against Christians existed before the fourth century.

[74] Wilson, *Related Strangers*, p. 181. Compare the general point of Gregory Nagy (with respect to Greek culture): "Ancient Greek institutions tend to be traditionally retrojected, by the Greeks themselves, each to a proto-creator, a culture hero who gets credited with the sum total of a given cultural institution. It was a common practice to attribute any major achievement of society, even if this achievement may have been realized only through a lengthy period of social evolution, to the episodic and personal accomplishment of a culture hero who is pictured as having made his monumental contribution in an earlier era of the given society;" Gregory Nagy, *Poetry as Performance Homer and Beyond* (Cambridge and New York, 1996), p. 76. We could imagine the Yavneh myth—with its "culture heroes," from Yohanan ben Zakkai to Aqiba—developing, then, on this pattern, in any case. It seems to me a fortiori that it is plausible in a case in which institutions—various modes of Judaism, including "Christianity"—are in direct competition (by which I do not mean necessarily competition for adherents but surely for legitimacy).

The first more or less datable mentions of the anathema against the heretics, in fact, occur in the same Rabbinic document, the mid-third century Tosefta, in which the first explicit mentions of disciples of Jesus are to be found. And while they themselves are almost certainly of somewhat earlier origin than the redacted text, they are with equal certainty not datable to the first century. There is a very important, if somewhat obscure, text in the Tosefta, that reads, "The eighteen blessings which the sages have said correspond to the eighteen mentions of [God's name] in [Psalm 29]. He shall include [mention] of the *minim* [heretics] in the blessing of the Pharisees [lit., Separatists]," T. Ber. 3:25.[75] Since "blessing" means curse here,[76] this text has been a real skandalon for scholars, because it seems to imply that the Pharisees were cursed in the early synagogue. There have been many attempts to emend this text, but as Saul Lieberman points out, it cannot be emended against all witnesses. Lieberman accordingly understands "Pharisees" here to mean those who "separate themselves from the public," and thus as the prototypical sect (the apparent etymological meaning), thereby endangering the unity of the people. He concludes that the Tosefta is referring to an early curse on them to which a curse on the minim was later appended or folded in.[77]

In contrast to my master, I would not be able to date this inclusion earlier than the third-century context in which the Tosefta was redacted or the immediately preceding decades, since the very term *minim* is attested only from the Mishnah at the end of the second century. Origen, roughly contemporary with the Tosefta, provides indirect evidence for the point that there was no early curse against Christians or Christianity as well. He writes that: "up till his own days the Jews curse and slander Christ" (Hom. Jer. X 8,2; XIX 12,31; Hom. Ps. 37 II 8). "But that is not what the Birkat ha-minim is about," comments P. W. van der Horst, "and in view of the fact that no Church father was better informed about Judaism than Origen, one may reasonably assume that curses against Christianity in a synagogual [sic] prayer would

---

[75] Saul Lieberman, *The Tosefta according to Codex Vienna, with Variants from Codices Erfurt, London, Genizah Mss. and Editio Princeps (Venice, 1521). Vol. 1: Order Zeraim* (New York, 1955), pp. 17–18.

[76] Not a euphemism, the "blessings" are that which Jews pray for; the curse is a curse on our enemies and thus a blessing to us, so to speak.

[77] It is not impossible to imagine, even, that it is the Qumran sectaries who were originally so designated.

certainly have been known to him and been mentioned by him. It is a telling fact that he fails to refer to any such prayer."[78]

An earlier curse of the sectarians [פרושים = Pharisees!] became the model for the curse of the heretics and did so, for all we can know, sometime in the third century. The most inviting context for the talmudic narrative is, in my opinion, the anathematizing of heretics that we find attested in the legend-encrusted councils of the late third and early fourth centuries, notably the Council of Antioch (260) in which Paul of Samosata and his followers were anathematized[79] and, more famously, the Council of Nicaea (325). It is perhaps going too far to suggest that the late stories of Yavneh were, in part, a kind of reflex of stories about Ecumenical Councils, but it is not, I think, extravagant to imagine that something was in the air of discourse at that time. I think that formal anathematization was of importance to both nascent Christianity and Judaism at this time and for similar reasons, namely the effort on the part of certain power groups and leaders to make a difference, to construct a binary opposition where none yet existed between them. It is of importance in this regard to remember to what extent the anathematized heretics of both the Rabbinic and Christian practices are marked, directly or indirectly, as virtual adherents of what will become, the other religion.

Once the evidence of and for a so-called curse of the heretics before the third century is removed from the picture, there is no warrant at all to assume an early Palestinian curse directed at any Christians.[80] I am not claiming to know that there was no such thing, but instead suggesting that we cannot know at all, and that it is certain, therefore, that we cannot build upon such a weak foundation an edifice of Jewish-Christian parting of the ways.[81]

In the historiography of early Judaism and Christianity, however, much weight indeed has been placed on the Council of Yavneh and its alleged institution of the "curse of the Christians." J. Louis Martyn's elegant and otherwise compelling hypothesis about the origins of the

---

[78] van der Horst, "Birkat-Haminim," p. 116.
[79] See Virginia Burrus, "Rhetorical Stereotypes in the Portrait of Paul of Samosata," in *Vigiliae Christianae* 43 (1989), pp. 215–225, with earlier literature.
[80] See also Martin Goodman, *State and Society in Roman Galilee, A.D. 132–212* (Totowa, 1983), p. 86, implying as well such a denial.
[81] Reuven Kimelman, "Birkat Ha-Minim," has suggested that the assumption that the so-called curse of the minim denotes automatically Christians "is behind the oft-repeated assertion that about the year 100 the breach between Judaism and Christianity became irreparable."

Johannine Community stands and falls on this assumption,[82] as does W. D. Davies's work on the Sermon on the Mount. In contrast to Davies's classic position that the "Sermon on the Mount" is "the Christian answer to Jamnia [Yavneh],"[83] it is possible to hypothesize that at least one version of "Yavneh" was produced in the talmudic imaginaire as a sort of Rabbinic answer to the conciliar formations of the Christian fourth century—themselves, as we have seen, the product of a certain imaginaire as well. While the retrospective construction of Nicaea by Athanasius and his followers involved the production of an imaginary enemy, "the Arians,"[84] the retrospective construction of Yavneh in late fourth-century (or even later!) Rabbinic texts involved the denial of real enmity and the production of an imaginary and utopian comity.

I abandon the quest for the historical Yavneh and instead embark on a quest for a New Historicist Yavneh,[85] or rather Yavnehs, a set of diachronically emplotted genealogies (essentially two) that will form the poles of what was surely a slow, almost imperceptible set of transformations. These transformations led Rabbinic Judaism to those textual practices which we take to be most characteristic of it, those that mark it as most insistently other to Western "Christian" textuality, midrash and Talmud.

---

[82] Daniel Boyarin, "The *Ioudaioi* in John and the Prehistory of 'Judaism,'" in *Festschrift for Calvin Roetzel* (2002).

[83] Davies, *The Setting of the Sermon on the Mount*, p. 315, and see Jacob Neusner, *Eliezer Ben Hyrcanus: The Tradition and the Man* (Leiden, 1973), vol. II, pp. 333–334.

[84] "'Arianism' as a coherent system, founded by a single great figure and sustained by his disciples, is a fantasy—more exactly, a fantasy based on the polemic of Nicene writers, above all Athanasius;" Rowan Williams, *Arius: Heresy and Tradition* (London, 1987), p. 82. Also, "the term 'Arian' seems to have been Athanasius' own coinage and his favored appellation for his opponents (unless he could call them 'Ariomaniacs'). Apparently it was only in 341, however, that the Eastern bishops learned that they were being called 'Arians,'" Joseph T. Lienhard, S. J., "The 'Arian' Controversy: Some Categories Reconsidered," in *Theological Studies* 48 (1987), p. 417. This, moreover, represents the consensus of present-day scholarship on the trinitarian controversies.

[85] Stephen D. Moore and Susan Lochrie Graham, "The Quest of the New Historicist Jesus," in *Biblical Interpretation* 5, no. 4 (1997), pp. 437–463.

Bibliography

Athanasius, *Athanasius Werke*. Edited by H. G. Opitz (Berlin, 1934).
Aune, David, "On the Origins of the 'Council of Yavneh' Myth," in *Journal of Biblical Literature* 110, no. 3 (fall, 1991), pp. 491–493.
Barnes, Michel René, "The Fourth Century as Trinitarian Canon," in Ayres, Lewis, and Gareth Jones, eds., *Christian Origins: Theology, Rhetoric, and Community* (London, 1998), pp. 47–67.
Baumgarten, Albert I., *The Flourishing of Jewish Sects in the Maccabean Era: An Interpretation* (Leiden, 1997).
Bloch, Marc, *The Historian's Craft: Reflections on the Nature and Uses of History and the Techniques and Methods of Those Who Write It* (New York, 1953).
Boyarin, Daniel, *Carnal Israel: Reading Sex in Talmudic Culture* (Berkeley and Los Angeles, 1993).
——, *Dying for God: Martyrdom and the Making of Christianity and Judaism* (Stanford, 1999).
——, "The Ioudaioi in John and the Prehistory of 'Judaism'," in *Festschrift for Calvin Roetzel* (2002).
——, "On the Status of the Tannaitic Midrashim," in *Journal of the American Oriental Society* 113 (1993), pp. 455–465.
Brent, Allen, "Diogenes Laertius and the Apostolic Succession," in *Journal of Ecclesiastical History* 44, no. 3 (July, 1993), pp. 367–389.
Bruns, Gerald, "The Hermeneutics of Midrash," in Schwartz, Regina, ed., *The Book and the Text: The Bible and Literary Theory* (Oxford, 1990), pp. 189–213.
Burrus, Virginia, *Begotten, Not Made: Conceiving Manhood in Late Antiquity* (Stanford, 2000).
——, "Rhetorical Stereotypes in the Portrait of Paul of Samosata," in *Vigiliae Christianae* 43 (1989), pp. 215–225.
Cohen, Shaye J. D., "The Significance of Yavneh: Pharisees, Rabbis, and the End of Jewish Sectarianism," in *Hebrew Union College Annual* LV (1984), pp. 27–53.
Daum, Robert, "Describing Yavneh: The Founding Myths of Rabbinic Judaism." Ph.D. Diss. (Berkeley: University of California, 2001).
Davies, William David, *The Setting of the Sermon on the Mount* (Cambridge, 1976).
Dunn, James D. G., *The Partings of the Ways between Christianity and Judaism and Their Significance for the Character of Christianity* (London and Philadelphia, 1991).
Eusebius, *Life of Constantine. Introduction, Translation and Commentary by Averil Cameron and Stuart G. Hall* (Oxford and New York, 1999).
Flusser, David, "Some of the Precepts of the Torah from Qumran (4QMMT) and the Benediction against the Heretics," in *Tarbis* LXI, no. 3–4 (April–September, 1992), pp. 333–374, ii.
Foucault, Michel, "What is an Author?" in Bouchard, Donald F., ed., *Language, Counter-Memory, Practice: Selected Essays and Interviews* (Ithaca, 1977), pp. 124–127.
Friedman, Shamma, "Literary Development and Historicity in the Aggadic Narrative of the Babylonian Talmud: A Study Based upon B.M. 83b–86a," in Waldman, Nahum W., ed., *Community and Culture: Essays in Jewish Studies in Honor of the 90th Anniversary of Gratz College* (Philadelphia, 1985), pp. 67–80.
Gafni, Isaiah M., *Land, Center and Diaspora: Jewish Constructs in Late Antiquity* (Sheffield, 1997).
Gallagher, Catherine, and Stephen Greenblatt, *Practicing New Historicism* (Chicago, 2000).
Goldberg, Arnold Maria, "Der Diskurs Im Babylonischen Talmud. Anregugengen Für eine Diskursanalyse," in *Frankfurter Judaistische Beiträge* 11 (1983), pp. 1–45.
Goodblatt, David, "The Beruriah Traditions," in *Journal of Jewish Studies* 26 (1975), pp. 68–86.

———, "From History to Story to History: The Rimmon Valley Seven," in Schäfer, Peter, ed., *The Talmud Yerushalmi and Graeco-Roman Culture* (Tübingen, 1998), vol. I, pp. 173–199.

Goodman, Martin, "The Function of Minim in Early Rabbinic Judaism," in Cancik, H., H. Lichtenberger, and P. Schäfer, eds., *Geschichte—Tradition—Reflexion: Festschrift für Martin Hengel zum 70 Geburtstag* (Tübingen, 1996), vol. 1, pp. 501–510.

———, *State and Society in Roman Galilee, A.D. 132–212* (Totowa, 1983).

Goshen-Gottstein, Alon, *The Sinner and the Amnesiac: The Rabbinic Invention of Elisha Ben Abuya and Eleazar Ben Arach* (Stanford, 2000).

Graham, William A., *Beyond the Written Word: Oral Aspects of Scripture in the History of Religion* (Cambridge, 1987).

Green, William Scott, "What's in a Name? The Problematic of Rabbinic Biography," in *Approaches to Ancient Judaism: Theory and Practice* (Missoula, 1978), vol. I, pp. 77–96.

Hall, Jonathan M., *Ethnic Identity in Greek Antiquity* (Cambridge, 1997).

Hasan-Rokem, Galit, *The Web of Life—Folklore in Rabbinic Literature: The Palestinian Aggadic Midrash Eikha Rabba* (Stanford, 2000).

Hopkins, Keith, "Novel Evidence for Roman Slavery," in *Past and Present* 138 (1993), pp. 3–27.

Josephus, Flavius, *Books XVIII–XX. Vol. IX of Jewish Antiquities*. Translated by L. H. Feldman. Loeb Classical Library (Cambridge, 1965).

Kalmin, Richard, *Sages, Stories, Authors, and Editors in Rabbinic Babylonia* (Atlanta, 1994).

Kellner, Hans, "Introduction: Describing Redescriptions," in Ankersmit, Frank, and Hans Kellner, eds., *A New Philosophy of History* (Chicago, 1995), pp. 1–18.

Kimelman, Reuven, "Birkat Ha-Minim and the Lack of Evidence for an Anti-Christian Jewish Prayer in Late Antiquity," in Sanders, E. P., A. I. Baumgarten, and Alan Mendelson, eds., *Aspects of Judaism in the Greco-Roman Period* (Philadelphia, 1981), vol. 2, pp. 226–244; 391–403.

LaCapra, Dominick, "History, Language, and Reading: Waiting for Crillon," in Fay, Brian, Philip Pomper, and Richard T. Vann. Malden, eds., *History and Theory: Contemporary Readings* (1998), pp. 90–118.

Lieberman, Saul, *The Tosefta according to Codex Vienna, with Variants from Codices Erfurt, London, Genizah Mss. and Editio Princeps. Vol.: Order Zeraim* (New York, 1955).

Lienhard, Joseph T., S. J., "The 'Arian' Controversy: Some Categories Reconsidered," in *Theological Studies* 48 (1987), pp. 415–437.

Lim, Richard, *Public Disputation, Power, and Social Order in Late Antiquity* (Berkeley and Los Angeles, 1994).

Macherey, Pierre, *A Theory of Literary Production* (London, 1978).

Meeks, Wayne A., "Breaking Away: Three New Testament Pictures of Christianity's Separation from the Jewish Communities," in Neusner, Jacob, and Ernest S. Frerichs, eds., *"To See Ourselves as Others See Us:" Christians, Jews, "Others" in Late Antiquity* (Chico, 1985), pp. 93–115.

———, "The Man from Heaven in Johannine Sectarianism," in *Journal of Biblical Literature* 91 (1972), pp. 44–72.

Moore, Stephen D., and Susan Lochrie Graham, "The Quest of the New Historicist Jesus," in *Biblical Interpretation* 5, no. 4 (1997), pp. 437–463.

Motyer, Stephen, *Your Father the Devil? A New Approach to John and "the Jews"* (Carlisle, 1997).

Nagy, Gregory, *Poetry as Performance Homer and Beyond* (Cambridge and New York, 1996).

Neusner, Jacob, "Beyond Historicism, after Structuralism: Story as History in Ancient Judaism," in Neusner, Jacob, *Method and Meaning in Ancient Judaism* 3rd series (1981), pp. 217–238.

———, *The Canonical History of Ideas: The Place of the So-Called Tannaite Midrashim* (Atlanta, 1990).

———, *The Documentary Foundation of Rabbinic Culture. Mopping up after Debates with Gerald L. Bruns, S. J. D. Cohen, Arnold Maria Goldberg, Susan Handelman, Christine Hayes, James Kugel, Peter Schaefer, Eliezer Segal, E. P. Sanders, and Lawrence H. Schiffman* (Atlanta, 1995).
———, *Eliezer Ben Hyrcanus: The Tradition and the Man* (Leiden, 1973).
———, "The Formation of Rabbinic Judaism: Yavneh (Jamnia) from A.D. 70 to 100," in Haase, Wolfgang, ed., *Aufstieg und Niedergang der Römischen Welt, Principat: Religion (Judentum: Pälastinisches Judentum [Forts.])* (Berlin, 1979), pp. 3–42.
———, "Judaism after the Destruction of the Temple: An Overview," in Neusner, Jacob, *Formative Judaism: Religious, Historical, and Literary Studies, Third Series: Torah, Pharisees, and Rabbis* (Chico, 1983), pp. 83–98.
———, *Reading and Believing: Ancient Judaism and Contemporary Gullibility* (Atlanta, 1986).
Pearson, Birger, "1 Thessalonians 2:13–16: A Deutero-Pauline Interpolation," in *The Emergence of the Christian Religion: Essays on Early Christianity* (Harrisburg, 1997), pp. 58–74.
Rosman, Moshe, *Founder of Hasidism: A Quest for the Historical Ba'al Shem Tov* (Berkeley and Los Angeles, 1996).
Sanders, E. P., *Jewish Law from Jesus to the Mishnah: Five Studies* (London, 1990).
Sanders, Jack T., *Schismatics, Sectarians, Dissidents, Deviants the First One Hundred Years of Jewish-Christian Relations* (Valley Forge, 1993).
Schäfer, Peter, "Research into Rabbinic Literature: The State of the Question," in *Journal of Jewish Studies* 37 (1986).
———, "Die Sogenannte Synode von Jabne. Zur Trennung von Juden und Christen Im Ersten/zweiten Jahrhundert n. Chr.," in *Judaica* 31 (1975), pp. 54–64, 116–124.
Schwartz, Seth, *Imperialism and Jewish Society from 200 B.C.E. to 640 C.E.* (Princeton, 2001).
Segal, Alan F., *Two Powers in Heaven: Early Rabbinic Reports About Christianity and Gnosticism* (Leiden, 1977).
Simon, Marcel, "From Greek Hairesis to Christian Heresy," in Grant, Mélanges R. M., *Early Christian Literature and the Classical Intellectual Tradition* (Paris, 1979), pp. 101–116.
Skarsaune, Oskar, *The Proof from Prophecy—A Study in Justin Martyr's Proof-Text Tradition: Text-Type, Provenance, Theological Profile* (Leiden, 1987).
Stemberger, Günther, "Die sogenannte 'Synode von Jabne' und das frühe Christentum," in *Kairos* 19 (1977), pp. 14–21.
Tanner, Kathryn, *Theories of Culture: A New Agenda for Theology. Guides to Theological Inquiry* (Minneapolis, 1997).
Taylor, Joan E., *Christians and the Holy Places the Myth of Jewish-Christian Origins* (Oxford and New York, 1993).
Trout, Dennis E., *Paulinus of Nola: Life, Letters, and Poems* (Berkeley and Los Angeles, 1999).
van der Horst, P. W, "The Birkat Ha-Minim in Recent Research," in *Hellenism-Judaism-Christianity: Essays on Their Interaction. Contributions to Biblical Exegesis and Theology* (Leuven, 1998), pp. 113–124.
Vann, Richard T., "Turning Linguistic: History and Theory and History and Theory, 1960–1975," in Ankersmit, Frank, and Hans Kellner, eds., *A New Philosophy of History* (Chicago, 1995), pp. 40–69.
White, Hayden, "The Historical Text as Literary Artifact," in Fay, Brian, Philip Pomper, and Richard T. Vann, eds., *History and Theory: Contemporary Readings* (Malden, 1998), pp. 15–33.
Williams, Rowan, *Arius: Heresy and Tradition* (London, 1987).
Wilson, Stephen G., *Related Strangers: Jews and Christians 70–170 C.E.* (Minneapolis, 1995).

ON THE QUALITY OF THE RABBINIC TEXT: THE OPENING OF THE MISHNAH

Dalia Hoshen
University of Manchester

In another study, in which I engaged in the construction of a theory of the Rabbinic text, I proposed characterizing the language of the rabbis as an interpretive language that is derived from, and returns to, the Bible.[1] This understanding is more suitable the more deeply we enter into the Rabbinic text. The dialectic between commenting on the Bible and continuing to be within it is present not only in the content of the texts, and in their targets, but also in the methods of thinking reflected within them. This dialectic appears, first of all, as a theoretical philosophical principle in the understanding of the Oral Law, as an interpretive system surrounding the Written Law,[2] and is expressed in the pair of synonyms for the Oral Law: Mishnah and Midrash.[3] Although these two nouns represent certain textual genres in the Rabbinic literature,[4] we shall attempt to view them, in their shared meaning of

---

[1] This article is based on my Ph.D. dissertation: "Agnon's Writing: An Additional Tier in the Talmudic-Aggadic Literature," Bar-Ilan University, 2000 (Hebrew); see pp. 89–104 (henceforth "Agnon's Writing").

[2] See H. Albeck, *Introduction to the Mishnah* (Jerusalem and Tel Aviv, 1959), p. 3 (Hebrew). Admittedly, this holistic conception of the Oral Law as an interpretive system of the Bible is not accepted by all scholars. See the forceful opposition by G. G. Porton, "Defining Midrash," in J. Neusner, ed., *The Study of Ancient Judaism* (New York, 1981), vol. 1, pp. 65–66; see also J. Neusner, *The Four Stages of Rabbinic Judaism* (London, 1999).

[3] For the Mishnah as a general name for the Oral Law, see Albeck, *Introduction*, p. 1; M. Friedmann (Ish-Shalom), in his introduction to Mekhilta (Vienna, 1870), p. 39; L. Finkelstein, "Midrash, Halakhot, and Aggadot," in S. W. Baron, et al., eds., *Y.F. Baer Jubilee Volume* (Jerusalem, 1960), p. 29 (Hebrew). As regards the midrash, however, one scholarly view regards it as part of the Mishnah, but not synonymous (see Albeck, *Introduction*, loc. cit.), or, in the expansive definition of L. Zunz, *Die Gottesdiensnlichen Vorträge der Juden Historisch Entwickelt* (Hebrew translation: *ha-Derashot be-Yisrael ve-Hishtalshalutan ha-Historit* [Jerusalem, 1974], p. 25), as a general term for both Laws (the Oral and the Written); but see the dictum by Yohanan in B. Qid. (n. 12, below).

[4] See D. Hoshen "Midrash and Genres," in J. Neusner and A. J. Auery-Peck, eds., *Encyclopedia of Midrash* (Leiden, 2004) p. 126, where I propose a theory and application for the distribution by genre of the various disciplines of the Oral Law that differ from the accepted view in that they are not based on the contrast between connection and separation from the Bible.

"study" (since both roots, *li-drosh* and *li-shnot*, mean "to learn"),⁵ as representing the Oral Law literature in its entirety as this was phrased by Finkelstein, "This is Mishnah, this is midrash."⁶

Talmudic scholars and those researching Rabbinic language concur that the designation "Mishnah," derived from the verb *shnh* (with the meaning of repetition), was given to the Oral Law not only under the influence of Aramaic but also "since there is added importance in the Oral Law to repetition—studying several times, so that it will be preserved in one's memory, and only the student who reviewed and studied [again] what he heard has truly learned it."⁷ In other words, the Mishnah—that is, the Oral Law—is learned by review, by repetition of what was studied, so that it would be preserved in one's memory. The exercises in memory are important for the culture that adheres to the principle of oral culture, as opposed to a culture that is written and that lends itself to being written. This matter can hardly be accepted in its entirety, for just as oral teachings are not to be written, so, too, written teachings are not to be transmitted orally.⁸ The zealous defense of the written book, that it not to be uttered orally, is no less intense than the spirited activity taken to ensure that oral teachings not be committed to writing. Consequently, it can hardly be accepted that the meaning of the principle on which the Oral Law is based—*shnah* (repetitive learning)—has its foundations in mnemonic exercises that are meant to serve an oral culture with a goal of undetermined importance. Additionally, a culture interested solely in oral repetition for the sake of mnemonic exercise necessarily undergoes essential change when

---

⁵ See Zunz, *Die Gottesdiesntlichen Vorträge*, loc. cit., for the primary meaning of the term "midrash" as study and *derishah* (interpretation); and in Albeck's notes in the Hebrew edition, p. 237, n. 18: "Study is called *midrash* (Avot, chapter 1) or *Mishnah* (Sifra, *Aharei Mot* 173:9:9)."

⁶ See Finkelstein, "Midrash, Halakhot, and Aggadot," p. 29, following the response of Judah bar Ilai in a *baraita* (B. Qid. 49a) to the question: "What is Mishnah? [. . .] R. Judah says, Midrash." Finkelstein apparently brings this identification in order to resolve the textual variant between Midrash and Mishnah. It is unclear, however, how this identification fits into his explanation of the midrash as Bible with a short explanation, or how it contributes to an understanding of Judah's unclear statement itself, as is mentioned by Albeck, *Introduction*, p. 2, n. 4. At any rate, he concurs with our view that "midrash" is used with the same general meaning in relation to the Oral Law as "Mishnah."

⁷ Albeck, *Introduction*, loc. cit. See A. Bendavid, *Biblical Hebrew and Mishnaic Hebrew* (Tel Aviv, 1967), vol. 1, p. 101 (Hebrew); for an additional possibility for the source of the term "Mishnah," see below, p. XX.

⁸ See B. Git. 60b; "Agnon's Writing," p. 93.

committed to writing, with the process of its textualization. Once it was written, there is no longer any need to exercise the memory, it is no longer to be repeated—but this is not the case. The common practice of concluding the study of every tractate with the recitation of "*Hadran alekh* [we have repeated]"[9] reflects the essence of the Rabbinic text, that repeated study is required; the question that demands an answer is: why is this so?

Our approach will direct the discussion into an onto-philosophical context, within which we will see the process of study that entails review and repetition not as exercises in memory but as ensuing from the relationship between the human and the divine logos, the relationship between dynamic and diverse thought and uniform and static thought, between thought that is to be explained and that which explains.[10] We understand the term "Mishnah" as a comprehensive term for the Oral Law that pertains, in the words of Albeck, to "all that is studied orally as complementing the Written Law," along with our understanding of the term "midrash"[11] as an exhaustive term for the Oral Law that is concerned with "the general explanation and examination of the Torah;" and in Bacher's formulation:

> Aus der Bedeutung suchen, forschen (Deut. 13, 15; 17, 4, 9) entwickelte sich mit Beziehung des Verbums auf die heilige Schrift die Bedeutung: den Sinn, den Inhalt des Schrifttextess erforschen, zu verstehen suchen; den Schrifttext auslegen, erklären. Schon von Esra wird ausgesagt (Esra 7, 10) dass er sein Herz darauf richtete, *lidrosh et torat hashem*. Im 119. Psalm (V. 45 und 155) [. . .] wird die mit *darash* bezeichnete Thätigkeit auf die göttlichen Gebote und Satzungen, also wohl auch auf die Schrifttexte, in denen dieselben enthalten sind, bezogen.[12]

---

[9] This formula appears in printed volumes from recent centuries; however, some of the passages appearing in it are earlier in origin. The text of the *hadran* itself apparently dates to the Geonic period.

[10] For the ontological-philosophical essence of the biblical text as viewed by the rabbis, see the extensive discussion in "Agnon's Writing," p. 64.

[11] For a general survey of the scholarly views regarding the meaning of the term, see Porton, "Defining Midrash," loc. cit.

[12] W. Bacher, *Die exegetische Terminologie der jüdischen Traditionsliteratur* (Leipzig, 1905), p. 25 (Hebrew edition: *Erkhei Midrash* [Tel Aviv, 1923]), q.v. *darash*. See also B. Qid. 49a, the statement by Yohanan, on the question of the Talmud as to the meaning of a betrothal condition such as "On condition that I am learned [*shoneh*] [. . .] R. Yohanan said: In Torah." The Talmud concludes, in accordance with the answer by R. Judah in a *baraita* to the same question: "What is Mishnah? [. . .] R. Judah says: Midrash." Afterwards, the *Stama de'gemara* seeks to be precise with the statement by Yohanan, by joining it with that of Judah, that Torah is the exegesis [midrash] of the Torah, thereby turning the midrash into a specific genre, and not a general term for Torah study.

Thus the Oral Law is connected to two parallel processes: explanation, commentary (the midrash), and the strategy of *shinun*—repetitive learning.[13] The relationship between these two processes reflects the essence of the Oral Law as the non-establishment of the interpretation as an independent entity, one that is absolute and total, but rather as being situated within a relative interpretive system, for further comprehension. The relativity of the interpretive process ensues from the linkage to the interpreted text, from the linkage of the *midrash* of the Torah to the Torah itself. The strategy of repetitive learning aims to prevent the erection of boundaries between them and to enable incessant flow between the two.

> "*Ve-shinantam le-vanekha*"—that they be sharply impressed in your mouth, so that if someone asks you something, you will not need to stammer, but tell him immediately. And similarly, it says (Prov. 7:4), "Say to Wisdom, 'You are my sister,' and call Understanding a kinswoman;" and it says (v. 3), "Bind them on your fingers; write them on the tablet of your mind;" and it says (Ps. 45:6), "Your arrows, sharpened (*shenunim*)"—what is the reward for this? (ibid.) "[they pierce] the breast of the king's enemies; peoples fall at your feet;" and it says (Ps. 127:4), "Like arrows in the hand of a warrior are sons born to a man in his youth." What is said regarding them (v. 5): "Happy is the man who fills his quiver with them; they shall not be put to shame when they contend with the enemy at the gate" (Sifre Deut. 34:7, p. 60).

The subject of the midrash's explanation of the commandment "*Ve-shinantam le-vanekha*" is unclear. Does it refer to the verb *shanan*, which means sharp impression, and the command relates to the level of comprehension of "these instructions"—the words of the Torah? Or, perhaps, this relates to the verb *shanah*, and the command is to repeat the words of the Torah? It is similarly unclear from the midrash if the command "*Ve-shinantam*" refers to the external form of the biblical verses, which must be correctly pronounced and not mumbled and for the same reason should be repeated. Or does this refer to the content of the verses, a possibility that transfers us from the Written Law to the Oral Law? *Tosafot*, in the parallel to this midrash in B. Qid. 30a–b, explain:

> If they ask him a halakhic teaching [*devar halakhah*], or if a tractate is to be learned from him, they must be distinct in his mouth and not mumbled.

---

[13] See the version appearing in several sources: "*li-shnot ba-midrash* [to learn the midrash]" (T. Ber. 2:12, p. 8); see also Rashi's version, B. Ber. 22a: "he arranges (lays before them) the Mishnah, but not the Midrash," in contrast with the printed version: "he arranges the Mishnah but not the Talmud [*Gemara*]."

According to this, the "*davar*" that one could be asked about, as well as the *devarim haele* of which the Torah speaks are either "*devar halakhah*" or "*devar Talmud*," and therefore the content of "*ha-devarim ha-eilu*" is the Oral Law.

Rashi on Qiddushin offers the following definition: "That they be sharply impressed in your mouth"—repeat them, and examine them in depth, "so that if someone asks you [regarding them] you will not need to stammer, but tell him immediately." Rashi's commentary indicates that this does not refer to the external aspect of the Torah, the purely vocal repetition of the verses in a clear manner. Nonetheless, the "*shinun*," in his explanation, connects the two roots of the verb: repetition and sharp impression, with *shinun* as repetition understood not only in the first sense of clarity but also as referring to the function of something sharp that penetrates deeply to the innermost depths. This understanding also incorporates the second meaning of *shinun* as repetition, not as a technical means to attain external fluency, or as mnemonic exercises, but rather as related to the content and inner meaning of these words. A reexamination of Sifre in light of this integrated interpretation offers an intriguing direction for understanding the plethora of verses it cites from Proverbs and Psalms to support its unclear interpretation of the command "*ve-shinantam*." The verses from Proverbs, concerning the Torah and wisdom,[14] make no mention of the sharpened arrows, nor do they contain the verb *shanah*.[15] Nevertheless, the method proposed by these verses, and the entire chapter, is the acquisition of the Torah and Wisdom by their total and constant adoption.[16]

---

[14] The clear parallelism between the Torah and Wisdom at the beginning of the chapter in Proverbs (and, before this, in an allusion: see Deut. 4:6) enables us to understand this comparison by the Rabbis; see the midrashim on the wisdom chapter (28) in Job (Y. Hag. 2:1, 77b; B. Shab. 89a, and more).

[15] Indeed, at the end of the chapter, in verse 23 we find: "until the arrow will split his liver" in regard to the strange woman who is metaphorically the counterpart of wisdom.

[16] It is written regarding the teachings of the Torah: "Bind them on your fingers; write them on the tablet of your mind" (Prov. 7:3), and regarding Wisdom: "Say to Wisdom, 'You are my sister,' and call Understanding a kinswoman" (v. 4). See the commentary *Ha'amek Davar* of the *Netziv* (Naphtali Zevi Judah Berlin, nineteenth century, Volozhin): "That you be accustomed to it, as with your sister, with whom you are always present." Rashi (B. Qid., loc. cit.) explains: "That you be as knowledgeable [as you know] that your sister is forbidden to you." The commentaries understood this as referring to clarity (see Rabbeinu Hillel on Sifre); but see the commentary by Rashi on the verse in proverbs: "'You are my sister'—draw her near to you," influenced by the continuation of the passage: "and call Understanding a kinswoman [*moda*];" see also the commentary by Gersonides on the verse.

Here we are exposed to the meaning of the *shinun* activity as repetition and habit. Since, however, Proverbs speaks of Wisdom, this can hardly be understood as external repetition, as a habit acquired by the technical repetition of the words. When we proceed to the texts from Psalms (chap. 45),[17] which speak of the sharpened arrows that excel in their ability to penetrate deeply, whether these are the arrows of seed that are fired and create the fruit of the womb (chap. 127) or whether they are the arrows of war that penetrate the heart of the king's foes, and, with a retroactive reading, connect these two Scriptural branches to the beginning of the midrash, we receive the interpretation of Rashi that reflects the two dialectic elements active in the Oral Law. The command to repeat the words of Torah so that they will be sharply impressed in your mouth is not a mere exercise but a way to acquire them, just as wisdom is acquired, so that a person will be accustomed to them, and so they will be bound to him forever. The action of *shinun* of the words of Torah, as constant repetition of them, acts in tandem with the action of penetration to the depth of the teachings and the expansion of our comprehension. Thus we are also to understand the element of comprehensional clarity not as a static target but as dynamic and incessant penetration within the flow between the written *ha-devarim ha-eileh* and their content "so that if someone asks you;" this is a flow that, thanks to the strategy of repetition, does not remain forever within the content or form of these teachings; rather, their essence remains as a profundity that can never be exhausted.

When we come to examine the manner in which the dialectic of interpretation and repetition is fashioned in the Rabbinic texts, in their various genres (*mikra* [Scripture], midrash, halakhah, haggadah), we are presented with an unfinished text. All the texts, beginning with the Mishnah in its concise style to the expanded Talmudic discussions do not reflect textual exhaustion, as if all that can be said has been stated. The incompleteness of the Rabbinic text is primarily established from the presence of intertextual elements that were innate in the various strata of the text. The realm of the text provides the context for the discourse that fashions those elements in a certain manner and creates the character of the specific text. At the same time, however, it does

---

[17] Ps. 45 was interpreted (B. Shab. 63a) as relating to the battling style of Torah study as was also Ps. 127. See Avot de-Rabbi Nathan, addendum 2 to Version A, chap. 6, p. 159 (ed. M. Kister, *Studies in Avot de-Rabbi Nathan: Text, Redaction and Interpretation* [Jerusalem, 1998]); see also Rashi on Ps. 45:6.

not limit them from an independent dialogue, beyond or beside the dialogue that it brings into existence. We refer here not to what is termed the textual subconscious, which suggests the existence of an essence unaware of the object in which it is expressed.[18] Rather, the text in its interpretive connective structure reflects an awareness that, inherent in the elements that populate it, abides an infinite potential that is qualitative and therefore also infinitely discursive. Since the text is incapable of simultaneously presenting this diversity, neither ontologically, that is, by reaching an exhaustive examination of this potential, nor methodologically, that is, by molding this potential in a wholly harmonious simultaneous thought, instead of an analytic linear thought, it lessens the interpretive connective that it presents and imparts to it a relative, secondary, fragmentary, and incomplete coloration.[19]

M. Ber. 1:1, the first passage in the Mishnah, exemplifies this:

> From what time in the evening may the *Shema* be recited? From the time the priests enter to eat of their *terumah* [heave-offering].

We would expect a qualitative cultural transition from this beginning of the document of the textualization of the Oral Law: a collection of exhaustive teachings with beginning and end that would exempt the student from the burden of repetition and memory. This, however, is not the textual quality to which we are exposed here. Rather, it is as if we have stumbled into the middle of a discussion whose beginning is not at all distinct.[20] In other words: what is this "*Shema*" that is to be read? Who said that it is to be read, and in the evening? Its end also is unclear: "From the time when the priests enter to eat of their *terumah*." Even if we accept the view that "it was the practice of even the pure [priests] to immerse every day upon sunset [...] [and] the time for their entry to eat the *terumah* was known and distinct,"[21] we nevertheless see that the parallel in a *baraita* (see below) also found it necessary to explain when the priests entered to eat, proving from verses in Nehemiah that this was the time of "the appearance of the stars."

---

[18] For this psychoanalytical approach in interpretation, see Z. Levy, *Hermeneutics* (Tel Aviv, 1986), chap. 11 (Hebrew).

[19] For the contrasting nature of Western thought and that reflected in the Bible and sages, expressed in the difference between linear and simultaneous thought, see "Agnon's Writing," p. 73.

[20] For a description of the beginning of the Mishnah from this perspective, see also J. Neusner, *The Mishnah: An Introduction* (Northvale, New Jersey, and London, 1989), pp. 1–2.

[21] S. Albeck, *Moda'ah: Babylonian Talmud* (Warsaw, 1913), p. 1 (Hebrew).

In any event, the question arises, why did the Tannaitic texts not speak in clear and unequivocal language, stating that the *Shema* is to be read when it gets dark or "when the stars have appeared"?

The "unsuccessful" opening of the Oral Law canon did not avoid being read by its interpretive text, that is, the Talmud, and it is at the center of the beginning of its discussion of the Mishnah, which is the beginning to all the tractates of the Talmud, that as time passed also became a canon in their own right.

"On what does the Tanna base himself?" the Talmud cries out; on what text or on what missing layer[22] does the Mishnah stand when it begins with an advanced phase of the discussion? The first phase, the "what," the very fact of the obligation of reading the *Shema*, is absent. If we were to ask the Talmud's question more directly, we would say: Is this how a respected canon, whose writing was delayed for generations, begins, halfheartedly, when the gist is lacking from the chapter? Although the Tanna opened with the essence, the reading of the *Shema*, in which one accepts the yoke of the kingship of Heaven, he does not trouble himself to present it, not even briefly.[23] His statement is reflective of the middle of a discussion, with the elements that populate it not passing over to the phase of presentation, and even the role that they play in it is presented only in partial fashion. The Talmud, however, does not engage in criticism of the Tanna but rather rises to the textual challenge posed for it by the Mishnah and begins the labor of reconstruction. Thus the incomplete Mishnaic text is transformed from a flawed text that lacks logic into a context for *shinun*. *Shinun*, not in its classic sense and as was understood by many scholars as "repetition," as a means for preservation in memory, but rather repetition as a method for deeper understanding and honing the content of the teaching; *shinun* as a method for revealing the intertextual and philosophical spaces located between the fragments of the incomplete text.

---

[22] See Rashi, B. Ber. 2a, q.v. "*Heikha Kai*;" Albeck, *Moda'ah*, p. 1, who seeks to demonstrate the connection between the wording of the Mishnah: "be recited [*korin*, literally, be read]" and the commandment: "Teach them [*ve-shinantam*] to your children and speak [*ve-dibarta*] of them:" "From this we learn that the commandment consists of repetition [*shinun*] and speaking with the mouth, that every individual is obligated to recite it."

[23] Even according to the view that maintains that the Mishnah is in essence a legal code (see M. Elon, *Jewish Law: History, Sources, Principles*, vol. 3 [Philadelphia and Jerusalem, 1994], p. 1057), it could have begun with the obligation itself of the acceptance of the yoke of the kingship of Heaven. In any event, the question "From what time" cannot constitute a logical starting point.

The passive function assigned by scholars to the element of repetitive study in the Oral Law[24] is, in actuality, a creative and active element that does not change not even when it undergoes a process of textualization and ceases to be an oral culture, understood by many as a culture of memory.

The question of "On what does the Tanna base himself?" in the Talmudic reading presents the Mishnah as an interpretive text, one that is part of a broader speculative textual system. Since the Mishnah does not present the system of interpretive relations with this expanse, the opposite process occurs, in which the interpretive text becomes a text in need of interpretation. This reversal does not leave the process presented above one-directional. The Mishnaic text, rather, in its incomplete form, creates a symbiotic essence whose reconstruction requires us to constantly progress from it and beyond it into the expanse where it is situated in an interpretive relationship. The Talmud itself, despite its cry of "On what does the Tanna base himself?," continues along the same path: it intends to explain but finds itself in need of explanation.

If we follow this textual character (regarding both the Mishnah and Talmud) in an analysis of the continuation of the passage, the Talmud suggests the missing layer of the Mishnah appears to be the Bible, stating: "The Tanna bases himself on Scripture. As it is written, 'when you lie down and when you get up' (Deut. 6:8)." The reference by the Talmud to the passage in Deuteronomy, aside from its declared aim of interpreting and explaining what the Tanna omitted, is itself in need of interpretation. This is not only because of the short quote style within which it is cited, for even if we ourselves refer to the verse in its entirety ("Teach them to your children and speak of them [. . .] when you lie down and when you get up"), it is unclear from which words the Mishnah learned of the obligation of reading the *Shema*: from "Teach them to your children"? From "and speak of them"? From both?[25] Or from neither?

Matters remain unclear even if we assume that the Talmudic text does not relate to the entire series of problems raised by the verse in Deuteronomy but focuses on the connection between the referenced biblical text and the Mishnah. Accordingly, the Talmud rephrases the

---

[24] See, e.g., A. Walfish, "Literary Phenomena in the Mishnah and Their Redactional-Ideational Significance," Master's thesis, Hebrew University, Jerusalem, 1994, p. 11; appendix, p. 127 (Hebrew).

[25] Albeck, *Moda'ah*, at the beginning of his commentary, holds that the Tanna learned from both of them, but this is by no means clear.

Mishnah's question as an explanation of the verse: "When is the time of the lying-down-recitation of *Shema*." The Mishnah does not make the stylistic choice of "From what time when lying down may the *Shema* be recited?" but rather "From what time in the evening;" despite the ideational similarity between the time of lying down and "evening," this is unsuitable for a focused interpretation in the Talmud, which neglected sections of verses and important questions in order to put forth an interpretation that merely offers a general connection.

At this unpolished point, the Talmudic discussion opens an additional textual window by revealing the inter-textual expanses in which the Mishnah is situated, namely, Gen. 1:5: "And there was evening and there was morning, a first day." The half-opening of this textual window is as problematic as its predecessor, because it is unclear if the linkage of the Talmud ensued from the question that arose when relating to the verse in Deuteronomy. That verse, according to the Talmud, is the source not only of the obligation of reading the *Shema* but also of the specification that it is to be recited in the morning and in the evening, giving rise to the question of why the Tanna spoke first of evening and only then of morning.[26] The first answer proposed by the Talmud is that the verse in Deuteronomy mentions evening first: "when you lie down and when you get up." The second answer ("And if you like, I can answer...") is that the Mishnah is based on the verse in Genesis[27] or that the connection indicates an independent and parallel textual focus upon which the Tanna bases his teaching. This possibility is strengthened not only because it is presented as the second possible solution: "the Tanna bases himself on the Bible" (although we cannot rule out the prospect, presented above, that this is a silent transition to a question that arose in the wake of the opening of the window in Deuteronomy), but also because when the entire verse in Genesis is opened: "God called the light Day, and the darkness He called Night.

---

[26] According to the order in the Talmudic passage, the two questions are raised separately. The first: "On what does the Tanna base himself?" and the second: "Furthermore, why does he first deal with the evening [*Shema*]? Let him begin with that of the morning." From the continuation, however, which returns to "On what does the Tanna base himself?" in the answer "The Tanna bases himself on Scripture," some redactor's hand appears to be at work here.

[27] See *Penei Yehoshua* (Jacob Joshua ben Zevi Hirsch Falk, Cracow eighteenth century), novellae on Tractate Berakhot, q.v. "*Be-Gam*," who maintains that the text in Genesis is cited in the Talmudic passage in accordance with the one who asserts that the verse in Deuteronomy does not speak specifically of the recitation of the *Shema*, but rather of Torah study in general (see B. Ber. 21b).

And there was evening and there we morning, a first day," we find that the word *erev* is linked to synonymous concepts. "Darkness" and "night" are related to the definition of *erev*, while, in parallel, the definition of day is also conceptually linked to "light" and "morning." These concepts appear in the parallel of the Mishnah in the Tosefta (see below) and also in the Talmudic passage. Consequently, the Mishnaic use of "in the evening" teaches the more profound connection to "evening" that is embraced in the verses describing the Creation.

It is difficult to decide upon a reconstruction of the interpreted elements raised in the Talmudic discussion that seem to be intermingled. Of importance, however, for our examination of the nature of the Rabbinic text is that it does not impose its textual fashioning upon the elements themselves. The Mishnaic text, in its unfinished form, transfers the arena of the textual contention beyond itself, where its strength is undoubtedly weaker and suffices to create an attenuated coloration of the expanse of hues in which it is located. The Talmudic text, despite its declared aim of interpreting and explaining, leaves the interpretive organization that it offers in a minor chord. The reflective and textual regions, whether the verses of the *Shema* in Deuteronomy, or whether the verses of the Creation in Genesis, are more complex and profound than "just any" exhaustive interpretive organization of theirs. The strength of the interpreted elements over the labor of interpretation itself is that which transforms the Rabbinic text from an interpretive text to one that requires interpretation. It should be noted, on the other hand, that the elements to be explained are elements and regions of biblical texts. Despite the reflective-textual expanse in which the Mishnah is situated, we are also witness to non-biblical formulations, such as parallel Mishnayot (*baraitot*) that disagree or not; at any rate, the biblical nuclei that are scattered throughout each of them constitute the interpretive context for the relationship between the different formulations that creates the expanse that unites them all.

This textual nature, as regards both the Mishnaic text (in its Talmudic reading) and the Talmudic text itself, is finely expressed in the continuation of the passage in Berakhot, concerning the answer of the Mishnah: "From the time the priests enter to eat of their *terumah*." The Talmud initially adopts the method of textual criticism, "Is this how one writes?", and when the labor of reconstruction begins, it changes from an interpretive text to one that requires explanation. "'From the time the priests [. . .]'—when do the priests eat of the *terumah*? From the time of the appearance of the stars. Therefore, let him say:

From the time of the appearance of the stars." From within the argument of the Talmud as to why the Tanna distorts the style of the Mishnaic text and engages in such a roundabout approach (if the time for the reading of the *Shema* is from the appearance of the stars, then say so—why involve the priests here?) we see the emergence of the perception of the Mishnaic text that was presented earlier, in the question "On what does the Tanna base himself?" The Mishnaic text is revealed to be not-simple,[28] and its not-simple style reveals its nature, which united within it textual windows and references that are within it to focal points active outside it. "This thing he incidentally wanted to teach us is that the priests may eat *terumah* from the time of the appearance of the stars; he also wants to teach us that the atonement offering is not indispensable [for the eating of *terumah*]."

Unlike the previous instance, the textual window that is opened now is presumably not connected to the subject of the Mishnah: the time of the reading of the *Shema* ("This thing he incidentally wanted to teach us"). Moreover, the textual foundation to which the Mishnah is connected is not biblical but Mishnaic, and it relates to a discussion among the rabbis concerning priestly purity; all this, however, is only seemingly so. The textual foundation to which the Mishnah is related is cited in the Talmudic passage, immediately, as a *baraita*:[29] "As it has been taught, 'As soon as the sun sets, he is clean' [Lev. 22:7]—the setting of the sun is indispensable [for his ability] to eat *terumah*, but the atonement offering is not indispensable for the eating of *terumah*." The Tannaitic discussion in this foundation is connected to the Bible (Lev. 22:7). The revealing of the biblical elements in the Mishnaic discussion, through its expansion in the *baraita*, infuses life into all the strata present in the Talmudic discussion.

The first to be affected by this process is the Mishnah, whose Tanna bases himself on the verse in Leviticus, where he regains his standing as explainer. "As soon as the sun sets, he is clean." According to the Talmudic reading, the Mishnah interprets the verse as "the cleansing of the day," that is, the day is cleansed of the sun, and the stars are seen, i.e., the appearance of the stars.[30] The wording of the Mishnah

---

[28] In contrast with those who are of the opinion that the redactive style is a "simple and lucid style" (see Elon, *Jewish Law*, p. 1078).
[29] See the same in Sifra, *Amor*, 4:4.
[30] See Hai Gaon, *Otzar ha-Gaonim, Brakhoth*, ed. B. Lewin (Haifa, 1928) p. 3; see the definition by Saadiah Gaon, Lewin's n. 3; Rashi, B. Ber. 2a.

does not mention the language of the verse, as it is cited in the parallel *baraitot*,[31] nor the conclusion of the Talmud, that this refers to the appearance of the stars. It merely refers halfheartedly, and in general language, to when the priests eat their *terumah*, and whoever seeks to know the time should go to Leviticus. But the Talmud, which "went" to Leviticus, while bearing the standard of simplicity and interpretive clarity ("Therefore, let him say: From the time of the appearance of the stars"), also retreats. The verses that are supposed to be an interpretive object start to exert a converse effect upon the interpretation and sow a fluid interpretive dynamic: "But how do you know that these words, 'As soon as the sun sets,' mean the setting of the sun, and that 'he is clean' means the clearing away of the day? Perhaps it means: When the [next morning's] sun appears, and 'he is clean' means that the man becomes clean?" That is to say, it is not clear that we can simply learn that this verse speaks of the "appearance of the stars," for it may refer to the sunrise ("the coming" of the light)[32] or to the beginning of the sunset, but not to total darkness (the "appearance of the stars");[33] while *ve-taher* may refer to the priest, and not to the day.

After an unsatisfying attempt by the Talmudic passage to make a distinction in the biblical language between "*ve-taher*" (and he was cleansed) to "*va-yitaher*" (and he will be cleansed),[34] and the conclusion that it means "the clearing away of the day" and not "the man becomes clean," the Talmud pins its hopes on the *baraita* in the Tosefta, which had been used already in the land of Israel: "They solved this from a *baraita*, it being stated in a *baraita*: The sign of the thing is the appearance of the stars." The sugya concludes: "You thereby learn that it is the setting of the sun [that makes the priest clean], and the meaning of '*ve-taher*' is the clearing away of the day." The summation, however,

---

[31] See B. Ber. 2b, "when the priests are cleansed (*metoharin*) to eat of their *teruma*;" the word *metoharin* was explained by Albeck, ibid., as: "they become clean, and this happened at the end of sunset when the stars appear." Accordingly, the verse "as soon as the sun sets, he is clean" refers to both: the day and the man/priest, but the Talmud viewed it diversely. See also Albeck there, p. 2, regarding the Tosefta's style: *zakain* as parallel to *metoharin*; if so, we should view it as another version to the same Beraita in the Talmud. At any rate both relate to the verse in Leviticus.

[32] Rashi, B. Ber. 2b, q.v. "*Dilma Biat Oro*:" "that the sun shines on the eighth day."

[33] As suggested by Tosafot, B. Ber. 2b, q.v. "*Dilma*," who disagree with Rashi.

[34] It is unsatisfying, as this grammatical function of the conversive waw is not an irregular phenomenon in the Bible. See Tosafot's comment, B. Ber. 2b, and Abraham Ibn Ezra's commentary, Leviticus, ibid. See also the continuation: "in the land of Israel they didn't hear (*la shmia laho*) that distinction, which could be understood as they didn't accept it (*la svira laho*)."

despite its intending to sound decisive and absolute, closing the interpretive dynamics that began to flow upon the opening of the textual window in Leviticus, is not closed. It is, on the contrary, opened. The interpretive non-exhaustion and the opening occur, once again, when the Tanna (this time of the *baraita*) becomes an interpreting commentator. In other words, the Talmud understood the statement by the Tanna in the *baraita* to relate to the time the priests are entitled to eat their *terumah*: "The sign of the thing is the appearance of the stars," as a commentary on Leviticus: "*ve-taher*." The interpretive solution, however, to the textual window in Leviticus is itself an additional textual window that addresses itself to Nehemiah.[35] This window is not opened at this juncture in the Talmudic discussion but rather is sealed with the fanfare of the summation of the Mishnah's textual question, that somewhat removes it from being a biblical quotation and incorporates it within the course of the Tanna's statement.

The window contains a reflective textual potential, and its opening overturns the interpretive fashioning of the Mishnah that is proposed by the Talmud. The direction in which the blocked window in Nehemiah is opened is provided by the Talmudic passage itself, in its second part, where the Talmudic discussion on the question of the priests and the reading of the *Shema* passes from interpretive textual accents to contentual emphases. With this transition, the Talmud seeks to anchor the Mishnah within the expanse of dissenting or parallel views. At this point it also touches upon that parallel *baraita* from the Tosefta that includes the text from Nehemiah:

> From what time in the evening may the *Shema* be first recited? [. . .] And the rabbis say, From the time when the priests are entitled to eat of their *terumah*. The sign of the thing is the appearance of the stars. And although there is no real proof for this, there is an allusion to this, as it is said, "And so we worked on, while half were holding lances, from the break of day until the stars appeared" [Neh. 4:15]. And it [further] says: "that we may use the night to stand guard and the day to do work" [Neh. 4:16].[36]

---

[35] See L. Ginzberg, *A Commentary on the Palestinian Talmud* (New York, 1941–1961), vol. 1, p. 13 (Hebrew), who holds that the expression "the appearance of the stars" in the *baraita* (see below) is a quotation from Nehemiah, and he would appear to be correct. Also see Albeck, *Moda'ah*: "And thus it is the practice of the rabbis, to give signs from Scripture." For our purposes, this sign is the textual window that sows an interpretive dynamic, and not as he continues: "For any law that has no root or allusion in the Written [Law], the rabbis agreed on some biblical passage that will be an indicative sign."

[36] We have chosen the version of the *baraita* that appears in B. Ber. 2b and not in our text of the Tosefta.

Why has the second verse been brought? If you object and say that the night really begins with the setting of the sun, but that they left late and came early, [I reply,] Come and hear: "that we may use the night to stand guard and the day to do work."

The question that arises is, Why does the *baraita* cite two verses from Nehemiah? The answer given is that it might be learned from the first verse that nighttime is from sunset, and only those engaged in the repair of the wall continued into the darkness, until the appearance of the stars.[37] The second verse therefore establishes a general definition of "night," which is "the appearance of the stars." The interpretation of the verses from Nehemiah does not go totally beyond the topic of the priests; on the contrary, echoes of the verse from Leviticus reverberate in it. For what connection does sunset[38] bear to the text in Nehemiah, which speaks of night and the "appearance of the stars," if it were not for the text in Leviticus connecting between "evening" and *be'at shemesh*? The verse in Leviticus reads: "The person who touches such shall be unclean until evening and shall not eat of the sacred donations [...] as soon as the sun sets, he shall be clean; and afterwards he may eat of the sacred donations" (Lev. 22:6–7). The preceding textual discussion also revolves around the question: is this same *be'at shemesh* (literally, the coming of the sun) absolute, that is, "the appearance of the stars," or sunset? Here as well, in the contentual discussion, the Talmud can ask, in the same style: "If you object and say that the evening (*erev*) really begins from the coming of the sun (*ba ha-shemesh*)," but it actually asks: "If you object and say that the night [*laylah*] really begins with the setting of the sun (*arva shemsha*)." It uses the term "*laylah*" (night) and not "*erev*" (evening) not only under the inspiration of the linguistic style of Nehemiah but also under the influence of the contentual context that this style offers, which also brings the "evening" of priestly purity and of the reading of the *Shema* into the general cosmic context of the determination of the times of day and night.[39]

---

[37] See the version in MS. Munich: "Because of the construction of the Temple [they work] early and late [until nightfall]." Albeck's rejection of this version (*Moda'ah*), merely because they engaged in the repair of the wall and not in the reconstruction of the Temple, seems incorrect, since these activities were interrelated. See the view of Maimonides (*Commentary on the Mishnah*, R.H. 4:1), who asserts that all Jerusalem was called "*Miqdash*."

[38] Certainly in this style, and in pure Rabbinical language, we would expect "*sheki'at ha-hamah*;" the style here, however, is influenced by the dynamics of "*erev*" and *bi'at ha-shemesh* based on Leviticus ibid.

[39] The headline of the second part of the Talmudic passage (within which the *baraita* in incorporated): "No. The poor man and the priest have the same time," and in the

This context returns us to the passage in Genesis mentioned at the beginning of the discussion in the Talmudic passage: "God called the light Day, and the darkness He called Night. And there was evening and there was morning, a first day." Only if we assume that there is a mutual textual relationship between the windows in Genesis and in Nehemiah can we understand the Talmud's conclusion, that we are to learn from Nehemiah that *"laylah"* is evening, that is, total darkness, meaning, the complete departure of the light.[40] At any rate, the return to the text in Genesis, with the opening of the window in Nehemiah, takes place over the head of the Talmudic passage (or below it). From this second reading, we have difficulty in accepting the abbreviated proposal that focuses upon the textual precedence afforded the evening over the morning ("And there was evening and there was morning").[41] The hypothesis that we put forth, that the passage in Genesis constitutes a window for an additional textual foundation on which the Tanna bases himself, now joins a broad and complex foundation of windows. The foundation to which we have been exposed upon the opening of the window in Nehemiah brings about the collapse of the proposal of the Talmudic discussion, that the issue of the priests is incidental in the Mishnah, and that the Mishnah could have stated clearly that the time of the reading of the *Shema* is "the appearance of the stars." Now, with the opening of the window in Nehemiah, we understand that priestly purity is used as an additional window to a textual foundation (Leviticus) for an examination of the temporal aspect of the recitation of the *Shema*, the determination of the times of day and night. The Mishnah could not simply teach: "the appearance of the stars," because the determination of "the appearance of the stars" pertains to the issue of purity, and this extends to the foundations of the world that are anchored in the Creation.[42]

Thus, it transpires that the basis on which the Tanna relies—"when you lie down and when you get up"—is connected, according to the

---

continuation: "Would you think that the poor man and the people have the same time," even though the specific interpretive context of the explanation of some Tanna's statement pertains to the roots of the general question of time.

[40] See also the novellae of Ha-Meiri on B. Ber., loc. cit. (p. 10): "Thus they accepted that as long as the light of the sun is dominant, even though hidden from us, this is not called '*ha-erev shemesh*.' [...] And what they said '*he'eriv shimsho*' [...] means the complete setting of the sun, namely, that all the light of day is gone."

[41] Rashi accepted this; see Albeck, *Moda'ah*, p. 1.

[42] For the Creation as related to the question of purity in the teachings of the Tannaim, see my article: "Zimzum and R. Aqiba's School," in *Daat* 34 (1995), p. 45 (Hebrew).

reconstruction in the Talmudic discussion, to an expanse that is not supported by only a single biblical passage (Deuteronomy) but rather stands in an expanse that opens windows to several reflective-textual focal points. The wording "From what time in the evening may the *Shema* be recited?," and not as it perhaps should be: "From what time when people lie down may the *Shema* be recited?," binds the specific time of lying down to the commandment of the acceptance of the yoke of the kingship of Heaven within a cosmic evening that is linked to the creation of heaven and earth, that is connected to purity, that is in turn associated with the construction of the Temple. The Talmud does not open these windows and the links between them. Its declared aim at the beginning of its discussion was to interpret, to reconstruct, but we quickly saw how the spilling into the biblical channel to which the Mishnah is connected overturns the Talmudic explanation. All that remains of its reconstruction are road-signs strewn with biblical cores that call the active reader to interpret the interpretation and, obviously, call for a renewed reconstruction. This reconstruction entails the opening of those biblical nuclei that open windows to textual expanses replete with details, that maintain a multidimensional dynamics: within the windows, interwindow, and even external to the windows.[43] It is the opening of the biblical channel by the Talmudic explanation that infuses the Rabbinic text itself with dynamism, instability, a multiplicity of meanings, and with its simple interpretive non-exhaustion. The last quality is patently the result of the ontological complexity of the biblical text. This maintains a system of windows of textual reference,[44] in which details are not rendered insignificant by the general rule but exist simultaneously in harmonious fashion.[45]

We learn from this introduction to the textualization of the Oral Law of the nature of the Rabbinic text, whose uniqueness does not lie solely in the fact that it is an interpretive text, one that is constantly in the shadow of the interpreted object, no matter how complicated. Rather, its uniqueness is expressed in the constant awareness, in the non-exhaustion of the interpretation, in the inferiority of the explanation.

---

[43] For an illustration of these intertextual transitions in the Rabbinic text, see "Agnon's Writing," p. 126, in the analysis of the genres in the passage in Baba Qamma.

[44] For an understanding of the quality of the biblical text as perceived by the rabbis, in comparison with the computer program "Windows," see "Agnon's Writing," p. 89.

[45] For this conception, in contrast with the Western one, see "Agnon's Writing," p. 73.

Perhaps this is the place to include the interpretation by the *Arukh*, q.v. "Mishnah:" "Like *mishneh*, meaning second [*sheniyah*] to the Torah. Why is it called Mishnah? Because it is second to the Torah that all Israel heard at Mount Sinai, this is the Written Law. Moses heard the Mishnah from on high, a second time, this is the Oral Law; we learn that it is second to the first."[46] The awareness of the Oral Law of its secondary nature is expressed in its open, unfinished, fragmentary style, which does not force the interpretive fashioning on the elements that are interpreted; on the contrary, the latter shape it. Although it is an interpretive text, either in essence or by declaration, it remains only as a directive text that contains windows to philosophical and textual focal points that open to some degree or other, but never in exhaustive fashion. These windows transform it into a text situated on the way to a drama that takes place beyond it, in which they unfold in all their detail; at that place, they mutually effect one another, and inherent within them are additional directions—windows that open to areas that extend from them onwards. The windows-text turns from a text that interprets and retreats to one that drops anchor, whose voice is heard there among many others, and whose coloration appears among many colorations that mutually converse with one another, simultaneously. This intermediate style of the Rabbinic text inscribes in its structure the mandate for infinite repetitive study of those directing signs, that lead the student/reader to reconstruction, to activity, to creative action, in the philosophical-textual substrate that they interpret, and in which they cast anchor.

If we ask the obvious textual question, What is the difference between the nature of the biblical text, as understood by the rabbis,[47] and the nature of their own text? The textual theory we have proposed for the rabbis undoubtedly draws the two closer. Despite the separation between the interpretation and what is interpreted, on the part of the rabbis, and despite the consciousness inherent in the various strata of their text regarding the inferiority of the explanation,[48] the qualities that are

---

[46] See also Albeck, *Introduction*, p. 1 and note, in the name of the early Christian Fathers; Albeck, however, identifies the pronunciation (of the early Christian Fathers): *mishneh* with *shinun*—repetitive learning, and not with the meaning of secondary; see Albeck, loc. cit., n. 2, on the interpretation of the wording *"Mishneh Torah."*

[47] For the Rabbinic perception of the biblical text as a fiery text connected to the revelation at Sinai, see "Agnon's Writing," p. 69.

[48] Zunz, *Die Gottesdiesntlichen Vorträge*, p. 24, seemingly was aware of this nature of the midrash but presented it from a negative viewpoint (as an adverse turning point that overshadows our national literature) of submission and the lack of freedom and national independence.

characteristic of the interpreted biblical text and that also adhere to the explanatory rabbinic text, and the dynamics, the openness, and the windows, bring them into a single qualitative context. Our examination leads us to conclusions contrary to those of Isaac Heinemann,[49] who maintained that the qualities typical of primitive peoples, as regards the abandonment of logic, concentration upon the detail, the tangible, withdrawal from the abstract, are characteristic of the rabbinic text. We, on the other hand, have indicated the ontological philosophical conception that the rabbis inherited from the Bible, regarding the inexhaustible nature of spirit, wisdom, and the truth. It was this conception that presumably fructified the order in the text, interrupted, introduced details that seem to those of totally linear thought as weak associations and supports, free of any logic, and inconsistent. Indeed, they reflect a different logic, one that is simultaneous, diverse, dynamic, and guided by the principle of inexhaustibility.

---

[49] Y. Heinemann, *Darkei ha-Aggadah* [The Ways of the Aggadah] (Jerusalem, 1954), pp. 8, 13, and passim (Hebrew). Although Heinemann relates mainly to Rabbinic aggadah, his observations concerning the nature of the Rabbinic text are applicable to all the genres included in the Rabbinic literature. For an opposing view, see D. Hoshen, "The Fire Symbol in Talmudic-Aggadic Exegesis," Ph.D. diss., Bar-Ilan University, 1989, Introduction (Hebrew).

THE CONSTRUCTION OF HOUSEHOLDS IN THE MISHNAH

Hayim Lapin
University of Maryland

At the center of the Mishnah's representation of Israelite society stands the household and, at its head, the householder.[1] That centrality can hardly be gainsaid, despite considerable debate as to whether that representation was "historical" (in the sense of how well it corresponds to the life course of a larger or smaller sector of the population of Roman Palestine), "ideological," or even "philosophical."[2] The pages that follow examine the makeup of households, evaluate the process of household formation, and study the stresses internal and external to the household as these are worked out in the Mishnah. The bulk of this study is devoted to an "internalist" reading of the Mishnah's treatment. In some cases such a strategy assumes heuristically—and not unproblematically—that "in practice" Mishnaic rules will have had a particular consequence (e.g., in connection with the marriage of sons). The point, however, is not to reconstruct the practiced world of the Mishnah but to draw attention to the logical underpinnings, social judgments and expectations, and areas of ideological tension in the seemingly "systemic" discourse of the Mishnah.

"Internalist" or not, it is neither helpful nor entirely possible to isolate the Mishnah from the wider set of texts that constitute its earliest and

---

[1] Readers will recognize similarities between the discussion that follows and J. Neusner, *The Economics of the Mishnah* (Chicago, 1990), pp. 51–71. At the broadest level, the differences between our approaches have to do with the respective assessment of the political economy "outside" the Mishnah (see H. Lapin, *Early Rabbinic Civil Law and the Social History of Roman Galilee* [Atlanta, 1995]; idem, *Economy, Geography, and Provincial History in Later Roman Palestine* [Tübingen, 2001]). In addition, and more specific to the question of households, my own approach begins with what I take to be units of domestic, ritual, or economic activity, rather than (as Neusner does) with the referents of *bayit* and *baʿal bayit* in the Mishnah.

[2] See, for example, in addition to Neusner, the role played by "households" in the respective treatments of C. M. Baker, *Rebuilding the House of Israel: Architectures of Gender in Jewish Antiquity* (forthcoming); M. B. Peskowitz, *Spinning Fantasies: Rabbis, Gender and History* (Berkeley, 1993); S. Safrai, "Home and Family," in *The Jewish People in the First Century* (Assen and Amsterdam, 1976), vol. 2, pp. 728–792.

most immediate layer of witnesses, comparanda, intertexts, commentaries, and appropriators (and whose discussion I have tried to relegate to the notes). At the same time, I have avoided reducing this wider body of material to a homogenized "Tannaitic" or "early Rabbinic" stratum. The Mishnah has a structural and redactional coherence all its own that sets it apart from other corpora produced in early Rabbinic circles. While there are manifest overlaps in legal detail, terminology, and citation of traditions, there are also differences in emphasis,[3] and the lines of development and interrelationship are neither entirely clear nor settled.[4]

Underlying this examination is an attempt to attend to what is sometimes referred to as the "cultural work" going on in the text of the Mishnah: the creation of a grammar of household organization and structure, of a quite deliberately gendered and hierachically organized model of economic production and social reproduction. But seeing "cultural work," if this is not merely to be identified with the rhetoric or fantasies of a text, requires that we look outside the confines of the text and attempt to situate the authors, audience, or setting of the work, to think carefully, in short, about the place of Mishnaic householders in the provincial Roman society of Palestine in the first and second century. Despite the exceedingly limited evidence available, which accounts in part for its brevity, the final section addresses the question of historicity (or, more properly, the historical contextualization of the Mishnah's ideological construction of households).

Dramatis Personae

We can begin by surveying the makeup of households. These are centered on that fixture of the Mishnah's social map, the adult, male husband and father, and, more often than not, the owner of slaves or

---

[3] See, e.g., the emphasis in Sifre Deut. (although echoing material in the Mishnah) on the appointment of "relations" (*qerôbîm*) as judges, Sifre Deut. 153, 190, 208, ed. Finkelstein, pp. 206–207, 230, 243; and particularly in connection with patronage, Sifre Deut. 17, 144, ed. Finkelstein, pp. 27–28, 198.

[4] My own view of the relationships is discussed in Appendix II of *Early Rabbinic Civil Law*, pp. 311–329. In particular, the relationship between the Tosefta and the Mishnah has seen renewed attention in recent years, e.g., S. Friedman, "The Primacy of Tosefta in Mishnah-Tosefta Parallels—Shabbat 16, 1, *kol kitbê qôdš*," in *Tarbiz* 62 (1993), pp. 313–338 (in Hebrew); J. Hauptman, "Mishnah as a Response to 'Tosefta,'" in S. J. D. Cohen, ed., *The Synoptic Problem in Rabbinic Literature* (Atlanta, 2000), pp. 13–34.

other property. There is a recurring roster of participants in the household as economic if not as domestic unit that can be expanded or contracted depending on whether the legal or cultic status of the individual members requires greater specification.[5] Thus, for instance, in contemplating death, a man might cede property to his sons (not, in this particular instance, his daughters), his wife, or to his slave (M. Pe. 3:7–8).[6] By contrast, M. B.M. 7:6, discussing the ability of a man to stipulate special terms in a labor contract that involves members of his household, distinguishes sons and daughters who have attained majority, male and female "Hebrew" slaves, and his wife, from minor sons and daughters, male and female "Canaanite" slaves, and domestic animals, the latter group having no legally effective *daat* (here in the sense of "will"). Notably, in at least two places the roster excludes or distinguishes day laborers (*pôalîm*; e.g., M. Ter. 3:4; M. Ma. 3:1) from the more usual list of household members.[7]

Also occasionally attached to the household is the undefined category of *ben bayit*, literally son/member of the house.[8] Apparently glossing a tradition that appears in M. Sheb. 7:8, the Tosefta itself suggests two kinds of referent for the term (T. Ket. 9:3). One appears to be an intimate of the householder; the other is a kind of manager or agent.[9]

---

[5] See further, e.g., M. Ter, 7:3; M. M.S. 4:4; M. Erub. 7:6; M. B.M. 1:5; 8:3; T. Pes. 7:4; T. B.Q. 10:21; T. Zeb. 13:19; T. Toh. 6:14. See also M. Ab. 2:7: the moral dangers of multiplying meat, property, wives, and male and female slaves; and M. Qid. 2:4.

[6] For such a gift contemplated for a daughter, cf. M. B.B. 9:2. For the practice of manumitting slaves and making them heirs, cf. the Roman practice, e.g., J. Crook, *Law and Life of Rome, 90 B.C.–A.D. 212* (Ithaca, 1967), p. 125. On the problem of a gift to a slave that withholds a portion for the owner (see too T. Pe. 1:13), see B. Cohen, *Jewish and Roman Law* (New York, 1966), p. 177, n. 109; Lieberman, *Tosefta Ki-Fshuta* (New York, 1955–1988) (hereafter, *TK*) vol. 1, pp. 143–144.

[7] Cf. T. Ter. 1:6, which does include a hired laborer (*sâkîr*) on a list that also includes son, slave, and wife.

[8] It has this generic meaning in M. Ber. 9:3, and possibly Sifre Deut. 306, ed. Finkelstein, p. 330. See Cohen, *Jewish and Roman Law*, p. 201, n. 111; S. Lieberman, *Hayerushalmi Kiphshuto* (rpt. New York, 1995), p. 31: a euphemism for wife in at least some passages; but see Lieberman, *TK*, vol. 1, p. 297.

[9] M. Sheb. 7:8, lists *ben bayit* together with partner, tenant farmer, manager, and wife engaged in trade with her husband's property. See also R. Hananel, ad loc. (in standard editions of the Babylonian Talmud, B. Sheb. 48b). Rashi, ad loc., followed by later commentaries and by Albeck, *Shishâ sidrê mishnâ* (Jerusalem and Tel Aviv, 1959.), p. 269 (hereafter, Mishnâ), sees the *ben bayit* in M. Sheb. 7:8 as a brother of the main householder, jointly holding inherited property. In Sifre Num. 131, ed. Horovitz, p. 171, the expression seems to refer to an intimate; in 78, 117, 119, ed. Horovitz, pp. 76, 135, 143, a favored client.

One might imagine either sharing in festal meals (cf. M. Shab. 23:2; T. Pes. 10:4) or participating in the agricultural or economic activities of the household (M. Ter. 3:4; M. Ma. 3:7), and either might, in theory at least, live with the household. It is presumably "intimacy" as a beneficence by the wealthier that underlies the admonition to "let poor people be your *benê bayit*" (M. Ab. 1:5); the inverse, the access of the *ben bayit* to the patron, is adumbrated in the famous story of Honi's prayer for rain (M. R.H. 3:8). At any rate, *benê bayit* are distinguished from both slaves (M. Ter. 3:4) and children (M. Hal. 4:11; M. Shab. 23:2; T. Ber. 2:15).

This highly conventional roster constitutes households as both insular and patriarchal. The households presupposed are two-generational, like the modern nuclear family, expanding either "vertically" to include members of additional generations (grandchildren, or grandparents) or "horizontally" (to include children's spouses or, as in a *frèreche*, co-resident adult siblings and their spouses and children). Like the nuclear household, too, households in the Mishnah are frequently depicted as autonomous ritual or economic units. The lists of members cited above typically arise in connection with the fulfillment of duties incumbent upon the householder or in places in which the householder interacts with other householders (as in contracting labor agreements). Autonomy and insularity emerge sharply in connection with the Mishnah's special Sabbath rules allowing the joint inhabitants of a courtyard or on an alley to create a shared "private" domain in which carrying is permitted to residents on the Sabbath (*erûb haserôt, shittûp mebô'ôt*).[10] For such a shared domain to become effective requires the participation (through the joint deposit of foodstuffs) of each inhabitant (almost certainly assumed to represent a household),[11] or according to an alternative view, each Israelite inhabitant (M. Erub. 6:1–2, 3; see also 2:6).

The underlying assumption that households are distinct from one another yields the somewhat paradoxical result that a householder who was engaged in some sort of partnership with the other inhabitants of the courtyard did not need a separate act creating a shared domain (M. Erub. 6:5; T. Erub. 5:9), because they already owned requisite foodstuffs in common, but "brothers in partnership who would eat at their father's table but sleep in their houses" did require such an act from each one except under certain conditions (M. Erub. 6:7), because

---

[10] The terminology distinguishes two different kinds of joining; for the possible significance see Albeck, *Mishnâ*, vol. 2, pp. 437–438.

[11] Compare M. Shab. 2:7, where a "person" (*adam*) is clearly a household head.

each brother constituted a separate household.[12] There is the general sense that the inhabitants of a village share a definable territory that can be used to mark the Sabbath boundary (the maximum distance that it is permissible to walk from one's residence on the Sabbath; 5:1–3, 8; see also M. Erub. 4:10; but cf., e.g., 5:7, the Sabbath boundary for an individual), but little sense that the inhabitants of a courtyard or an alley participate in a "natural" social unit, and contacts between them needed to be mediated by real or fictive legal acts.[13] Indeed, manipulating the insularity of households, the centrality of the autonomous household heads, and the independent legal agency of some members of a household, the Mishnah allows a household head to constitute a shared domain with other neighbors without direct contact with other villagers (M. Erub. 7:6).[14]

However, unlike in the nuclear-family paradigm, the households we have been discussing are organized not around the husband-wife dyad (indeed, they can, in principle and unlike most contemporary Western households, include more than one wife),[15] but rather around the male household head. It is in that sense that we can describe such households as "patriarchal." As noted, households can include fully independent legal persons (notably, "adult" [*gedôlîm*] sons or daughters; sons in particular would have the same ritual obligations and legal privileges as their fathers), who are nevertheless subordinated to the household head.[16]

---

[12] For the text, particularly the expression *ha-aḥîm ha-shuttapîm*, see J. N. Epstein, *Mabo le-nusaḥ ha-mishna* (Jerusalem, 1948), pp. 1097–1098 (hereafter, *Nusaḥ*). The word *ha-shuttapîm* (translated "in partnership") is omitted in some witnesses (as in the Paris MS.). Others have *we-* preceding *ha-shuttapîm*, which Epstein takes to be *waw explicativum*, introducing an appositive gloss.

[13] For the limited role assigned to villages in early Rabbinic texts (and Palestinian Jewish society more generally), see S. Schwartz, *Imperialism and Jewish Society, 200 B.C.E. to 640 C.E.* (Princeton, 2001), pp. 222–227. The view of Judah in M. Erub. 7:11 suggests an inchoate sense of "community" between joint occupants of a "courtyard."

[14] If this interpretation is correct, M. Erub. 7:6 partially elides the issue of intention on the part of other inhabitants. Cf. M. Erub. 7:7; 8:1. The issue of intention is complicated in the later interpretive tradition in part by the dispute in M. Erub. 7:11 and by the *baraîtâ* at B. Erub. 80a (cf. T. Erub. 6 [Erfurt MS. 9]:1); see, e.g., Rashi, 80a, *s.v. Sarîk le-hôdîa*; and to M. Erub. 7:7, at B. Erub. 80b; Maimonides, *Commentary*, followed by Bertinoro, both to M. Erub. 7:7; and see Albeck, *Mishnâ*, vol. 2, p. 438; A. Goldberg, *The Mishnah Treatise Erubin* (Jerusalem, 1986), pp. 209–211 [Hebrew]; Lieberman, *TK*, vol. 3, p. 416.

[15] E.g., T. Egan, "The Persistence of Polygamy," in *New York Times Magazine*, Feb. 28, 1999, p. 51.

[16] The age of majority is keyed to the onset of secondary sex characteristics, at which point a man or woman "is obligated with respect to all the commandments stated in the Torah" (M. Nid. 6:11; see too 5:7–8; Mekhilta Neziqîn 3, ed. Horovitz,

There is relatively little attention to legal situations in which household members other than wives have entirely independent property or sources of income.[17] At least once they have attained majority, sons or daughters (and "Hebrew" slaves, since they are not technically unfree) can acquire property for themselves, for instance, if they find it (e.g., M. B.M. 1:5; cf. M. Git. 5:8; Sifra Emor, Par.1:[7], 94a). Elsewhere, the Mishnah assigns the ownership of what a daughter finds or produces to her father. In one passage this is explicitly said to be the case if she is a minor; if she has come fully of age, she acquires what she finds or produces (M. Nid. 5:7; cf. M. Ket. 4:4; see also T. Sot. 2:7).[18] For the most part, however, the Mishnah and related literature is concerned with the property of sons or daughters when it comes from the estate of their deceased parents or when daughters are married off (i.e., upon major transitions in the structure of households).

As noted above, wives are exceptional members of households in that the very creation of the marital relationship involves property

---

Rabin, p. 254). Interestingly M. Nid. 5:6 explicitly specifies a girl's twelfth year and a boy's thirteenth as the transition to the ability to undertake a vow. In general, the traditional view is that majority began at a fixed age: for a boy, thirteen (see M. Ab. 5:21, apparently a later supplement to the Mishnah, see Meiri to M. Ab. 5:[23], *Bêt ha-beḥîrâ*, ed. B. Z. Prag [Jerusalem, 1973/1974], pp. 100–101; Epstein, *Nûsaḥ*, p. 978; A. Schremer, "'Eighteen Years to the *Huppah*'? The Marriage Age of Jews in *Eretz Israel* in the Second Temple, Mishna and Talmud Periods," in I. Bartal and I. Gafni, eds., *Sexuality and the Family in History* [Jerusalem, 1998[, p. 52, n. 26, a revision of idem, "Men's Age at Marriage in Jewish Palestine of the Hellenistic and Roman Periods," in *Zion* 61 [1995/1996], p. 53, n. 26); for a girl, generally, twelve and one half years, but see M. A. Friedman, *Jewish Marriage Law in Palestine* (Tel Aviv and New York, 1980), vol. 1, p. 217, n. 3; cf. Cohen, *Jewish and Roman Law*, p. 214; and C.E. Fonrobert, *Menstrual Purity: Rabbinic and Christian Reconstructions of Biblical Gender* (Stanford, 2000), pp. 143–144 and nn. 29–31, which refers to T. Nid. 6:8–9. For discussion of the talmudic and post-talmudic texts, see *Encyclopedia Talmudica* (Jerusalem, 1947–), vol. 2, pp. 377–379, s.v. *bôgeret*.

[17] Note M. Ket. 4:4: fathers do not have right of usufruct over possessions belonging to a daughter (the rule is a bit obscure; the Babli apparently assumed that it dealt with a daughter below legal age, B. Ket. 46b; and as early as the Geonic period it was assumed that the daughter had inherited the property from her maternal kin; see the extracts from *Halakôt gedôlôt* and *Sheîltôt*, cited in B. M. Lewin, ed., *Otzar ha-Geonim* (Jerusalem, 1938), vol. 8, responsa 126 (and see S. K. Mirsky, ed., *Sheeltot de Rab Ahai Gaon* [Jerusalem, 1959–1977], vol. 3, pp. 180–181, *Mishpatîm* 67; and see E. Hildesheim, ed., *Sefer Halakhot Gedolot* [Jerusalem, 1971–1983], vol. 2, pp. 254–255, n. to line 30, citing Warsaw edition) and cf. M. Ket. 6:1, where inheritance (by a wife) is specified. As with a wife, T. Arak. 3:8 can at least imagine a scenario in which the monetary value of what a slave produces is used for his maintenance.

[18] J. R. Wegner, *Chattel or Person? The Status of Women in the Mishnah* (New York, 1988), pp. 116–117; Peskowitz, *Spinning*, pp. 118–120.

transfers promised or real. To be sure, the Mishnah's construction of the primary property relationship between spouses as the *ketûbâ* obligation, treated as in theory a payment by the groom to the bride or her father, but in practice held in trust for the bride and only paid upon divorce or death,[19] severely contracts the potential scope of a woman's autonomy of economic activity within her marital household. Nevertheless, the Mishnah does recognize other forms of property or income belonging to the wife, precisely because these pose problems for a view of the household as an economic and ritual entity organized around the householder. These forms include the wife's dowry and/or trousseau,[20] property she might inherit or be given as gift,[21] and the products of her labor.[22] In each case, the Mishnah is generally concerned to subordinate a wife's economic agency to her husband (see, e.g., M. Ket. 4:4–5).

---

[19] On the history of this institution, see Friedman, *Jewish Marriage Law*, pp. 238–262; M. Satlow, "Reconsidering the Rabbinic *Ketubah* Payment," in S. J. D. Cohen, ed. *The Jewish Family in Antiquity* (Atlanta, 1993), pp. 133–151; idem, *Jewish Marriage in Antiquity* (Princeton, 2001), pp. 200–204, and the literature cited there.

[20] My differentiation here between dowry (the settlement of property on the bride by the bride's family) and trousseau (clothing, goods, or ornaments to be used by the woman or the marital household) risks artificially distinguishing between aspects of what may well be, in Rabbinic legal thought, a single institution (see Satlow, *Jewish Marriage*, p. 333, n. 27, and the discussion of dowry, pp. 204–213, and my forthcoming discussion in "Maintenance of Wives and Children in Early Rabbinic and Documentary Texts from Roman Palestine;" cf. more generally, J. Goody, *The Development of the Family and Marriage in Europe* [Cambridge, 1984]; J. L. Comaroff, "Introduction," in idem, ed., *The Meaning of Marriage Payments* [London, 1980], pp. 1–48). Trousseau: M. Ket. 5:2; see also T. Ket. 4:17; 6:1, with Friedman, *Jewish Marriage Law*, vol. 1, p. 378; M. Ket. 6:5. Dowry: see, e.g., M. Ket. 6:2–6; M. Yeb. 7:1–2 (cf. T. Ket. 9:1). For the distinction between *ṣon barzel* and *melôg* in M. Yeb. 7:1–2 (cf. T. Ket. 9:1) see Cohen, *Jewish and Roman Law*, vol. 1, p. 363; Friedman, *Jewish Marriage Law*, pp. 291–292; Satlow, *Jewish Marriage*, p. 350, n. 51, and 351, n. 64, in general treating the former as constituting the dowry (see Rashi, B. Yeb. 61a, to M. Yeb. 7:1; cf. Maimonides, *Code, Laws of Marriage (îšût)*, 16:1, as opposed, say, to his commentary to M. Yeb. 4:3, ed. Qafiḥ); the Mishnah does not make such a distinction explicit. See also M. Yeb. 4:3 (= M. Ket. 8:6), "property that comes in and goes out with her," typically treated as referring to non-dotal, i.e., *melôg*, property, but which may well mean simply "dowry," as noted by Cohen, *Jewish and Roman Law*, p. 347, n. 6.

[21] Inheritance or gift (see T. Ilan, *Jewish Women in Greco-Roman Palestine* [rpt. Peabody, 1996], pp. 167–172): M. Yeb. 4:3; M. Ket. 6:1; 8:1–6; T. Ket. 8:1 (and see the discussion in Peskowitz, *Spinning*, pp. 27–48); note also strategies for keeping property out of the control of the husband (see Satlow, *Jewish Marriage*, pp. 208–209): M. Ned. 11:8 (cf. Satlow, who sees the vow as the important element here); M. Ket. 6:6; M. Ket. 9:1.

[22] Products of labor: see e.g., M. Yeb. 11:1; M. Ket. 4:4; 5:9; 6:1; 11:1; M. Git. 8:5; T. Yeb. 2:3, 4; 13:2; T. Ket. 5:2; 8:1; T. Git. 7:4; T. Mak. 2:8; see also T. Ned. 7:1, 7; Peskowitz, *Spinning*, pp. 101–105.

Patriarchy, Marriage, and Household Formation

The "household," then, as the Mishnah constructs it, is a more or less static set of radial relationships around the central figure of the householder. The constituent presence of slaves ("gentile" or "Hebrew") and of benê bayît makes it difficult to conceive of such a construction, despite its "nuclearity," as entirely analogous to a modern ideal of "family," made up of people linked through biological reproduction. Their presence reminds us that the fundamental relationships constituting a household might be those of domination or patronage and dependency. Relationships between householders, too, are generally structured around legal obligations, duties, or rights, rather than "natural" norms of behavior towards those people deemed "closest" to one. Sons and fathers have reciprocal duties that are spelled out in the Tosefta (M. Qid. 1:7; T. Qid. 1:11).[23] Husbands have obligations such as maintenance and sexual intimacy toward their wives, and wives, in turn, have to perform labor and services in the household (e.g., M. Ket. 5:5, 6, 8–9; T. Ket. 5:4, 8–10). These sets of obligations could also explicitly be construed as reciprocal (M. Ket. 5:9).[24] By contrast, reciprocality fails in the connection between the rights of a father over his daughter: he certainly has rights over her person and what she finds or produces (e.g., M. Ket. 4:4–5), but although she is entitled to maintenance after his death, the idea that her father is obligated to maintain her during his lifetime is rejected outright in the Mishnah, and even her right to maintenance from his estate is treated ambivalently (M. Ket. 4:6, with 4:11; M. B.M. 8:8; M. Ket. 13:3).[25]

---

[23] The Mishnah's inclusion of daughters in the sons' obligation is also ambivalently handled in the Tosefta: "but a man has sufficient power (?) to perform it, but a woman does not have sufficient power, for the authority (reshût) of others is upon her," T. Qid. 1:11; see also Sifra, Qedôshîm, Par. 1:3, 86d, to Lev. 19:2, glossing îš, "a man."

[24] Friedman, *Jewish Marriage Law*, pp. 167–178. For "reciprocity" in relations between spouses, by which I mean specifically the articulation of them as balancing one another, whether or not that articulation covers over or even structures an underlying inequality, see Peskowitz, *Spinning*, pp. 96–105, 115–117; Satlow, *Jewish Marriage*, pp. 219–223.

[25] For the obligation to maintain daughters, cf. T. Ket. 4:8 (with B. Ket. 49a–b) expressed once as miṣwâ and once as ḥôbâ. Both Talmuds mention the tradition of an enactment at Usha requiring maintenance; only the version in the Babli refers explicitly to daughters (Y. Ket. 4:8, 28d; B. Ket. 49b). See Peskowitz, *Spinning*, pp. 118–127; Friedman, *Jewish Marriage Law*, pp. 356–360. Ilan, *Jewish Women*, p. 50, n. 16, rejects out of hand the reciprocal, if negative, linkage between a daughter's productive activity and her maintenance drawn by L. Archer, *Her Price Is Beyond Rubies* (Sheffield, 1990), p. 63; cf. T. Ket. 10:2 (where such a linkage is prohibited); Y. Ket. 12:1, 34d.

That it is the householder who is at the center of these static relationships makes it difficult to reconstruct from within the Mishnah any single coherent paradigm of household formation. Points of transition (marriage, death, divorce) are treated casuistically and push at the limits of legal or social assumptions.[26] More generally, the Mishnah has an interest in posing puzzles at the boundaries of legal categories.[27] This recurrent interest makes it difficult, for instance, to pin down a specific preference or bias in the Mishnah and related texts for age of males at first marriage.[28] The one exception, probably a post-Mishnaic addendum, is itself interesting for its focus solely on the life-trajectory of the ideal male, in which marriage (at eighteen years) is mentioned as one of the (appropriate? inevitable?) life stages, among which the rearing of children in due course is not explicitly included (M. Ab. 5:21).[29] Legal situations in which boys are said to marry young are discussed precisely because of the technical inability of a minor—a non-householder more or less by definition—to perform a valid act of marriage or betrothal. "A minor," for instance, "whom his father married off, her *ketûbâ* is valid (*qayyemet*), for it is on that condition that he upheld her (?) (*qiyyemah*)" (M. Ket. 9:9).[30] The father's role in creating

---

[26] Particularly in terms of women, the interest of the Mishnah in transitions of this sort has already been noted by J. Neusner, *Judaism: The Evidence of the Mishnah*, pp. 137–143.

[27] E.g., M. Yeb. 3, entire; for a more elaborate example cf. T. Yeb. 3:1, working out a rule in M. Yeb. 2:3.

[28] For the age of men at marriage, see Schremer, "Eighteen Years," pp. 43–68; idem, "Men's Age at Marriage," pp. 45–66; Satlow, *Jewish Marriage*, pp. 104–109; Safrai, "Home and Family," pp. 748, 755.

[29] Schremer, "Eighteen Years," p. 52 and n. 28; "Men's Age at Marriage," p. 53 and n. 28 reads this as stating the age at which marriage becomes appropriate.

[30] The proper reading in the Mishnah is *ketûbatah*, "her *ketûbâ*;" see M. Hershler, J. Hutner, eds., *The Babylonian Talmud with Variant Readings: Tractate Kethuboth* (Jerusalem, 1977), vol. 2, p. 332. However, the corresponding material in the Tosefta reads *ketûbatô*, "his *ketûbâ*" (T. Ket. 9:7), underscoring the boy's agency (i.e., the document written by or for him and transmitted to the wife, Friedman, *Jewish Marriage Law*, p. 240, n. 5; cf. Satlow, *Jewish Marriage*, p. 312, n. 92) as what is at issue. M. Ket. 9:9 continues with the analogous case involving a proselyte who converted together with his wife and who, like the minor, is already in a non-legally constituted but nonetheless marital relationship at the moment he enters into the status of adult, male, Israelite person. For other examples involving a minor, see M. Yeb. 10:9–11; M. B.B. 8:7 (*qatan*, here, presumabably a relative term, not a legal specification, but note the issue of financing of marriage from the estate of the deceased father). See also T. Yeb. 5:9–10. The strong statement of Mekhilta Nezîqîn 3 (ed. Horovitz, Rabin, p. 258): "From here they said: 'A man is obligated to marry off his minor son [or: his son while a minor],'" followed by an exhortation to do so, does not, to my knowledge, find an echo in the Mishnah.

marriages for his offspring and the son's assumption of status and obligations as a householder in his own right, apparently upon his own entry into adulthood, are dealt with here. On the other hand, at least one passage in the Mishnah, Schremer has noted, implies later first marriage for men.[31]

Similarly, the Mishnah is not particularly forthcoming about the point in his marital life at which a husband became an autonomous householder. A number of texts suggest a neolocal model of marriage (the bride and groom establish a new household upon marriage) with the groom drawing on the property of his paternal household. One tradition, mentioning a contract "to build... a house of marriage for his son, or a house of widowhood for his daughter" (M. B.M. 6:4) reads well in terms of a pattern of creating (spatially and socially) contiguous dwellings for married sons, possibly of extending the paternal household itself, but this reading is not necessitated by the text itself. More narrowly, the passage implies the husband's father's participation in establishing the living situation of his newly married son. Elsewhere the Mishnah considers the claim of younger, unmarried heirs that they be entitled to the same marriage settlement that their older brothers received from their father or from his estate (M. B.M. 8:7).[32] It is in the context of assumptions about paternal funding of a new, possibly close-by, marital household, and not child marriage, that we might interpret the balance of texts in which a father betroths or marries off his son where no age is specified (e.g., M. Ned. 5:6; 9:2; see also T. Erub. 5:11; T. Pes. 2:1; T. Qid. 1:11, 2:1; Sifre Deut. 253, ed. Finkelstein, 279).

The above suggests a fundamental tension. On the one hand we have the Mishnah's highly schematized world of autonomous households that might in theory be formed by men at any age above majority. On the other hand, in practice—again, within the schematized world of the Mishnah—the formation of households may require the ceding

---

[31] M. Ber. 2:5 (the marriage of Gamaliel), although no age is mentioned. The implication for later age and life stage is even stronger in T. Sot. 7:20. Schremer, "Eighteen Years," pp. 62, 64–65; "Men's Age at Marriage," pp. 60–61, 62–63 (for the text of M. Ber. 2:5, see n. 68 in both versions; and see N. Sacks, ed., *The Mishnah* (Jerusalem, 1971–), vol. 1, pp. 20–21.

[32] See also T. Ket. 6:8, a fatherless groom supported from charity: provision of a (rented) house and bed—or even, the text continues, a slave or horse. See also Y. Ket. 5:1, 29c; Y. B.B. 9:4, 16d; B. Git. 14a; B. B.B. 144a. See Friedman, *Jewish Marriage Law*, 298; Safrai, "Home and Family," p. 753, has the new couple as part of the groom's father's household; but marriage is described as the transfer of the bride "to the groom's house," p. 756 (in neither passage does Safrai quote M. B.B. 6:4).

of property by fathers to their sons, a factor that might delay marriage or give fathers a continued hand in their sons' households. It is only a slight over-reading to see this concern in the possibility raised that a formally adult groom might make his act of betrothal dependent upon paternal consent (M. Qid. 3:6). The case cited earlier of "brothers in partnership who would eat at their father's table but sleep in their houses" (M. Erub. 6:7) may be read in two ways: as an example of happy commensality between siblings and father, or one of the dependency of nominally independent householders.[33]

Again, it is the rights of the householder (i.e., the father or the new husband) that are the central preoccupation of the passages in which the Mishnah presupposes that daughters are married off, or at least betrothed, as fully minors (qetanôt) or at the pre-majority intermediate stage when they are na'arôt (presumably approximately coordinate with puberty).[34] This preoccupation is clearly the case in a text that compares the incomplete rights of father and groom to nullify the vows of

---

[33] T. Ket. 9:6, where a widow may have returned (ḥazrâ) "from the grave [of her husband] . . . to her father-in-law's house," may assume the dependence of married sons on, or their coresidence with, their fathers. The potential dependence of adult sons on their father is addressed in a gloss to M. B.M. 1:5 attributed to Yohanan (regarding possession of that which one's adult son finds): "When they are not dependent upon their father, but if they were dependent upon their father that which they find is his [the father's]," Y. B. Mes. 1:5, 8a; paralleled also at Y. Pe. 4:6, 18b; Y. Ket. 6:1, 30c; and see B. Ket. 47a; B. B.M. 12b. The ideal of a groom's financial autonomy as well as, it seems, of its elusiveness (parnasâ, "sustenance," comes to him almost as a windfall: nitmantâ lô, "it was assigned to him") is expressed in the instructions of T. Sot. 7:20 (Venice ms. and editio princeps; cf. Erfurt ms.).

[34] Qetanôt: e.g., M. Yeb. 13:1-9, 11-12; M. Ned. 11:10, end; M. Git. 5:5 [cf. M. Ed. 7:9, 8:2], 6:2-3; M. Qid. 3:8; na'arôt: M. Ket. 3:3; M. Ned. 10:1; M. Git. 6:2; M. Qid. 2:3. My impression is that such examples tend to cluster around cases involving explicitly biblical rules (vows, penalties paid in the case of rape or seduction, and so on). For the question of age of girls or women at marriage, see Ilan, Jewish Women, pp. 65-69; Schremer, "Eighteen Years," pp. 68-70; Satlow, Jewish Marriage, pp. 104-109. R. Katzoff, "The Age of Marriage for Jewish Women in the Talmudic Period," in M. A. Friedman, ed., Marriage and the Family in Halakhah and Jewish Thought [Hebrew] (Tel Aviv, 1997), pp. 9-18. Satlow has argued plausibly that age of first marriage for women in Palestine was likely to be in the middle teens or later, but that argument is driven primarily by analogy with better documented areas of the empire (cf. Katzoff; and see below), and his citations in support from the Mishnah and related literature remain inconclusive (pp. 107-108, and especially 309-310, nn. 56-58, 61-62). (Thus, for instance, examples having to do with physical blemishes on the bride and their ability to be inspected, M. Yeb. 7:7-8; M. Qid. 2:5, seem to be applicable equally to children and mature women; T. Nid. 6:9 raises female attendance of baths—precisely the setting where the Mishnah expects a potential bride to be inspected by the groom's relations—as the cause of the differential onset of secondary sex characteristics between urban and village girls.)

a *naʿarâ* who has been betrothed but remains unmarried (M. Ned. 10:1). In connection with a *qetanâ*, we are told, if she is married off by her father and divorced she is effectively emancipated also from her father's authority (she is "like an orphan in the lifetime of her father;" M. Yeb. 13:6; cf. also M. Ket. 3:3). This example is the third of three dealing with suitability of divorcées for levirate marriage should the husband have "taken back" the wife before his death, the first two being a "normal" case of divorce, remarriage, and the death of the husband, and one of a fatherless girl, presumably married off by her brother or mother (cf. M. Yeb. 13:2; M. Ket. 6:6). Examples specifying a rough age at marriage are thus embedded in a series of other judgments about the rights and statuses of the men in the orbit of whom women or girls may fall. Other passages—no less implicated in such male-centered connections—imply that brides can have attained legal majority by the time they marry (e.g., M. Ned. 10:5; M. Qid. 3:8–9; see also T. Qid. 4:11).[35]

Where the interest is particularly in marriage as a contractual arrangement, marriage can be conceived of as taking place between a man and a woman (of unspecified age) without the bride's father's intervention. This is the case, for instance, in connection with the offer of betrothal, the terms of the marriage or betrothal document ("he wrote *for her* . . ."), and stipulations of dowry ("*she* agreed to bring in . . .").[36] Even more clearly than with sons, the Mishnah here seems to operate with a fundamental but not fully articulated tension. With males, the tension appeared to be between an ideal of households formed by and

---

[35] By contrast, M. Yeb. 6:4 singles out high priests as specifically enjoined to avoid brides who have attained majority. For the text of M. Ned. 10:5, see Epstein, *Nûsaḥ*, pp. 329–331, who argues that reading "and one (*we-*) who has waited" (as in the Kaufmann and Parma MSS.) is based on a Babylonian emendation. M. Ned. 10:5 intersects with M. Ket. 5:2. The verbal and thematic overlaps are quite clear, with one notable difference: where M. Ket. 5:2 deals with a "virgin," *betûlâ*, with age unspecified, M. Ned. 10:5 has *bôgeret*, "woman who has attained majority." T. Ket. 5:1 (Erfurt MS.), glossing M. Ket. 5:2, may harmonize these two passages: "coming of age (*hebger*) is like demanding [by the groom for completion of the marriage]: one gives her twelve months." For the continuation of T. Ket. 5:1, see Lieberman, *TK* 6, p. 255, and Friedman, *Jewish Marriage Law*, vol. 1, pp. 193–194. The Tosefta thus appears to treat the *bôgeret*/*betûlâ* (and if it makes good sense of the Mishnah, the Mishnah as well) as quite close to puberty.

[36] Offer of betrothal: e.g., M. Qid. 2:2–7; 3:1–7, 10–11. Marriage document clauses: M. Yeb. 15:3 (M. Ed. 1:12); M. Ket. 4:7–10; 5:1; 9:1, 5; see also T. Ket. 4:6, 11; 6:5, 6; 9:3; 11:5; 12:1 (note here the direct involvement of the father despite the fact that the document is written "for her"); T. Ed. 1:6. Dowry stipulations: M. Ket. 6:3–4; see also T. Ket. 6:5–6 (but note that the father is engaged in making stipulations in the passages that frame these, M. Ket. 6:2, 5; T. Ket. 6:4, 7).

around autonomous householders, and paternal dependence. With females, the tension is between marriage as a consensual (and "reciprocal") contract between husband and wife and marriage as the transfer of women from the domain of the father to the domain of the husband. The latter appears in perhaps its strongest legal formulation in M. Ket. 4:5: "She is ever (*le-ôlam*) in the domain of the father until she enters the domain of the husband for marriage...." The context is a discussion of the distinction between fathers and husbands with respect to the women in their charge (M. Ket. 4:4). The cited statement is followed by discussion of precisely when in the process of the transfer of the bride that change of domain takes place.

There are several intersections with other passages in the Mishnah that invite a redactional and compositional study that cannot be undertaken here. What is of interest for the present purposes is the fact that no age is specified (see also T. Sot. 2:7). Elsewhere, as noted above, the question of the father's rights over his daughter's vows or to what she produces or finds is keyed to her age or maturation (M. Nid. 5:6–8), and a logical, if harmonizing, reading would take the present passage as simply assuming that daughters are married near their age of majority.[37] A similar harmonizing reading would assume that the father's entitlement to contract the daughter's betrothal (see also M. Sot. 3:8) refers to the period before she comes of age even where that is not specified (as it is in M. Qid. 2:1). Rhetorically, however, the passage just quoted makes a rather more extensive claim, namely that a father's authority over his daughter extends as long as she is living with him, however old she is, up until the moment she is transferred into her husband's domain.

It might be noted, as an aside, that assumption of majority is less straightforward than one might suppose. The Mishnah can manipulate the meaning of *na'arâ*—which usually refers to a woman in the intermediate status between "minority" and "majority"—by using it to include women in the status of *bôgeret* (woman who has attained majority),[38] a manipulation that might, in theory (but not, so far as I have been

---

[37] Note that M. Ket. 4:1 explicitly deals with a *na'arâ* and the consequences of her attaining majority for the payment of the biblical penalties for her seduction. That passage also raises the issue of possession of her productive labor and what she finds. Note too that the verse quoted in M. Ket. 4:3 uses the language of *na'arâ* (Deut. 22:21, but cf. 22:13–14).

[38] M. Ned. 11:10 (note also the curious locution *na'arâ bôgeret* for a girl who has attained majority). However, that passage works in the opposite direction to the possibility suggested above: at least for the purposes of vows, it rules that some *ne'arôt* have the same status as *bôgerôt*. See also T. Nid. 6:3, which uses *tinôqet* (small girl, infant) for a woman of twenty or eighteen, although in this case she has not matured physically.

able to determine, utilized within the Mishnah itself) allow fathers to extend the range of their daughters' "youth." Moreover, by making the change in status dependent upon physical maturity rather than any particular chronological age[39] (and by presenting the precise definition of physical maturation as subject to dispute), the Mishnah effectively transforms the point of transition to majority into a more or less indeterminate band.[40] "Majority" would then depend not only upon the age of maturation of any particular girl or woman but on the domestic and social practices of marking (or hiding) physical changes.[41] This definition of maturity and legal personhood performs the further cultural work of drawing (male, Rabbinic) attention, far more than for maturing boys, to the developing female body, and consequently to sexual difference and its social and legal consequences.[42]

To return to the tension between marriage as contract and marriage as patriarchal transfer, it seems to me that this tension is effectively that diagnosed by Wegner as between woman as "person" or "chattel" in the Mishnah.[43] But whereas Wegner stressed the either/or position of women, depending upon whether their sexuality was at issue, I would underscore the fundamental hybridity of women—as both agents and the objects of transactions by other agents—in the Mishnah's constructed world. The two constructions of marriage underwrite one another, and the movement of women, as agents or as objects, plays a role in maintaining the double construction. The Mishnah's normative construction of households around autonomous male householders entails notions of rights, duties, property, and membership (including the "emancipation" of children through, e.g., the attainment of majority) and thus requires

---

[39] See above, n. 16. In the Mishnah, age limits are raised in specific legal circumstances having to do with the maturation of girls (see M. Nid. 5:6, and 5:9, next note). T. Nid. 2:5 believes that girls in their twelfth year are susceptible to (for them, particularly life-threatening) pregnancy; note also T. Nid. 6:2, which both correlates physical changes of puberty in boys and chronological age, and rules on deviations from that correlation.

[40] See, e.g., M. Nid. 5:9, where the dispute centers on when (at eighteen or twenty years) a young woman who has not attained puberty becomes classed as *aylônît* (and disqualified as a sexual adult for, e.g., fulfillment of the levirate obligations); cf. T. Nid. 6:2 on males.

[41] See, for instance, the practice of physical inspection of young women, T. Nid. 5:4; 6:8–9 and Fonrobert, *Menstrual Purity*, pp. 137–147.

[42] Fonrobert, *Menstrual Purity*, pp. 144–145, 148. See also Satlow, "Rabbinic Texts of Terror," in *AJS Review* 21 (1996), pp. 273–297, on the "pornographic" in Rabbinic texts. See also Peskowitz, *Spinning*, 8 (and *passim*) on Joan Scott's identification of gender as "knowledge of sexual difference."

[43] Wegner, *Chattel or Person*.

or shapes the imagined negotiations and agreements between households to effect the transfer of women (together with the transfer or property). It is thus at the same time instrumental in giving marriage as contract the particular cast that it has in the Mishnah. The construction of marriage as contractual, in turn, validates the unequal terms of those agreements. Particularly where the bride is an "adult" party to the contract she is presented as willingly assenting to a contractual agreement where her autonomy of economic activity, sexuality, and comportment are subject to another's authority.[44]

Stresses on the Fabric of the Household

The presence of slaves and *benê bayit* in households, I have suggested above, implies that the household is more complicated than a simply "natural" form of reproduction. Slippage between the autonomy and dependency of sons as they form their own marital households, or between marriage as transfer or contract as daughters enter into marriage suggest areas in which the Mishnah's exposition may obscure underlying ideological (and possibly social) tensions at work in that exposition. The concerns in the Mishnah with property as it was played out in the household—most notably inheritance and the property of wives, and in the quotidian interactions between and among households—are consistent with analyses of households as material rather than affective institutions.[45]

---

[44] T. Ket. 12:3 explicitly implicates women's desire for marriage in the structuring of its uneven terms:
    R. Judah says in the name (?) of R. Simeon: "Why did they say 'The *ketûbâ* of a woman [collects] from the least [valuable property of the husband]'? More than a man wishes to marry, a woman wishes to be married; and moreover, the shame of a woman [unmarried?] is more than a man's."
    If so, let her not have a *ketûbâ* [at all]? It is because a woman goes out [of a marriage] whether in accord with her [own] will or not in accord with her will, but a man puts [a woman] out only in accord with his will.
Cf. M. Git. 5:1; T. Ket. 6:8, with Lieberman, *TK*, vol. 6, p. 371. Ilan, *Jewish Women*, p. 124, reads the first paragraph (and its partial parallel, T. Ket. 6:8) in terms of concerns over chastity and child marriage.

[45] See Satlow, *Jewish Marriage*, pp. 233–242; idem, "'One Who Loves His Wife like Himself': Love in Rabbinic Marriage," in *Journal of Jewish Studies* 49 (1998), pp. 67–86; and P. Veyne, "La famille et l'amour sous le haut empire romain," in *Annales, ESC* 33 (1978), pp. 35–63; S. Dixon, "The Sentimental Ideal of the Roman Family," in B. Rawson, ed., *Marriage, Divorce, and Children in Ancient Rome: New Perspectives* (Oxford, 1991), pp. 99–113; R. P. Saller, *Patriarchy, Property and Death in the Roman Family* (Cambridge, 1994), pp. 4–8.

Yet such a reconstruction of Mishnaic households is insufficient. If fullfledged examples of domestic bliss are hard to find (somewhat surprisingly, the best example of mourning in the Mishnah is that of the unexpected observance of mourning practices by Gamaliel for his servant Tabi, M. Ber. 2:6),[46] it is also not true that emotions are absent. The Mishnah repeatedly mentions shame or its absence in characterizing relationships between household members. On the one hand, "shame" severely circumscribes the range of emotions the Mishnah deems relevant to its discussions. On the other, it hints at internal tensions (based on class, gender, social pressures, and so on), and sexual desires to be controlled or inculcated.[47]

What this suggests is that the Mishnah's more or less formal conceptualization of households is not entirely adequate to encompassing the social processes of their formation, function, and perpetuation that the Mishnah itself considers. The Mishnah's organization of Israelite society into households structured around relationships with the head of household is thus something of a static and ragged fiction. One way of identifying some of the stresses that pull on the household and undermine its fabric is to point to some of the conflicting interests that emerge when the household head is removed by death. The Mishnah specifies that built into the marriage contract (and presumed to be operative even when the clauses are omitted) are the stipulations that sons of the wife inherit her marriage settlement and that daughters are entitled to maintenance (M. Ket. 4:10–11).[48] The heirs of one man but of multiple wives might therefore be understood to be engaged in conflicts that

---

[46] Note also the exposition of the love that a ["Hebrew"] slave must feel for his master if the ritual making him permanently enslaved is to be carried out: Mekhilta Nezîqîn 2 (ed. Horovitz, Rabin, p. 252); Sifre Deut. 121 (ed. Finkelstein, p. 179); and see Exod. 21:5; Deut. 15:16.

[47] Note the concern with the comportment of household members, particularly of wives (e.g., M. Ket. 7:6; T. Sot. 5:10), and with the "shame" that a mother-in-law might feel were the gifts of food sent to her son-in-law not properly tithed (M. Dem. 3:6). Note too the attention to texts specifying the absence of shame (particularly care with respect to displays of nakedness or sexuality) born of familiarity. Connected with presumed sexual activity: M. Yeb. 4:10, with M. Ket. 1:5 (see also T. Ket. 1:6, and T. Ilan, "Premarital Cohabitation in Ancient Judaea: The Evidence of the Babatha Archive and the Mishnah," in *Harvard Theological Review* 86 [1993], pp. 247–264); M. Git. 8:9; M. Ed. 4:7. Absent before female slaves, M. Git. 7:4; her young children, T. Git. 5:4; T. Qid. 5:9 (Lieberman, *TK*, vol. 8, pp. 871–872, 978–979; according to the Vienna and Erfurt mss. T. Qid. 5:9 might refer to lack of shame before any child); male slaves, M. Sot. 1:6. Note also T. Ket. 7:6; T. Sot. 5:9 (the text needs clarification), "swollen heartedness" (i.e., a lack of shame) can extend even to female neighbors.

[48] See on these stipulations Friedman, *Jewish Marriage Law*, pp. 356–360, 379–391.

could only be appropriately resolved by court involvement (M. Ket. 10:2). Brothers and sisters, even of the same parents, are assumed to be at odds with one another where the father's estate was small; the Mishnah's formulation suggests a certain amount of internal Rabbinic struggle against received tradition, in favor of improving the position of sons (M. Ket. 13:3; M. B.M. 9:1).[49] Older and younger daughters might be in conflict over the level of maintenance or dowry they might receive after their father's death (M. B.M. 8:8) as might older and younger sons over these issues and their share in the inheritance (M. B.M. 8:7, 9:3)[50]

Widows constitute a particular locus of tension.[51] In general, a woman's marital settlement in the case of widowhood puts her at odds with the husband's heirs (including, potentially, her own sons), who can require her to verify by oath that she has not already received her settlement (M. Ket. 9:7–8; M. Git. 4:3). The two *ketûbâ* stipulations mentioned above are themselves a formal compromise between the technical merging of the wife with the husband's household (assumed to be based on biblical rules) and the assumption that the wife, her natal family, and her sons have an interest in the property that is settled upon or falls to her. A third stipulation states that a widow was entitled to maintenance in her deceased husband's house (M. Ket. 4:12). This right, or at least the presumption that a widow might continue to live with her husband's heirs, is seen to shape the relationship between the parties: she is partly reduced to the same "reciprocal" relationship of production and consumption she had with her husband (M. Ket. 11:1); and her entitlement to maintenance is seen as dependent on her actually living in her husband's house (M. Ket. 12:3, 4). Indeed, according to one view (Meir), after twenty-five years in her deceased husband's house,

---

[49] On this tradition see J. Neusner, *Rabbinic Traditions about the Pharisees before 70* (Leiden, 1971, rpt. Atlanta, 1999), vol. 1, pp. 350–351, 387; Ilan, *Jewish Women*, p. 170; Satlow, *Jewish Marriage*, p. 208; and especially Peskowitz, *Spinning*, pp. 124–127 (and note the general observation by Wegner, *Chattel or Person*, p. 233, n. 151). T. Ket. 6:1, 2, on the other hand, extends the Mishnah's rule in the opposite direction, adding the daughters' entitlement to dowry or trousseau, Lieberman, *TK*, vol. 6, p. 272.

[50] See also T. B.B. 8:18, and Epstein, *Nûsaḥ*, pp. 660–661; Lieberman, *TK*, vol. 10, pp. 431–432. Here Lieberman (as opposed to in T. Ket. 6:1, 2, previous note) takes *mitparnesîn* to mean "provisioning" (the traditional commentaries understood this to refer to the clothing and other needs that older sons need more of than younger, e.g., Maimonides to M. B.B. 8:8; Rashi, s.v. *mitparnesîn*, to Mishnah, B. B.B. 139a).

[51] See also M. Ket. 11:2–4, on the potential limits on a widow's ability to sell her husband's property to pay for her maintenance or to fund her marriage settlement.

her right to collect the marital settlement lapses. The Mishnah explains this view in terms of long term, uncompensated benefits received at the expense of the heirs: "because it happens in twenty-five years that she will receive benefit (?) to offset (*ke-neged*) her *ketûbâ*" (M. Ket. 12:4).[52] Still, the Mishnah considers other possibilities: namely that the wife might be made the manager of her deceased husband's estate (M. Ket. 9:6; see also 9:4).

One last example, this time dealing with a divorced rather than a widowed woman, will help us make the transition from stresses internal to the structure of the household to external pressures. Where a bride stipulated with more than one husband in series that they maintain her existing daughter for a set period, the daughter may be entitled to maintenance from more than one husband; where the daughter herself has married she continues to have this entitlement in addition to support from her own husband (M. Ket. 12:1–2).[53] For present purposes, it is significant that the Mishnah imagines that one marriage may produce ripples that affect other people outside the "nuclear," householder-centered structure of the household: here, a situation in which householders may be involved in the maintenance of women not their wives or daughters, and moreover who might be the wives of other householders.

A primary area in which we might expect to explore the involvement of "outsiders" is the domain of kinship. This would necessitate a study of its own, one made more difficult by the Mishnah's own emphasis on the "nuclearity" of autonomous households.[54] Still, there are enough hints of kinship ties affecting the household that we should hesitate before taking the Mishnah as simply attesting to the attenuation of kinship. The Mishnah has at least one passage in which a man is

---

[52] This seems to be the understanding of the Mishnah in the Yerushalmi: "Against the benefit that she managed her [non-dotal, independent?] property as in the life of her husband," (Y. Ket. 12:5, 35b). The commentaries generally read the text of the Mishnah differently and see the wife as "performing favors" (at the expense of the heirs) in giving gifts to friends or the poor (e.g., Meiri, to B. Ket. 104a, in A. Sofer, ed., *Bêt ha-beḥîrâ al masseket ketûbôt* [Jerusalem, 1947], p. 478, who mentions both categories).

[53] Note that the Mishnah attempts to foreclose the result outlined above: "The clear-sighted would write: 'On condition that I maintain your daughter for five years, as long as you are with me'" (M. Ket. 12:2).

[54] It is made difficult, too, by the misgivings of recent generations of anthropologists about the entire enterprise of studying kinship. See J. Carsten, "Introduction: Cultures of Relatedness," in idem, ed., *Cultures of Relatedness: New Approaches to the Study of Kinship* (Cambridge, 2000), pp. 1–36.

under pressure to marry his sister's daughter; it is plausibly kin (i.e., not uninterested outsiders) who are applying pressure in favor of this form of close-kin endogamy, precipitating his vow that the niece have no benefit from him (M. Ned. 8:7).[55] More widely presupposed, at least for casuistic purposes, is marriage of men to their brother's daughters (e.g., M. Yeb. 1:2).[56] Elsewhere, in a somewhat obscure passage, the Mishnah follows the rule that a man can, by his own vow, make his (minor?) son a Nazirite (see Num. 6:1–21), with the qualification "[if] he shaved [his head] or [if] his relations (qerôba(y)w) shaved him, he protested or his relations protested [for] him" that the sacrifice the father had set aside is invalidated (M. Naz. 4:6).[57] This is one of the few cases in which a father's authority can be nullified by other relatives.

Unfortunately just who the "relations" are is not specified. Some indication of how that term might be unpacked may perhaps be derived from a passage specifying the "relations" (qerôbîm) prohibited from serving as witnesses or judges in a case (M. San. 3:4; see also 3:1). As I understand this passage, there are at least two modes of constructing proximity.[58] One, putatively older ("the first mishnâ"),[59] maps "relationship" for judicial

---

[55] See also M. Ned. 9:10; T. Qid. 1:4: "Let a man not marry until his sister's daughter comes of age, or until he finds [a woman] appropriate to him. See S. Krauss, "Die Ehe zwischen Onkel und Nichte," in D. Philipson, et al., eds., *Studies in Jewish Literature Issued in Honor of Kaufman Kohler* (Berlin, 1913; rpt. New York, 1980), pp. 165–175; A. Schremer, "Kinship Terminology and Endogamous Marriage in the Mishnaic and Talmudic Periods," in *Zion* 60 (1995), pp. 5–35 [Hebrew]; Satlow, *Jewish Marriage*, pp. 157–158. That choice of an "appropriate" wife may be tied to the estimation with which she is held by a man's kin is made explicit in the description (attributed, in the Yerushalmi, to a late Palestinian rabbi) of a ritual staged by qerôbîm ("relations") on the occasion that a man marries such a woman, or when he divorces her (see Y. Ket. 2:10, 26d; Y. Qid. 1:5, 30c; both glossing the baraîtâ at T. Ket. 3:3; see also B. Ket. 28b, on which see Satlow, *Jewish Marriage*, pp. 152–153).

[56] Schremer, "Kinship Terminology," pp. 16–18, views the pattern as widespread, and as underlying the paradigmatic Hillelite-Shammaite dispute of M. Yeb. 1:4; it clearly plays a central role in the understanding of the tradition about Dosa b. Hyrkanos in Y. Yeb. 1:6, 3a; B. Yeb. 16a.

[57] See also M. Sot. 3:8. T. Naz. 3:17 may assume that a minor is intended (see also Y. Naz. 4:6, 53c; B. Naz. 29b), but this is not made explicit in the Mishnah. Epstein, *Nûsah*, p. 1037; Lieberman, *TK*, vol. 7, pp. 536–537, to T. Naz. 3:17.

[58] Just how to disentangle the first two views in the Mishnah (particularly the extent of Yose's comment) is not clear; cf. Sifre Deut. 280, ed. Finkelstein, p. 297, to 24:16. See Maimonides, *Commentary, ad loc.*; Rashi (*ad loc.* at B. San. 27b; with *Tos. yom tob*, M. San. 3:4, s.v., *we-kol ha-raûy*, and others; but cf. *Meleket shelomoh, ad loc.*); *Tiferet yisrael*, n. 26; Albeck, *Mishnâ*, vol. 4, p. 444. I am reading the material attributed by Yose to the "first Mishnah" as extending at least to the phrase "and anyone suitable to inherit him."

[59] For *mišnâ* here as recited tradition rather than corpus, see M. Jaffee, *Torah in the Mouth* (Oxford, 1999), p. 68.

purposes onto the rules of inheritance: a "relation" is someone who can inherit from one, primarily agnatic kin.[60] The other mode casts the net more widely: it includes cognates on both the father's and mother's side and affines (people related to the person in question through marriage: e.g., step-son, wife's sister's husband, and the sons-in-law of nearly every relation mentioned). At the very least, this second mode suggests that kinship may be operationalized in different ways for different purposes, for inheritance, for example, as opposed to for giving of evidence. Certainly, this mode of kinship sees marriage as constructing patterns of relations and relatedness: one's wife's immediate relations (father, brother, son) are too close to testify or judge. As the Mishnah constructs a wider relatedness, however—in the context of a male-focused assessment of which *men* are too close—the resulting picture does not merely reflect a generic notion of "relation through marriage" but a quite specific replacement of every female relation with a husband who stands in for her. This is a complex picture, in which the Mishnah's peculiar brand of thoroughgoing patriarchy (in which wives belong to the households of their husbands, who may otherwise be "unrelated") is tied to presuppositions that marriage creates ties of proximity between men.

Kinship can, however, link women as well. One set of affinal ties, linking a wife to her husband's female relations ("her mother-in-law, her mother-in-law's daughter, her co-wife, her husband's brother's wife, and her husband's daughter"), appears to be marked in the Mishnah by a presumption of hostility (see M. Yeb. 15:4; M. Sot. 6:2). Hostility and kinship are mobilized, too, in a passage that rules on the consequences of a wife's vow not to benefit by her productive labor her own or her husband's father or brother (M. Ned.11:4). On the other hand, positive connections on the part of a wife with her paternal home is an occasionally recurring theme (M. Ter. 11:10; M. Ket. 7:4).[61] All of this

---

[60] See M. B.B. 8:1–2. Based on the individuals listed in M. B.B. 8:1, "those suitable to inherit him" would include: son, and, where there is no son, father, and brother through his father; and for a woman, her husband or son. However, 8:2 allows that in the absence of other heirs fathers' brothers (and in theory more distant agnatic kin) inherit (see the biblical setting, Num. 27:7–11 and also 36:5–12), and see Maimonides, *Code, Inheritance* 1:3, which traces succession back to relations of ascendants of the father. For the complications involved in applying M. B.B. 8:1–2 to M. San. 3:4 see, e.g. *Nimûqê yôsep, ad loc. s.v. Zô mishnat r. aqîbâ.*

[61] Note also the mother-in-law's sending food to her son-in-law's house, M. Dem. 3:6, discussed above. A father might sacrifice a Passover sacrifice with his married daughter in mind; where the couple was celebrating the first festival after their wedding with her father, the husband's sacrifice did not necessarily take precedence, M. Pes. 8:1. T. Yeb. 6:6, in which a widow or divorcée might be anxious to return to her father's house, may reflect this convention as well.

suggests that nuclear households—even within the schematic framework of the Mishnah—are more complex institutions than appears on the surface.

Historical Context

The Mishnah, we have seen, organizes its view of the household in terms of relationships to the head of household. As a consequence, for instance, it is extremely attentive to the issue of the movement of females in and out of households, and in and out of such relationships, while the transfer of males, or a son's transition to independent householder, is given far less focused attention. Given the Mishnah's concern with property and household ritual there is fairly little evidence for affective relationship within households; indeed, based on the Mishnah's own discussion, it is far easier to envision the household as the locus of competition, frequently over property: between siblings, between wife and children, or between wives and an extended circle of female relations. At the same time, the Mishnah's focus on the "nucleated" household is only occasionally explicitly mediated by pressures external to that household, notably kinship relationships.

The relative blind spots suggest that the Mishnah's schematic framework does not amount to a description of lived household practices, even if we were to agree that it reflects or effectively legislates legal principles that "real" households operated with. But this too is problematic. Documents from the Judaean Desert produced by and for Jews suggest a rather more complex relationship between the Mishnah and actual practice, at least in connection with one group of Palestinian Jews. On the one hand, there is overlap in terminology (e.g., *ketûbâ* for the monetary obligation of the husband).[62] Documents in Greek and Aramaic have clauses that look very much like those presupposed in

---

[62] Y. Yadin, J. C. Greenfield, A. Yardeni, B. A. Levine, *The Documents from the Bar Kokhba Period in the Cave of Letters: Hebrew, Aramaic, and Nabatean-Aramaic Papyri* (Jerusalem, 2002), hereafter *P. Yadin* II, no. 10.11, 17, Babatha's Aramaic marriage document. Note also "according to the laws of Moses and the Jews" in *P. Yadin* II 10 (partial letters) and *P. Mur.* 20 (almost entirely restored), and an analogous expression presupposed in M. Ket. 7:6 (possibly connected with documentary practice already in Tobit 7:14, ed. Rahlfs, p. 1025, according to Codex Sinaiticus; but cf. the text of Vaticanus and Alexandrinus; for the text of this passage see V. T. M. Skemp, *The Vulgate of Tobit Compared with Other Ancient Witnesses* [Atlanta, 2000], pp. 252–257).

M. Ket. 4:10–12.⁶³ Even the Mishnah's assumption of both polygamy and the occupation by husband and wife of separate domiciles seems attested in the documents, the latter with rather less certainty.⁶⁴

On the other hand, where the Mishnah's marriage is effected through a (nominal, M. Qid. 1:1; M. B.M. 4:7) bridegift, and the main property obligation is the husband's promise to pay the *ketûbâ* in case of divorce or death, the documents seem to assume dowry (brought by the bride into the marriage) as the primary property transfer and obligation.⁶⁵ In a number of documents both Greek and Aramaic the maintenance of the wife and her children seems to be linked to the dowry (*P. Yadin* I 18, 37 [= *P. Hev.* 65]; *P. Hev.* 69); while the Mishnah articulates such an assumption (M. Ket. 6:4⁶⁶) it makes a stronger linkage between maintenance and a wife's productive labor (M. Ket. 5:8–9). Moreover, it seems to be precisely in response to differing conventions of maintenance that two documents stipulate specifically that the husband will maintain the wife "according to Greek custom [or: law]" (*P. Yadin*

---

⁶³ See Hannah Cotton's discussion of the obligation with respect to sons and daughters, with bibliography, in the excursus to *P. Hev.* 69 (*DJD* XXVII), pp. 270–273. *P. Yadin* II. 10.10–11 has a clause dealing with redemption from captivity; arguably, this is to be restored in *P. Mur.* 20, 21 as well (following Friedman, *Jewish Marriage Law*, p. 348; the former is followed in Yardeni, *A Textbook of Aramaic, Hebrew, and Nabataean Documentary Texts from the Judaean Desert and Related Material* [Jerusalem, 2000], A, pp. 125–126). See also Friedman, *Jewish Marriage Law*, pp. 347–391, 427–443, more generally.

⁶⁴ Polygamy seems to be the most straightforward explanation of N. Lewis, *The Documents from the Bar Kokhba Period in the Cave of Letters: Greek Papyri* (Jerusalem, 1989), hereafter *P. Yadin* I, no. 26.7–8, 13–4; 34 (fr. 3).5; see the introduction to *P. Yadin* I, pp. 22–24. If Babatha was already married to Judah Khthousion at the time of the property registration where he serves as her legal guardian (as the editor, N. Lewis, believes), they may have maintained separate domiciles, *P. Yadin* I 16.14, 16–17 (each is said to be "domiciled on their private property").

⁶⁵ This is true of the Greek documents (*P. Yadin* I 18, 37 = *P. Hev.* 69; *P. Mur.* 115, 116; *P. Hev.* 65); the situation of the Aramaic documents is unclear, but Cotton, Excursus to *P. Hev.* 69, pp. 266–268, and Satlow, *Jewish Marriage*, pp. 201–202, argue that the payment or obligation called *ketûbâ* in *P. Mur.* 21 and *P. Yadin* II10 refers to dowry; cf. Y. Yadin, J. C. Greenfield, and A. Yardeni, "Babatha's *Ketuba*," in *Israel Exploration Journal* 44 (1994), p. 87, which takes the amount to be the biblical *mohar* or bridegift. (Although favored by Yadin in the restoration of line 5, the word *mohar* was not in the reading adopted by the initial 1994 publication; Yardeni, *Textbook*, pp. 125–126, and the official publication in *P. Yadin* II equivocate; see *P. Yadin* II 10, and Commentary, p. 133). The position of Satlow and Cotton is strengthened, but by no means proved, by the fact that even in early Rabbinic texts *ketûbâ* can mean "dowry" (see Cohen, *Jewish and Roman Law*, pp. 353–354; Friedman, *Jewish Marriage Law*, pp. 310–311; Satlow, "Reexamining *Ketubah*," pp. 142–144; idem, *Jewish Marriage*, pp. 213–216).

⁶⁶ See Epstein, *Nûsaḥ*, pp. 494–495; Lieberman, *TK*, vol. 6, pp. 276–277.

I 18.16, 51; *P. Hev.* 65.9–10 [= *P. Yadin* I 37]).[67] Finally, although this is contested, at least one document from the Judaean Desert seems to refer to a bill of divorce delivered by the wife, something that, whatever other methods women may have had within Rabbinic law for effecting divorce, the Mishnah does not acknowledge (*P. Hev.* 13 esp. ll. 6–7).[68]

In the limited case in which we can "test" its influence, the Mishnah does not appear to reflect what "people" did in any simple sense, although the Mishnah does comment on, or appropriate, what may have been more or less conventional practice (notably documentary practice) for its own purposes. Those purposes included articulating a model of a particular kind of highly nucleated household organized around a dominant male head of household. There is no direct evidence for the broad distribution of household patterns in Palestine. Egypt census returns indicate that a substantial proportion of households there were "extended" in some form or another; if this were true of Roman Palestine as well, the Mishnah's emphasis on "nuclearity" might be understood as an ideological preference rather than "natural."[69] The model of a household as consisting of wife (or wives), children, and slaves is, in any case, utterly conventional, comparable to that of Aristotle in the *Politics* (1.2.1) and to the so-called *Haustafeln* in New Testament epistles ascribed to Paul (Eph. 6:1–9; Col. 3:18–22). Even if a common lived pattern, such a household was, given the demographic context of the Roman world, extraordinarily fragile (and the

---

[67] I discuss this issue more fully in a forthcoming paper, "Maintenance of Wives and Children in Early Rabbinic and Documentary Texts from Roman Palestine."

[68] See, in addition to the publication in *P. Hev.*, the treatments by T. Ilan, "Notes and Observations on a Newly Published Divorce Bill from the Judaean Desert," in *Harvard Theological Review* 89 (1996), pp. 195–202; A. Schremer, "Divorce in Papyrus Seelim 13 Once Again: A Reply to Tal Ilan," in *Harvard Theological Review* 91 (1998), pp. 193–202; T. Ilan, "The Provocative Approach Once Again: A Response to Adiel Schremer," in *Harvard Theological Review* 91 (1998), pp. 203–204; H. Cotton and E. Qimron, "XHev/Se ar 13 of 134 or 135 C.E.: A Wife's Renunciation of Claims," in *Journal of Jewish Studies* 49 (1998), pp. 108–118; R. Brody, "Evidence for Divorce by Jewish Women?" in *Journal of Jewish Studies* 50 (1999), pp. 230–234.

[69] R. S. Bagnall, B. W. Frier, *Demography of Roman Egypt* (Cambridge, 1994), pp. 60–69; but cf. R. P. Saller and B. D. Shaw, "Tombstones and Roman Family Relations in the Principate: Civilians, Soldiers and Slaves," in *Journal of Religious Studies* 74 (1984), pp. 124–156; B. D. Shaw, "The Cultural Meaning of Death: Age and Gender in the Roman Family," in D. I. Kertzer and R. P. Saller, eds., *The Family in Italy from Antiquity to the Present* (New Haven, 1991), pp. 66–90; Saller, *Patriarchy*, pp. 74–101; and the criticism of Saller and Shaw in D. Martin, "The Construction of the Ancient Family: Methodological Considerations," in *Journal of Religious Studies* 86 (1986), pp. 40–60.

Judaean Desert documents certainly give evidence of households without a male head).⁷⁰ We might interpret the recurrent Rabbinic assumption of marriage of daughters at or near puberty—not clearly attested among Jews outside of Rabbinic texts, attested in only a very few *cases* in early Palestinian Rabbinic texts themselves, and probably relatively uncommon in the Roman world—as, at least in part, an assertion, in the face of contrary evidence, of a world in which men do directly control the fate of their daughters.⁷¹ Given this presumptive demographic fragility, the relative lack of attention to the succession of men to the status of married householders in their own right seems striking and not without poignancy. Yet demography will not "explain" everything, least of all the tendency of the Mishnah to devalue dowry (both as a requirement of marriage and in the sense of pitching it as fairly small, M. Ket. 6:5), and to insist on marriage based on *ketûbâ* payment. This paradigm isolates marriage in technical terms (whatever else the Mishnah allows may have happened in practice in the formation of the new household) as a legally constituted acquisition effected unilaterally by the groom, and disentangles a man (a household head) from potential dependence upon the wife's natal family (or, upon another Roman stereotype, the *uxor dotata*, the well-dowered woman).⁷²

Paradoxically, the Mishnah, with its intra-communal self-referentiality and its traditionalizing, is in many ways best contextualized in terms of the incorporation of Palestine into the system of Roman provinces.

---

⁷⁰ Saller, *Patriarchy*, pp. 25–68; see also Bagnall, Frier, *Demography*, passim (and pp. 64–65 for "life cycle" of households). Based on Saller's computer simulation (which generally conforms in terms of fertility and mortality to Bagnall and Frier's reconstruction based on Egyptian census returns, Saller, *Patriarchy*, p. 68, table 3.4), already at age fifteen over one third of children (boys or girls) would have had no living father (Saller, *Patriarchy*, tables 3.1b, 3.1e); by age twenty that proportion rises to about one half.

⁷¹ For age of marriage see the preceding note and K. Hopkins, "The Age of Roman Girls at Marriage," in *Population Studies* 18 (1965), pp. 309–327; idem, "Brother-Sister Marriage in Roman Egypt," in *CSSH* 22 (1980), pp. 333–334, suggesting a later age for women than for the western empire, and than Bagnall, Frier, *Demography*, pp. 111–121 (and p. 133 n. 82) for Egypt; B. D. Shaw, "The Age of Roman Girls at Marriage: Some Reconsiderations," in *Journal of Religious Studies* 77 (1987), pp. 30–46, using a different method than Hopkins, argues for a later age, in the late teens to early twenties, comparable to the Egyptian evidence. For discussion of the rabbinic context see above n. 34; and Ilan, *Jewish Women*, p. 84, for cases of daughters married as minors "refusing" their husbands; but cf. Katzoff, "Age of Marriage." The significance of "cases" is not that they happened but that someone at least claimed they did. My suggestion is quite close to that of Satlow, *Jewish Marriage*, pp. 109–111.

⁷² See S. Treggiari, *Roman Marriage* (Oxford, 1991), pp. 329–331; cf. Saller, *Patriarchy*, p. 221.

This process began outright in the early years of the first century C.E. and was by no means complete when the second revolt against Rome in 132–135 was suppressed.[73] The process was thus precisely contemporaneous with the development of the Mishnah. Thus, for instance, I have argued elsewhere that the Mishnah was the product of moderately wealthy landed men resident in larger settlements and that rabbis constituted a largely urban group by some time in the third century.[74] Urbanization, a feature of provincialization, may perhaps be connected to the emphasis on the "nuclearity" of the household in the Mishnah, which, it has been argued for other regions of the empire, fostered the formation of nuclear households.[75]

In addition, the Judaean Desert documents make it clear that provincials, even provincials who became embroiled in a revolt against Rome, availed themselves of what they labeled "Greek" law or custom and of the court system of the then newly-formed Roman province of Arabia (e.g., most strikingly, *P. Yadin* I 28–30). It is worth remembering therefore that a substantial proportion of the preserved documents, especially in Greek, relate to households and their constitution and property structure, presumably relying on provincial courts for results not otherwise available "traditionally."[76] It is probably not too much to suggest that precisely what the household looked like was among the issues about which Palestinian (Jewish) provincials differed under Roman rule. In lower Galilee, where the Mishnah seems to have been produced, urbanization and other forms of provincial administration may have progressed faster than in the Dead Sea area, and such differences may have been even more accentuated there. Seen in those terms, the staking out of a claim to legislating the form of proper Israelite households in the

---

[73] See, for a general overview, E. M. Smallwood, *The Jews under Roman Rule from Pompey to Diocletian*, 2 ed. (Leiden, 1981). My own somewhat idiosyncratic view is briefly discussed in *Economy*, pp. 155–162.

[74] Lapin, *Early Rabbinic Civil Law*; idem, "Rabbis and Cities: The Literary Evidence," in *Journal of Jewish Studies* 50 (1999), pp. 187–207; "Rabbis and Cities: Some Aspects of the Rabbinic Movement in its Greco-Roman Environment," in P. Schäfer and C. Hezser, eds., *The Talmud Yerushalmi in Greco-Roman Culture II* (Tübingen, 2000), pp. 51–80.

[75] See both Bagnall and Frier, *Demography*, pp. 66–70, table 3.2; Shaw, "Death," pp. 85–90.

[76] See, e.g., H. M. Cotton and J. C. Greenfield, "Babatha's Property and the Law of Succession in the Babatha Archive," in *Zietschrift für Papyrologie und Epigraphik* 104 (1994), pp. 211–224; but with reservations expressed in H. M. Cotton, "The Law of Succession in the Documents from the Judaean Desert Again," in *SCI* 17 (1998), pp. 115–123.

Mishnah becomes part of a contest over local authority and normative practice under Roman rule. In this sense, the very phenomenon of the Rabbinic movement—wealthy, literate provincials claiming the authority of tradition to shape the proper practices of "the people"—may be understood as the product of provincialization.

THE MISHNAH IN HISTORICAL AND RELIGIOUS CONTEXT

Jacob Neusner
Bard College

The Mishnah is to be interpreted in the context of the crisis of the mid-second century, a crisis of both a historical-political and a religious-theological character. For a moment, Israel lost its autonomous polity in its own land, and, for the foreseeable future, the institutional embodiments of Israel's religious way of life and theological world view lay in ruins. Then, in the aftermath of the calamity brought about by the Bar Kokhba rebellion, the Temple was replaced by a pagan temple, and Jerusalem closed off to Israelite entry. From the return to Zion and the restoration of Israelite polity in the Land of Israel in the fifth century B.C.E., the events of 70–135 embodied the one disaster that represented a crisis in the interior life of Judaism. The former date, 70, asked a familiar question, the latter one, 135, gave an unprecedented answer.

To be more explicit, in August, 70 C.E., after four years of fighting, from 66 forward, the Roman army captured Jerusalem, restored Roman rule over the Land of Israel, and burned the Temple. That was a disaster. But the defeat provoked no crisis, for people knew what to expect. Scripture had told them about the exile of 586 B.C.E. and the return to Zion "three generations later," realized in ca. 530 B.C.E. and fully accomplished in the next century by Ezra and Nehemiah. They could explain what had happened and knew what to expect. So Israel could look forward to the recapitulation of the same established pattern and understood the disaster in context. But that is not how matters turned out. "Three generations" later, in 135, after three years of a second and still more catastrophic war for Israel's freedom from Rome, Jerusalem fell once more. Again the Romans retook Jerusalem, this time plowing over the Temple site and forbidding Jews to enter the city. This time, then, loss and destruction of the Temple was not followed by recovery and restoration but by utter ruin. And that event violated the established pattern.

Here we identify how a disaster becomes a crisis. That transformation takes place when people can make no sense of what has happened and find no reason to take courage in the future. The first of the two events—the destruction that happened in 70—could find its place in the established pattern of exile and return. The Temple had been destroyed before, but restored in the aftermath of Israel's suffering as punishment for its sin, repentance, atonement, and reconciliation with God. The restored Temple stood for that reconciliation. No wonder, three generations beyond 70, people fought to realize the ancient, reliable pattern.

Then what was to be said now, when the established pattern failed to repeat itself? The second destruction—definitive defeat, no prospect of recovery—could not find its explanation in the familiar pattern of exile and return. And that failure of the received Judaic account of Israel, its exile and return, defined the crisis to which the Mishnah represented the response and new beginning. For the Mishnah responded to the failure of the established pattern with a message of restoration and reconstruction all its own.

Content of the Historical-Political Crisis and Its Resolution

The Temple, destroyed in 586 B.C.E. and rebuilt three generations later, by the time of its second destruction had stood for five hundred years, as long a spell as separates us from Columbus. And, because of the message of the Judaism of the Torah of Moses, people regarded the fate of the Temple as a barometer of the relationship of their unique people-family to God. With its destruction by the Romans, the foundations of Israel's national and social life in the land of Israel were shaken. For the Temple had constituted one of the primary, unifying elements in that common life. People related the movement of the seasons and the sun in heaven to the cult in the Temple. They associated the first full moon after the vernal equinox with the rite of the Passover, the first full moon after the autumnal equinox with that of Tabernacles. They attained personal atonement for their sins of inadvertence (so they believed; how many did it God alone knows) by minor offerings, and they believed that, in the rite of the Day of Atonement, they reconciled themselves with God.

The Temple, moreover, had served as the basis for those many elements of autonomous self-government and political life left in the

Jews' hands by the Romans. The government of the country appealed for legitimacy to the Temple and the priesthood, with which it associated itself. The structure not only of political life and of society, but also of the imaginative life of the country, depended upon the Temple and its worship and cult. It was there that people believed they served God. At the Temple the lines of structure—both cosmic and social—converged. The altar was the point at which the transfer of life from heaven to earth took place: the transaction that sustained the world. Consequently, the destruction of the Temple meant not merely a significant alteration in the cultic or ritual life of the Jewish people, but also a profound and far-reaching crisis in their inner and spiritual existence.

When the Temple was destroyed, two distinctive groups survived, the scribes with their learning, and the priests with their memories, their sense of what God required for service, and their notion that all Israel, every Jew, stood in relationship to all others within the grid of holiness. What happened was that, over the next half century or so, these two groups began to forge that system that, through and beyond the Mishnah, would become Rabbinic Judaism. The period from 70 to the Bar Kokhba War, ca. 132–135, yielded the foundations of the Mishnaic system, system derived from the combination of three distinct political forces: [1] Roman rule, [2] a local Jewish authority, called the patriarch, recognized by Rome as legitimate Jewish administrator of Israel's affairs, and [3] the administration of the patriarch, staffed by knowledgeable clerks, called sages. The system took shape from 70 forward, originally, it would appear, in Yavneh, a coastal town.

We recall that the Persians, ruling a diverse empire, under Cyrus adopted the policy of identifying local groups and ruling through them, a standard imperial procedure followed when the ruling empire did not choose to settle its own population in a conquered area (e.g., the policy of the British in Nigeria but not in Kenya). Fortunately for the Jewish people, the several successor-empires, from the Persians, through the Macedonians under Alexander and then the inheritor states of Ptolemies and Seleucids, and, finally, the Romans, determined to leave the land of Israel in the hands of loyal regents. The Romans first supported the Maccabees, then Herod and his family. That policy—essentially a millet-system—remained in effect even after the Jewish wars against Rome in 66 and again in 132. Roman policy involved finding, in native populations, trustworthy leaders, who would keep the peace and execute Roman policy.

After 70, the Romans gave up on the policy of depending on the family of Herod, which had manifestly failed. They accorded some sort of limited recognition to a Jewish ruler of a different family, a Pharisaic one. Our knowledge of the new ruling figure scarcely extends beyond his name, Gamaliel, though we know that his heirs later on sustained the institution of Jewish rule that he began.

How and why the Romans turned to Gamaliel, we can only guess. He was the son of Simeon b. Gamaliel, a leading figure among the Pharisees before 70, and grandson of yet another such figure. That means that Gamaliel got Roman recognition as a promising local authority of a distinguished family prepared to cooperate with the government. As *nasi*, Gamaliel associated with himself two sorts of survivors of the war. One, as we realize, represented the pre-70 Pharisees, of which he was probably an adherent. The other derived from the important state officials of the period before 70, who, in the aggregate, are known as scribes: people who knew and administered the laws. Whatever sages associated themselves with the patriarchal regime contributed the know-how of government, and such administration, on a local basis, as the Jews of the land of Israel would know, derived from that group.

The patriarchal government with its scribal staff from the Roman perspective enjoyed only modest success, because they could not prevent the war of Bar Kokhba from breaking out. But once more the Romans after Bar Kokhba's defeat turned back to the system of ethnarchies and restored the ruling regime, this time with complete success. It endured into the fifth century, at which time the Christian government of Rome determined not to accord it further recognition. An equivalent system employed by the Parthian, then the Sasanian, rulers of Iran, across the eastern frontier from Rome, led to the development there of a Jewish ethnarchy, the exilarchate. Both regimes adopted as their constitution and law the Mishnah produced by Judah the patriarch, on account of which the document enjoyed immediate acceptance as the Jews' law code after Scripture. So much for the first and most important reason for the development of Judaism: the political choices made by outsiders. Judaism in the same form endured in part for the same reason, that is, Christendom and Islam tolerated it. But the other part of the reason matters far more: the Jews wanted to form their world within the structure of that Judaism, in that form. The reason is that that was the Judaism that asked the questions they found urgent and provided answers they deemed self-evidently valid.

The Religious-Theological Crisis and Its Resolution: The System of the Mishnah

From the political context that defined the foundations of the Mishnah's system, we turn to its method and doctrine—the world view, the way of life of that system. Our task, is to describe, analyze, and interpret that system as a religious and theological response to the critical turning of Israel in the second century in the land of Israel.

To understand the fundamental ontological structure of the Judaic system set forth by the Mishnah, we have to review what we know about one of the principal groups that contributed to the document, the Pharisees. These were Jews who, before the destruction of the Temple, had kept the laws of purity at home, and not only in the Temple, where people generally understood that those laws were to be kept. The Pharisees had tried to live a life of holiness, of sanctification, as if they were priests in the Temple. The relevance of the character of Pharisaic Judaism before 70 to the success of the Judaism they helped to shape is simple. When the Temple was destroyed, it turned out that the Pharisees had prepared for that tremendous change in the sacred economy. Lay people pretending to be priests, even after the destruction of the Temple to which those laws had applied, could continue in the paths of holiness the Temple had shown for centuries. Israel the people was holy, not only the place of the Temple and Jerusalem, not only the rite of the cult in the Temple. The Pharisees' (like the Essenes') doctrine of Israel as the holy people living the holy life proved remarkably congruent to the urgent issue posed by the destruction of the Temple.

The self-evident answer to the question of the destruction—who is Israel now? is Israel yet holy now?—was that Israel remains holy and effects sanctification through its act of intentionality. But that meant, with enormous emphasis, *Israel as a whole* and not solely the priesthood, Israel in its every day life and not only the priests in the Temple. The destruction of the Temple as a real place found compensation in the pretense that the Pharisees before 70 had maintained. True, the buildings are gone, but the critical issue was holiness, and holiness endures: a powerful and acutely pertinent message, an answer to the question of the day. That remarkable congruity between the Pharisaic view of Israelite life and the circumstances prevailing after the destruction of the Temple in 70 accounts for the success of the Judaism to which the Pharisees made a major contribution. For the political advantages accorded to the Pharisees through Gamaliel after 70 should not obscure the doctrinal ones they enjoyed.

The Mishnah's system, inheriting important components from the Pharisaism of the period before 70, therefore would maintain that the holiness of the life of Israel, the people, a holiness that had formerly centered on the Temple, now endured and transcended the physical destruction of the building and the cessation of sacrifices. Israel the people was holy, was the medium and the instrument of God's sanctification. The system then instructed Israel to act as if there was a new Temple formed of Israel, the Jewish people. Joined to the Pharisaic mode of looking at life, now centered in the doctrine of the holiness of Israel the people, was the substance of the scribal ideal, the stress on learning of Torah and carrying out its teachings. The emerging system would claim, like the scribes of old, that it was possible to serve God not only through sacrifice, but also through study of Torah. So the question is the question of the priests and Pharisees: how to serve God? But the answer is the answer of the scribes: through Torah-learning.

The union of scribe and priest yielded the sage, bearing the honorific title, Rabbi. To spell this out: a priest is in charge of the life of the community, just as the priests had said. But the new priest now qualified not by birth in the priestly caste. Rather, the validation derived from learning in the Torah: the new priest was a sage. The old sin-offerings too still may be carried out. But today it would be the sacrifice of deeds of loving-kindness in that tradition of wisdom that the rabbi would teach. Like the prophets and historians in the time of the first destruction, the sages or rabbis further claimed that it was because the people had sinned, had not kept the Torah, that the Temple had been destroyed. Then the disaster itself was made to vindicate the Rabbinic teaching and to verify its truth. When the people lived up to the teachings of the Torah as the rabbis expressed them, the Temple would be restored in response to the people's repentance and renewal.

To summarize the history of the formation of Judaism in the aftermath of the crisis of the second century: selecting its materials from the entire inherited repertoire, the system of Rabbinic Judaism began its formative history with the destruction of the second Temple of Jerusalem. The important figures derived from two groups before 70, the Pharisees, on the one side, sponsored as they were by Gamaliel, and the scribes or sages, necessary for the reconstitution of a Jewish government and administration, on the other. These groups do not really compare to one another, because the one constituted a religious sect, the other was made up of a profession, people who had mastered the Torah and applied its rules to the practical life of the people. Each made its contribution to the Judaism that would emerge.

The method, the way of life, of that system of Judaism as it would reach its final definition was the Pharisaic method, with its stress on the everyday sanctification of all Israel.

The world-view, the substance of that Judaism, was the scribal message, with its stress on the Torah.

Pharisaism lay stress upon universal keeping of the law, obligating every Jew to do what only the elite—the priests—were normally expected to accomplish. The professional ideal of the scribes stressed the study of Torah and the centrality of the learned person in the religious system. But there was something more. It was the doctrine of Israel and that made all the difference. If the world view came from the scribes, the way of life from the Pharisees, the doctrine of who is Israel—and the social reality beyond the doctrine—was fresh and unpredictable. It was surviving Israel, the Jewish people beyond the caesura marked by the apparently-permanent destruction of the Temple. What made the Judaic system aborning after 70 and fully realized beyond 135 more than the sum of its primary components, Pharisaism and scribism, was that very doctrine, which neither Pharisaism nor scribism can have contributed. The crisis of the failure of the ancient paradigm—destruction, repentance, reconstruction and reconciliation—is what centered attention on what had endured, persisting beyond the end. It was the people itself. Why focus attention on that people is not a difficult question to answer. We recall the established conviction that Israel was special, what happened to Israel signified God's will. What was unpredictable in fact marked a recapitulation of the most typical and fundamental characteristic of the original, and generative, paradigm. That is, Israel because of its (in its mind) amazing experience of loss and restoration, death and resurrection, had attained remarkable self-consciousness. In the life of a nation that had ceased to be a nation on its own land and then once more had regained that condition, the present calamity represented once more the paradigm of the death and resurrection. Consequently, the truly fresh and definitive component of the new system, after 70, in fact restated in contemporary terms the fixed and established doctrine with which the first Judaism, the Judaism of the Torah of "Moses" after 450, had commenced.

The religious system, Rabbinic Judaism, that begins with the Mishnah, its first document beyond Scripture, vastly transcended its original components, Pharisaism and Scribism, sanctification, on the one side, stress on mastery of the Torah, on the other. The unpredictable, final element in the synthesis of Pharisaic stress on widespread law, including ritual-law, observance and scribal emphasis on learning, is what makes Judaism distinctive. That is the conviction that the community now stands in the place of the Temple. The ruins of the cult did not mark the end of the collective, holy life of Israel. What survived was the holy people. It was the genius of the Judaic system of sanctification, that took shape after 70 and reached its full expression in the Mishnah, to recognize that the holy people might reconstitute the Temple in the sanctity of its own community life. Therefore the people had to be made holy, as the Temple had been holy. The people's social life had to be sanctified as the surrogate for what had been lost. That is why the Rabbinic ideal for Judaism further maintained that the rabbi served as the new priest, the study of Torah substituted for the Temple sacrifice, and deeds of loving-kindness were the social surrogate for the sin-offering—personal sacrifice instead of animal sacrifice. All things fit together to construct out of the old Judaisms the world-view and way of life of the new and enduring system that ultimately became Rabbinic Judaism. And that brings us to the Mishnah, its contents, character, and system.

THE MISHNAH'S RELIGIOUS SYSTEM FOR THE ISRAELITE SOCIAL ORDER

The Mishnah sets forth its statement through six systematic topical divisions, each devoted to a fundamental component of an encompassing theory of Israel's social order. These deal with agriculture, the seasons, the family ("Women"), civil law, Holy Things, and Purities. Let us review the main emphases and principal messages of each:

Agriculture

The religious system—Israel's power of effective sanctification through proper intentionality—of the Division of Agriculture, on the tithing laws, is expressed by Richard S. Sarason in the following language:

> The Mishnah's primary concern is with the process of sanctification of the various agricultural offerings. and. particularly. in the part which man plays in the process of sanctification. A careful analysis of these tractates will show that The Mishnah's theory of the holiness of produce which

grows from the soil of the Land of Israel is transactional. That is to say, holiness does not naturally inhere in produce. Rather, God and man are the agents of sanctification. God, as owner of the Land, has a prior claim on its produce. But man must acknowledge God's ownership, and validate God's claim through actively designating and separating God's portion. Additionally, holiness is to be understood primarily in functional rather than substantive terms, i.e., that which is deemed holy belongs to God (and frequently is allotted by God to his priests), and must not be used by ordinary Israelites. Sacrilege thus is conceived as a violation of God's property rights. The authorities behind The Mishnah primarily are interested in spelling out the role of human action and, particularly intention in the process of sanctification. That role is determinative throughout the process.

The Mishnah's theory of holiness in Seder Zeraim is transactional. Nothing (except perhaps for God) is inherently sacred. The land of Israel is sanctified through its relationship to God. The produce of the Lord is sanctified by man, acting under God's commandment, through verbal designation and separation of the various offerings. Man, through his action and intention, additionally determines what is susceptible to sanctification (i.e., liable to tithing as human food), and the point at which it is susceptible (i.e., edible, at the point of completion of processing or harvesting, or the point of intention to make a fixed meal). The Mishnah's primary concern is that people should separate properly that which is due to God, so that non-priests will not eat produce bonded or consecrated to God. The Mishnah's authorities further wish to examine in detail the human role in the process of sanctification and to specify the power of will, word, and deed.

Appointed Times

The advent of a holy day, like the Sabbath of creation, sanctifies the life of the Israelite village through imposing on the village rules on the model of those of the Temple. The purpose of the system, therefore, is to bring into alignment the moment of sanctification of the village and the life of the home with the moment of sanctification of the Temple on those same occasions of appointed times. The underlying and generative theory of the system is that the village is the mirror image of the Temple. If things are done in one way in the Temple, they will be done in the opposite way in the village. Together the village and the Temple on the occasion of the holy day therefore form a single continuum, a completed creation, thus awaiting sanctification.

The village is made like the Temple in that on appointed times one may not freely cross the lines distinguishing the village from the rest of the world, just as one may not freely cross the lines distinguishing the Temple from the world. But the village is a mirror image of the Temple. The boundary lines prevent free entry into the Temple, so they restrict free egress from the village. On the holy day what one may do in the Temple is precisely what one may not do in the village. The advent of the holy day thus affects the village by bringing it into sacred symmetry in such wise as to effect a system of opposites; each is holy, in a way precisely the opposite of the other. Because of the underlying conception of perfection attained through the union of opposites, the village is not represented as conforming to the model of the cult, but of constituting its antithesis. The world thus regains perfection when on the holy day heaven and earth are united, the whole completed and done: the heaven, the earth, and all their hosts. This moment of perfection renders the events of ordinary time, of "history," essentially irrelevant. For what really matters in time is that moment in which sacred time intervenes and effects the perfection formed of the union of heaven and earth, of Temple, in the model of the former, and Israel, its complement. It is not a return to a perfect time but a recovery of perfect being, a fulfillment of creation, which explains the essentially ahistorical character of the Division on Appointed Times. Sanctification constitutes an ontological category and is effected by the creator.

This explains why the Division in its rich detail is composed of two quite distinct sets of materials. First, it addresses what one does in the sacred space of the Temple on the occasion of sacred time, as distinct from what one does in that same sacred space on ordinary, undifferentiated days, which is a subject worked out in Holy Things. Second, the Division defines how for the occasion of the holy day one creates a corresponding space in one's own circumstance and what one does, within that space, during sacred time. The issue of the Temple and cult on the special occasion of festivals is treated in tractates Pesahim, Sheqalim, Yoma, Sukkah, and Hagigah. Three further tractates, Rosh Hashanah, Taanit, and Megillah, are necessary to complete the discussion. The matter of the rigid definition of the outlines in the village, of a sacred space, delineated by the limits within which one may move on the Sabbath and festival, and of the specification of those things which one may not do within that space in sacred time, is in Shabbat, Erubin, Besah, and Moed Qatan. While the twelve tractates of the Division appear to fall into two distinct groups, joined merely by a common theme, in fact they relate through a shared, generative metaphor. It is, as I said, the comparison, in the context of sacred time, of the spatial life of the Temple to the spatial life of the village, with activities and restrictions to be specified for each, upon the common occasion of the Sabbath or festival. The Mishnah's purpose therefore is to correlate the sanctity of the Temple, as defined by the holy day, with the restrictions of space and of action which make the life of the village different and holy, as defined by the holy day.

Family/Women

The Division of Women defines the role and rights of women in the social economy of Israel's supernatural and natural reality. Women acquire definition wholly in relationship to men, who impart form to the Israelite social economy. The status of women is effected through both supernatural and natural, this-worldly action. What man and woman do on earth provokes a response in heaven, and the correspondences are perfect. So women are defined and secured both in heaven and here on earth, and that position is always and invariably relative to men. The principal interest for the Mishnah is the point at which a woman becomes, and ceases to be, holy to a particular man, that is, enters and leaves the marital union. These transfers of women are the dangerous and disorderly points in the relationship of woman to man, therefore, the Mishnah states, to society as well.

The formation of the marriage comes under discussion in Qiddushin and Ketubot, as well as in Yebamot. The rules for the duration of the marriage are scattered throughout, but derive especially from parts of Ketubot, Nedarim, and Nazir, on the one side, and the paramount unit of Sotah, on the other. The dissolution of the marriage is dealt with in Gittin, as well as in Yebamot. We see very clearly, therefore, that important overall are issues of the transfer of property, along with women, covered in Ketubot and to some measure in Qiddushin, and the proper documentation of the transfer of women and property, treated in Ketubot and Gittin. The critical issues thus turn upon legal documents—writs of divorce, for example—and legal recognition of changes in the ownership of property, e.g., through the collection of the settlement of a marriage contract by a widow, through the provision of a dowry, or through the disposition of the property of a woman during the period in which she is married. Within this orderly world of documentary and procedural concerns a place is made for the disorderly conception of the marriage not formed by human volition but decreed in heaven, the levirate connection. Yebamot states that supernature sanctifies a woman to a man (under the conditions of the levirate connection).

What it says by indirection is that man sanctifies too: man, like God, can sanctify that relationship between a man and a woman, and can also effect the cessation of the sanctity of that same relationship. Five of the seven tractates of the Division of Women are devoted to the formation and dissolution of the marital bond. Of them, three treat what is done by man here on earth, that is, formation of a marital bond through betrothal and marriage contract and dissolution through divorce and its consequences: Qiddushin, Ketubot, and Gittin. One of them is devoted to what is done by woman here on earth: Sotah. And Yebamot, greatest of the seven in size and in formal and substantive brilliance, deals with the corresponding heavenly intervention into the formation and end of a marriage: the effect of death upon both forming the marital bond and dissolving it through death. The other two tractates, Nedarim and Nazir, draw into one the two realms of reality, heaven and earth, as they work out the effects of vows, perhaps because vows taken by women and subject to the confirmation or abrogation of the father or husband make a deep impact upon the marital life of the woman who has taken them.

The Division and its system delineate the natural and supernatural character of the woman's role in the social economy framed by man: the beginning, end, and middle of the relationship. The whole constitutes a significant part of the Mishnah's encompassing system of sanctification, for the reason that heaven confirms what men do on earth. A correctly prepared writ of divorce on earth changes the status of the woman to whom it is given, so that in heaven she is available for sanctification to some other man, while, without that same writ, in heaven's view, should she go to some other man, she would be liable to be put to death. The earthly deed and the heavenly perspective correlate. That is indeed very much part of larger system, which says the same thing over and over again.

The system of Women thus focuses upon the two crucial stages in the transfer of women and of property from one domain to another, the leaving of the father's house in the formation of a marriage, and the return to the father's house at its dissolution through divorce or the husband's death. There is yet a third point of interest, though, as is clear, it is much less important than these first two stages: the duration of the marriage. Finally, included within the Division and at a few points relevant to women in particular are rules of vows and of the special vow to be a Nazir. The former is included because, in the Scriptural treatment of the theme, the rights of the father or husband to annul the vows of a daughter or wife form the central problematic. The latter is included for no very clear reason except that it is a species of which the vow is the genus.

Civil Law/Damages

This Division comprises two subsystems, which fit together in a logical way. One part presents rules for the normal conduct of civil society: commerce, trade, real estate, and other matters of everyday intercourse, as well as mishaps, such as damages by chattels and persons, fraud, overcharge, interest, and the like, in that same context of everyday social life. The other part describes the institutions governing the normal conduct of civil society, that is, courts of administration, and the penalties at the disposal of the government for the enforcement of the law. The two subjects form a single tight and systematic dissertation on the nature of Israelite society and its economic, social, and political relationships, as the Mishnah envisages them.

The main point of the first of the two parts of the Division is expressed in the sustained unfolding of the Baba Qamma, Baba Mesia, and Baba Batra. Society must maintain perfect stasis, preserve the prevailing situation, and secure the stability of all relationships. To this end, in the interchanges of buying and selling, giving and taking, borrowing and lending, it is important that there be an essential equality of interchange. No party in the end should have more than at the outset, and none should be the victim of a sizable shift in fortune and circumstance. All parties' rights to, and in, this stable and unchanging economy of society are to be preserved. When the condition of a person is violated, so far as possible the law will secure the restoration of the antecedent status.

An appropriate appendix to the Babas is at Abodah Zarah, on the orderly governance of transactions and relationships between Israelite society and the outside world, the realm of idolatry, relationships which are subject to certain special considerations. These are generated by the fact that Israelites may not derive benefit (e.g., through commercial transactions) from anything that has served in the worship of an idol.

Consequently, commercial transactions suffer limitations on account of extrinsic considerations of cultic taboos. While these cover both special occasions, e.g., fairs and festivals of idolatry, and general matters, that is, what Israelites may buy and sell, the main practical illustrations of the principles of the matter pertain to wine. The Mishnah supposes that gentiles routinely make use, for a libation, of a drop of any sort of wine to which they have access. It therefore is taken for granted that wine over which gentiles have had control is forbidden for Israelite use and also that such wine is prohibited for Israelites to buy and sell. This other matter—ordinary everyday relationships with the gentile world, with special reference to trade and commerce—concludes what the Mishnah has to say about all those matters of civil and criminal law which together define everyday relationships within the Israelite nation and between that nation and all others in the world among whom, in Palestine as abroad, they lived side by side.

The other part of the Division describes the institutions of Israelite government and politics. This is in two main aspects, first, the description of the institutions and their jurisdiction, with reference to courts, conceived as both judicial and administrative agencies, and, second, the extensive discussion of criminal penalties. The penalties are three: death, banishment, and flogging. There are four ways by which a person convicted of a capital crime may be put to death. The Mishnah organizes a vast amount of information on what sorts of capital crimes are punishable by which of the four modes of execution. That information is alleged to derive from Scripture. But the facts are many, and the relevant verses few. What the Mishnah clearly contributes to this exercise is a first-rate piece of organization and elucidation of available facts. Where the facts come from we do not know. The Mishnah tractate Sanhedrin further describes the way in which trials are conducted in both monetary and capital cases and pays attention to the possibilities of perjury. The matter of banishment brings the Mishnah to a rather routine restatement by flogging and application of that mode of punishment conclude the discussion.

These matters, worked out at Sanhedrin-Makkot, are supplemented in two tractates, Shebuot and Horayot, both emerging from Scripture. Lev. 5 and 6 refer to various oaths that apply mainly, though not exclusively, in courts. Lev. 4 deals with errors of judgment inadvertently made and carried out by the high priest, the ruler, and the people; the Mishnah knows that these considerations apply to Israelite courts too. What for Leviticus draws the chapters together is their common interest in the guilt offering, which is owing for violation of the rather diverse matters under discussion. Now in tractates Shebuot and Horayot the materials of Lev. 5–6 and 4, respectively, are worked out. But here is it from the viewpoint of the oath or erroneous instruction, rather than the cultic penalty. In Shebuot the discussion in intellectually imaginative and thorough, in Horayot, routine. The relevance of both to the issues of Sanhedrin and Makkot is obvious. For the matter of oaths in the main enriches the discussion of the conduct of the courts. The possibility of error is principally in the courts and other political institutions. so the four tractates on institutions and their functioning form a remarkable unified and cogent set.

The goal of the system of civil law is the recovery of the prevailing order and balance, the preservation of the established wholeness of the social economy. This idea is powerfully expressed in the organization of the three Babas, which treat first abnormal and then normal transactions. The framers deal with damages done by chattels and by human beings, thefts and other sorts of malfeasance against the property of others. The Babas in both aspects pay closest attention to how the property and person of the injured party so far as possible are restored to their prior condition, that is, a state of normality. So attention to torts focuses upon penalties paid by the malefactor to the victim, rather than upon penalties inflicted by the court on the malefactor for what he has done. When speaking of damages, the Mishnah thus takes as its principal concern the restoration of the fortune of victims of assault or robbery. Then the framers take up the complementary and corresponding set of topics, the regulation of normal transactions. When we rapidly survey the kinds of transactions of special interest, we see from the topics selected for discussion what we have already uncovered in the deepest structure of organization and articulation of the basic theme.

The other half of this same unit of three tractates presents laws governing normal and routine transactions, many of them of the same sort as those dealt with in the first half. Bailments, for example, occur in both wings of the triple tractate, first, bailments subjected to misappropriation, or accusation thereof, by the bailiff, then, bailments transacted under normal circumstances. Under the rubric of routine transactions are those of workers and householders, that is, the purchase and sale of labor; rentals and bailments; real estate transactions; and inheritances and estates. Of the lot, the one involving real estate transactions is the most fully articulated and covers the widest range of problems and topics. The Babas all together thus provide a complete account of the orderly governance of balanced transactions and unchanging civil relationships within Israelite society under ordinary conditions.

The character and interests of the Division of Damages present probative evidence of the larger program of the philosophers of the Mishnah. Their intention is to create nothing less than a full-scale Israelite government, subject to the administration of sages. This government is fully supplied with a constitution and bylaws (Sanhedrin, Makkot). It makes provision for a court system and procedures (Shebuot, Sanhedrin, Makkot), as well as a full set of laws governing civil society (Baba Qamma, Baba Mesia, Baba Batra) and criminal justice (Sanhedrin, Makkot). This government, moreover, mediates between its own community and the outside ("pagan") world. Through its system of laws it expresses its judgment of the others and at the same time defines, protects, and defends its own society and social frontiers (Abodah Zarah). It even makes provision for procedures of remission, to expiate its own errors (Horayot).

The (then non-existent) Israelite government imagined by the second-century philosophers centers upon the (then non-existent) Temple, and the (then forbidden) city, Jerusalem. For the Temple is one principal focus. There the highest court is in session; there the high priest reigns. The penalties for law infringement are of three kinds, one of which involves sacrifice in the Temple. (The others are compensation, physical punishment, and death.) The basic conception of punishment, moreover, is that unintentional infringement of the rules of society, whether "religious" or otherwise, is not penalized but rather expiated through an offering in the Temple. If a member of the people of Israel intentionally infringes against the law, to be sure, that one must be removed from society and is put to death. And if there is a claim of one member of the people against another, that must be righted, so that the prior, prevailing status may be restored. So offerings in the Temple are given up to appease heaven and restore a whole bond between heaven and Israel, specifically on those occasions on which without malice or ill will an Israelite has disturbed the relationship. Israelite civil society without a Temple is not stable or normal, and not to be imagined. And the Mishnah is above all an act of imagination in defiance of reality.

The plan for the government involves a clear-cut philosophy of society, a philosophy that defines the purpose of the government and ensures that its task is not merely to perpetuate its own power. Within the Mishnaic fantasy, the Israelite government is supposed to preserve that state of perfection that, within the same fantasy, the society to begin with everywhere attains and expresses. This is in at least five aspects. First of all, one of the ongoing principles of the law, expressed in one tractate after another, is that people are to follow and maintain the prevailing practice of their locale. Second, the purpose of civil penalties, as we have noted, is to restore the injured party to his prior condition, so far as this is possible, rather than merely to penalize the aggressor. Third, there is the conception of true value, meaning that a given object has an intrinsic worth, which, in the course of a transaction, must be paid. In this way the seller does not leave the transaction any richer than when he entered it, or the buyer any poorer (parallel to penalties for damages). Fourth, there can be no usury, a biblical prohibition adopted and vastly enriched in the Mishnaic thought, for money ("coins") is what it is. Any pretense that it has become more than what it was violates, in its way, the conception of true value. Fifth, when real estate is divided, it must be done with full attention to the rights of all concerned, so that, once more, one party does not gain at the expense of the other. In these and many other aspects the law expresses its obsession with the perfect stasis of Israelite society. Its paramount purpose is in preserving and ensuring that that perfection of the division of this world is kept inviolate or restored to its true status when violated.

Holy Things

The Division of Holy Things presents a system of sacrifice and sanctuary: Matters concerning the praxis of the altar and maintenance of the sanctuary. The praxis of the altar, specifically, involves sacrifice and things set aside for sacrifice and so deemed consecrated. The topic covers these among the eleven tractates of the present Division: Zebahim and part of Hullin, Menahot, Temurah, Keritot, part of Meilah, Tamid, and Qinnim. The maintenance of the sanctuary (inclusive of the personnel) in dealt with in Bekhorot, Arakhin, part of Meilah, Middot, and part of Hullin. Viewed from a distance, therefore, the Mishnah's tractates divide themselves up into the following groups (in parentheses are tractates containing relevant materials): (1) Rules for the altar and the praxis of the cult—Zebahim Menahot, Hullin, Keritot, Tamid, Qinnim (Bekhorot, Meilah); (2) Rules for the altar and the animals set aside for the cult—Arakhin, Temurah, Meilah (Bekhorot); and (3) Rules for the altar and support of the Temple staff and buildings—Bekhorot,

Middot (Hullin, Arakhin, Meilah, Tamid). In a word, this Division speaks of the sacrificial cult and the sanctuary in which the cult is conducted. The law pays special attention to the matter of the status of the property of the altar and of the sanctuary, both materials to be utilized in the actual sacrificial rites, and property the value of which supports the cult and sanctuary in general. Both are deemed to be sanctified, that is: "holy things."

The Division of Holy Things centers upon the everyday and rules always applicable to the cult: the daily whole offering, the sin offering and guilt offering which one may bring any time under ordinary circumstances; the right sequence of diverse offerings; the way in which the rites of the whole, sin, and guilt offerings are carried out; what sorts of animals are acceptable; the accompanying cereal offerings; the support and provision of animals for the cult and of meat for the priesthood; the support and material maintenance of the cult and its building. We have a system before us: the system of the cult of the Jerusalem Temple, seen as an ordinary and everyday affair, a continuing and routine operation. That is why special rules for the cult, both in respect to the altar and in regard to the maintenance of the buildings, personnel, and even the hold city, will be elsewhere—in Appointed Times and Agriculture. But from the perspective of Holy Things, those Divisions intersect by supplying special rules and raising extraordinary (Agriculture: land-bound; Appointed Times: time-bound) considerations for that theme which Holy Things claims to set forth in its most general and unexceptional way: the cult as something permanent and everyday.

The Division of Holy Things thus in a concrete way maps out the cosmology of the sanctuary and its sacrificial system, that is, the world of the Temple, which had been the cosmic center of Israelite life. A later saying states matters as follows: "Just as the navel is found at the center of a human being, so the land of Israel is found at the center of the world . . . and it is the foundation of the world. Jerusalem is at the center of the land of Israel, the Temple is at the center of Jerusalem, the Holy of Holies is at the center of the Temple, the Ark is at the center of the Holy of Holies, and the Foundation Stone is in front of the Ark, which spot is the foundation of the world" (Tanhuma Qedoshim 10).

Purities

The Division of Purities presents a very simple system of three principal parts: sources of uncleanness, objects and substances susceptible to uncleanness, and modes of purification from uncleanness. So it tells the story of what makes a given sort of object unclean and what makes it clean. The tractates on these several topics are as follows: (1) sources of uncleanness—Ohalot, Negaim, Niddah, Makhshirin, Zabim, Tebul Yom; (2) objects and substances susceptible to uncleanness—Kelim, Tohorot, Uqsin; and (3) modes of purification—Parah, Miqvaot, Yadayim. Viewed as a whole, the Division of Purities treats the interplay of persons, food, and liquids. Dry inanimate objects or food are not susceptible to uncleanness. What is wet is susceptible. So liquids activate the system. What is unclean, moreover, emerges from uncleanness through the operation of liquids, specifically, through immersion in fit water of requisite volume and in natural condition. Liquids thus deactivate the system. In all, water in its natural condition concludes the process by removing uncleanness, while water in its unnatural condition, that is, deliberately affected by human agency, imparts susceptibility to uncleanness to begin with. The uncleanness of persons, furthermore, is signified by body liquids or flux in the case of the menstruating woman (Niddah) and the zab (Zabim). Corpse uncleanness is conceived to be a kind of effluent, a viscous gas, which flows like liquid. Utensils for their part receive uncleanness when they form receptacles able to contain liquid. In sum, we have a system in which the invisible flow of fluid-like substances or powers serve to put food, drink, and receptacles into the status of uncleanness and to remove those things from that status. Whether or not we call the system "metaphysical," it certainly has no material base but is conditioned upon highly abstract notions. Thus in material terms, the effect of liquid is upon food, drink, utensils, and man. The consequence has to do with who may eat and drink what food and liquid, and what food and drink may be consumed in which pots and pans. These loci are specified by tractates on utensils (Kelim) and on food and drink (Tohorot and Uqsin).

The human being is ambivalent. Persons fall in the middle, between sources and loci of uncleanness, because they are both. They serve as sources of uncleanness. They also become unclean. The zab, suffering the uncleanness described in Leviticus Chapter 15, the menstruating woman, the woman after childbirth, and the person afflicted with the skin ailment described in Leviticus Chapters 13 and 14—all are sources of uncleanness. But being unclean, they fall within the system's loci, its program of consequences. So they make other things unclean and are subject to penalties because they are unclean. Unambiguous sources of uncleanness never also constitute loci affected by uncleanness. They always are unclean and never can become clean: the corpse, the dead creeping thing, and things like them. Inanimate sources of uncleanness and inanimate objects are affected by uncleanness. Systemically unique, man and liquids have the capacity to inaugurate the processes of uncleanness (as sources) and also are subject to those same processes (as objects of uncleanness). The Division of Purities, which presents the basically simple system just now described, is not only the oldest in the Mishnah. It also is the largest and contains by far the most complex laws and ideas.

Viewed whole, the Mishnah's stress lies on sanctification, understood as the correct arrangement of all things, each in its proper category, each called by its rightful name, just as at the creation: Everything having been given its proper name, God called the natural world very good and God sanctified it. For the Mishnah makes a statement of philosophy, concerning the order of the natural world in its correspondence with the supernatural world. Later on, the Midrash-compilations and the Talmud of the Land of Israel would make a statement of theology, concerning the historical order of society in its progression from creation through salvation at the end of time. Rabbinic Judaism then constitutes a complete statement about philosophy and nature, theology and history, the one in the oral, the other in the written Torah. All together the two components would constitute that "one whole torah of Moses, our rabbi." But we have gotten ahead of our story. Let us return to the Mishnah and its focus upon its modes of sanctification and the orderly rules descriptive of the natural life of Israel in its holy land.

The system of philosophy expressed through concrete and detailed law presented by the Mishnah consists of a coherent logic and topic, a cogent world view and comprehensive way of living. It is a world view which speaks of transcendent things, a way of life in response to the supernatural meaning of what is done, a heightened and deepened perception of the sanctification of Israel in deed and in deliberation. Sanctification thus means two things, first, distinguishing Israel in all its dimensions from the world in all its ways; second, establishing the stability, order, regularity, predictability, and reliability of Israel in the world of nature and supernature in particular at moments and in contexts of danger. Danger means instability, disorder, irregularity, uncertainty, and betrayal. Each topic of the system as a whole takes up a critical and indispensable moment or context of social being. Through what is said in regard to each of the Mishnah's principal topics, what the Halakhic system as a whole wishes to declare is fully expressed. Yet if the parts severally and jointly give the message of the whole, the whole cannot exist without all of the parts, so well joined and carefully crafted are they all.

The Mishnah's System in Response to the Crisis of the Failed Paradigm

How does the Mishnah represent a response to the crisis of 135, the collapse of the ancient paradigm? It is one thing to state the system as a whole. It is quite another to address the issue of the circumstance addressed by the authorship of the Mishnah. For the Mishnah's authorship does not think it urgent to speak to a particular time or place. They provide no account of the history or authority of their code. They rarely refer to specific circumstances subject to legislation. They speak in the language of general, descriptive rules, implicitly applicable everywhere and any time. From the first line to the last, discourse takes up questions internal to a system which is never introduced. The Mishnah provides information without establishing context. It presents disputes about facts hardly urgent outside of a circle of faceless disputants.

If then we turn to the contents of the document, we are helped not at all in determining the place of the Mishnah's origination, the purpose of its formation, the reasons for its anonymous and collective plane of discourse and monotonous tone of voice. For the Mishnah covers a carefully defined program of topics, as I shall explain presently. But the Mishnah never tells us why one topic is introduced and another is omitted, or what the agglutination of these particular topics is meant to accomplish in the formation of a system or imaginative construction. Nor is there any predicting how a given topic will be treated, why a given set of issues will be explored in close detail, and another set of possible issues ignored. Discourse on a theme begins and ends as if all things are self-evident—including, as I said, the reason for beginning at one point and ending at some other. This appears on the surface to be a book lacking all traces of eloquence and style, revealing no evidence of system and reflection, serving no important purpose. First glance indicates in hand is yet another shard from remote antiquity—no different from the king-lists inscribed on the ancient shards, the random catalogue of (to us) useless, meaningless facts: a scrapbook, a cook-book, a placard of posted tariffs, detritus of random information, accidentally thrown up on the currents of historical time. Who would want to have made such a thing? Who would now want to refer to it? How does it solve the acute crisis of the age?

How, for the Faithful, the Mishnah Resolved the Crisis of 135

For the sages who wrote the document and the patriarchate that sponsored it and the social world formed by those components of all Israel, the Mishnah defined the way forward. The crisis precipitated by the destruction of the Second Temple followed by the defeat of Bar Kokhba and the closure of Jerusalem affected both the nation and the individual, since, in the nature of things, what happened in the metropolis of the country inevitably touched affairs of home and family. What connected the individual fate to the national destiny was the long-established Israelite conviction that the fate of the individual and the destiny of the Jewish nation depended upon the moral character both of the one and of the other. Disaster came about because of the people's sin, so went the message of biblical history and prophecy. The sins of individuals and of nation alike ran against the revealed will of God, the Torah. So reflection upon the meaning of the recent catastrophe inexorably followed paths laid out long ago, trod from one generation to the next. But there were two factors that at just this time made reflection on the question of sin and history, atonement and salvation, particularly urgent.

First, with the deep conviction of having sinned and the profound sense of guilt affecting community and individual alike, the established mode of expiation and guilt and of atonement for sin proved not inadequate but simply unavailable. The sacrificial system, which the priestly Torah describes as the means by which the sinner attains forgiveness for sin, lay in ruins. So when sacrifice turned out to be acutely needed for the restoration of psychological stability in the community at large, sacrifice no longer was possible.

Second, in August, 70 C.E., minds naturally turned to August, 586 B.C.E. From the biblical histories and prophecies emerged the vivid expectation that, through the suffering of the day, sin would be atoned, expiation attained. So, people supposed, just as before, in three generations whatever guilt had weighed down the current generation and led to the catastrophe would be worked out through the sacrifice consisting of the anguish of a troubled time. It must follow that somewhere down the road lay renewal. The ruined Temple would yet be rebuilt, the lapsed cult restored, the silent Levites' song sung once more.

Now these several interrelated themes—suffering, sin, atonement, salvation—from of old had been paramount in the frame of the Israelite consciousness. A famous, widely known ancient literature of apocalyptic prophecy for a long time had explored them. The convictions that events carry preponderant weight, that Israelites could control what happened through their keeping, or not keeping, the Torah, that in the course of time matters will come to a resolution—these commonplaces were given concrete mythic reality in the apocalyptic literature. Over many centuries in that vast sweep of apocalyptic-prophetic writings all of the changes had been rung for every possible variation on the theme of redemption in history. So it is hardly surprising that, in the aftermath of the burning of the Temple and cessation of the cult, people reflected in established modes of thought upon familiar themes. They had no choice, given the history of the country's consciousness and it Scriptural frame of reference, but to think of the beginning, middle, and coming end of time as it was known.

The second stage in the formation of the earlier phases of Rabbinic Judaism coincided with the flowering, in the second century, of that rather general movement, both within Christianity and also outside of its framework, called Gnosticism. It is as important as the apocalyptic movement in establishing a base for comparison and interpretation of earlier Rabbinic Judaism. One principal theme of the Mishnah, and of the Judaism beyond it, involved the affirmation of God's beneficence in creating the world and in revealing the Torah. A principal motif of diverse Gnostic systems was God's malevolence in creating the world, or the malicious character of the creator-god, and the rejection of the Torah. In these two critical aspects of the Judaism of the sages represented in the Mishnah and later writings, we see a direct confrontation on paramount issues of the day between Rabbinic Judaism and the family of systems we call, for convenience' sake, Gnosticism.

Gnostics, second-century Church Fathers tell us, believed, among other things, that salvation came from insightful knowledge of a god beyond the creator-god, and of a fundamental flaw in creation revealed in the revealed Scriptures of Moses. Insight into the true condition of the believer derives not from revelation but from self-knowledge, which is knowledge of God. Now in introducing the viewpoint of second-century Gnostics and juxtaposing their principal emphases with those of the Mishnah, I must emphasize that we know no writings of Gnostics who were Jews. We cannot claim that the viewpoint of Gnostic thinkers on two questions of fundamental importance to the Mishnah—creation, revelation—derives from Israelites of the land of Israel. The only certainty is that the Mishnah takes up a position both specifically and totally at variance with the position framed, on identical issues, by people writing in exactly the same period. No one can claim that Gnostic and Mishnaic thinkers addressed, or even knew about, one another. But they did confront precisely the same issues, and when placed into juxtaposition with one another, they present a striking and suggestive contrast. It is that contrast that we now shall briefly contemplate.

If the apocalyptic prophets focused upon historical events and their meaning, the Gnostic writers of the second century sought to escape from the framework of history altogether. For Israel, Jerusalem had become a forbidden city. The Temple had long stood as the pinnacle of creation and now was destroyed. The Gnostic thinkers deemed creation, celebrated in the cult, to be a cosmic error. The destruction of the Temple had evoked the prophetic explanations of the earlier destruction and turned attention in the search for meaning in the destruction to the Torah of God revealed to Moses at Mount Sinai. The Gnostic thinkers declared the Torah to be a deceit, handed down by an evil creator. It is as if the cosmic issues vital to the first-century apocalyptic prophets were taken up one by one and declared closed, and closed in a negative decision, by the second-century Gnostics.

The thinkers of the Mishnah for their part addressed two principal issues also important to Gnostic thought, the worth of creation and the value of the Torah. They took a quite opposite position on both matters. The Mishnah's profoundly priestly celebration of creation and its slavishly literal repetition of what clearly is said in Scripture gain significance specifically in that very context in which, to others, these are subjected to a different, deeply negative, valuation. True, as I said, we have no evidence that Gnostics were in the land of Israel and formed part of the people of Israel in the period in which the Mishnah reaches full expression and final closure. So we speak of a synchronic debate at best. In fact what we know in Gnostic writings is a frame of mind and a style of thought characteristic of others than Israelites, living in lands other than the Land of Israel. What justifies our invoking two ubiquitous and fundamental facts about Gnostic doctrine in the description of the context in which the Mishnah took shape is the simple fact that, at the critical points in its structure, the Mishnaic system counters what are in fact two fundamental and generative assertions of all Gnostic systems.

Whether or not there were Gnostics known to the Mishnah's philosophers, who, specifically in response to the destruction and permanent prohibition of the Temple, declared to be lies and deceit the creation celebrated in the Temple and the Torah governing there, we do not know. But these would be appropriate conclusions to draw from the undisputed facts of the hour in any case. The Temple designed by the Torah for celebrating the center and heart of creation was no more. Would this not have meant that the creator of the known creation and revealer of the Torah, the allegedly one God behind both, is either weak or evil? And should the elect not aspire to escape from the realm of creation and the power of the demiurge? And who will pay heed to what is written in the revelation of creation, Temple, and Torah? These seem to me conclusions distinctively suitable to be drawn from the ultimate end of the thousand-year-old-cult: the final and total discrediting of the long-pursued, eternally fraudulent hope for messianic deliverance in this time, in this world, and in this life. So it would have been deemed wise for those who know to seek and celebrate a different salvation, coming from a god unknown in this world, unrevealed in this world's revelation, not responsible for the infelicitous condition of creation.

In so far as Gnosticism incorporated a cosmic solution to the problem of evil, the Gnostic mode of thought had the power to confront the disaster of Israel's two wars against Rome and their metaphysical consequences. The Gnostic solution is not difficult to discern. These events proved beyond doubt the flaw in creation, for the Temple had been the archetype of creation. The catastrophes demonstrated the evil character of the creator of this world. The catastrophes required the conclusion that there is another mode of being, another world beyond this one of creation and cult. So, whatever positive doctrines may or may not have found adherents among disappointed Israelites of the later first and second centuries, there are these two negative conclusions that anyone moving out of the framework of the cult, priesthood, and Temple, with its Torah, celebration of creation and the creator, and affirmation of this world and its creations, would have had to reach. First, the creator is not good. Second, the Torah, the record of creation and the will of the creator, is false. Such conclusions yield, for one Gnostic-Christian thinker after another, the simple proposition that redemption is gained in escape; the world is to be abandoned, not constructed, affirmed, and faithfully tended in painstaking detail. It is in the context of this widespread negative judgment on the very matters on which, for their part, the Mishnah's sages register a highly affirmative opinion, that the choices made by the framers of the Mishnah become fully accessible.

Characterizing the Mishnah's ultimate system as a whole, we may call it both locative and utopian, in that it focuses upon Temple but is serviceable anywhere. In comparison to the Gnostic systems, it is, similarly, profoundly Scriptural; but it also is deeply indifferent to Scripture, drawing heavily upon the information supplied by Scripture for the construction and expression of its own systemic construction, which in form and language is wholly independent of any earlier Israelite document. It is, finally, a statement of affirmation of this world, of the realm of society, state, and commerce, and at the same time a vigorous denial that how things are is how things should be, or will be. For the Mishnaic system speaks of the building of a state, government, and civil and criminal system, of the conduct of transactions of property, commerce, trade, of forming the economic unit of a family through transfer of women and property and the ending of such a family-economic unit, and similar matters, touching all manner of dull details of ordinary and everyday life.

So the Mishnah's framers deemed the conduct of ordinary life in this world to be the critical focus and central point of tension of all being. At the same time, their account of these matters drew more heavily upon Scripture than upon any more contemporary and practical source. The philosophers designed a government and a state utterly out of phase with the political realities of the day, speaking, as we have seen, of king and high priest, but never of sage, patriarch, and Roman official. They addressed a lost world of Temple cult as described by the Torah, of cleanness, support of priesthood, offerings on ordinary days and on appointed times in accord with Torah law, and so mapped out vast tracts of a territory whose only reality lay in people's imagination, shaped by Scripture. The Mishnah's map is not territory.

Accordingly, for all its intense practicality and methodical application of the power of practical reason and logic to concrete and material things, the Mishnah presents a made-up system that, in its way, is no more practical or applicable in all ways to ordinary life than are the diverse systems of philosophy and myth, produced in its day in other parts of the world, that fall under the name Gnostic. What the framers of the Mishnah have in common with the framers of the diverse world constructions of the Gnostic sort thus is, first, a system building, and, second, confrontation with two issues addressed in the diverse Gnostic systems of antiquity, the nature of creation and the creator and the character of the revelation of the creator-god. If I may state in a few simple words the position of the Mishnah on these two burning issues of the day, it is that creation is good and worthy of humanity's best consideration and that the creator of the world is good and worthy of our deepest devotion. So out of creation and revelation will come redemption. The Torah is not only not false but the principal source of truth. A system that intersects with the rules of the Torah therefore will patiently and carefully restate, and, so, blatantly reaffirm, precisely what Scripture has to say about those same points in common. A structure coming in the aftermath of the Temple's destruction that doggedly restated rules governing the Temple so reaffirmed, in the most obvious possible way, the cult and the created world celebrated therein. For as soon as we speak of sacrifice and Temple, we address the questions of creation and the value of the created world and of redemption. When, therefore, a document emerges rich in discourse on these matters and doggedly repetitive of precisely what Scripture says about exactly the same things, the meaning in context is clear.

The real crisis of the age therefore was located in that middle range of life between the personal tragedy of individuals, who live and die, and the national catastrophe of the history of Israel. The pivot had wobbled; everything organized around the Temple and in relationship to it had shifted and shaken. Left out were those two things at the extremes of this middle world: private suffering, and national catastrophe in the context of history, the encompassing history of Israel and of the world alike. That is why, when we contemplate how others of the same time framed the issues of the day, we are struck by the contrast. The obvious and accessible dilemmas of Israel's suffering at the hand of gentiles, the deeper meaning of the age in which the Temple had been ruined and Israel defeated, the resort for expressing public sorrow to evocative symbols of private suffering and its mystery, the discourse on the meaning of human history in the light of this awful outcome for Israel—none of these to us accessible and sympathetic themes and modes of thought comes to the surface in those themes and topics which the precursors of the Mishnaic system deem the appropriate focus of discourse. It is as if before us in the Mishnah are bystanders. These are people taken up with the result of the catastrophe and determined to make a quite distinctive statement about what was important in it. But the miserable world of the participants—the people who had fought, lost, and suffered—seems remote. It would stand to reason that before us is the framing of the issue of 70 by the priests, alongside people who, before the wars, had pretended to be priests and imitated their cultic routines. To such people as these, the paramount issues of

70 were issues of cult. The consequences demanding sustained attention, as I said, therefore were the effects of the wobbling of the pivot for the continued life of the cult in those vast stretches of the Israelite land that remained holy, among those sizable Israelite populations of the country that remained vital. Israel had originally become Israel and sustained its perpetual vocation through its living on the holy Land and organizing all aspects of its holy life in relationship to the conduct of the holy Temple, eating like priests and farming in accord with the cultic taboos and obsessions with order and form, dividing up time between profane and holy in relationship to the cult's calendar and temporal division of its own rites. Now Israel remained Israel, loyal to its calling, through continuing to live in the mirror and under the aspect of that same cult.

The truly stunning change effected after the wars was the formation of the book itself, the Mishnah, which brought together the ideas and principles and laws in circulation before its time, and put them all together into something far more than the components, the paltry corpus of conceptions available to the framers of the document. Now we see with full clarity the ponderous movement from one orbit to the other, the shift of the previous culture of, if not a millennium, then at least nearly seven or eight hundred years (from the second century backward to the sixth). That old, reliable, priestly way of life and world view from the Temple mountain came to be subsumed by, and transformed into, a social vision, as I said, framed on the plane of Israel. What is stunning is the shift in perspective, not the change in what was to be seen. Merely seeing the Temple and its altar from a vantage point other than the Temple mount itself is a remarkable movement in perspective. Only framing a code of law framed in rules made of words in place of practice codified in gesture and studied act constitutes an astonishing shift in focus. From interests limited to the home and hearth the opening lens of social thought takes in a larger frame indeed: from home to court, from eating and drinking, beds and pots and pans, to exchanges of property and encounters of transactions in material power. What moved the world on its axis, the ball of earth in its majesty? The answer is self-evident: seventy years of wars and the tumult of wars. These shattered a hope which, to begin with, had had little to do with the Temple at all. There was then a moment of utter despair about things which, from the perspective of the philosophers of the Mishnah, might as well have taken place on yet another planet (but, alas, things wholly within their experience). The previous culture of somewhat less than a millennium spun into another orbit, not because of the gravity of yet a new civilization of impressive density, though.

The Mishnah's principal message, which makes the Judaism of this document and of its social components distinctive and cogent, is that humans are at the center of creation, the head of all creatures upon earth, corresponding to God in heaven, in whose image humanity is made. The way in which the Mishnah makes this simple and fundamental statement is to impute power to humans to inaugurate and initiate those corresponding processes, sanctification and uncleanness, which play so critical a role in the Mishnah's account of reality. Human will, expressed through deed, is the active power in the world. Will and deed constitute those actors of creation that work upon neutral realms, subject to either sanctification or uncleanness: the Temple and table, the field and family, the altar and hearth, woman, time, space, transactions in the material world and in the world above as well. An object, a substance, a transaction, even a phrase or a sentence is inert but may be made holy, when the interplay of human will and deed arouses or generates its potential to be sanctified. Each may be treated as ordinary or (where relevant) made unclean by the neglect of the will and inattentive act of man. Just as the entire system of uncleanness and holiness awaits human intervention, which imparts the capacity to become unclean upon what was formerly inert, or which removes the capacity to impart cleanness from what was formerly in its natural and puissant condition, so in the other ranges of reality, humans are at the center on earth, just as is God in heaven. Humanity is counterpart and partner and creation, in that, like God, people have power over the status and condition of creation, putting everything in its proper place, calling everything by its rightful name.

So, stated briefly, the question taken up by the Mishnah and answered by Judaism is, What can a human being do? And the answer laid down by the Mishnah is, humans, through will and deed, are master of this world, the measure of all things. Since when the Mishnah thinks of humanity, it means the Israelite, who is the subject and actor of its system, the statement is clear. This human being is Israel, who can do what he wills. In the aftermath of the two wars, and the end of the established paradigm, the message of the Mishnah cannot have proved more pertinent—or poignant and tragic.

THE STRUCTURE AND IMPLICIT MESSAGE OF MISHNAH TRACTATE NAZIR

Simcha Fishbane
Touro College

This analysis concerns the implicit message of the Mishnaic redactor of Tractate Nazir. Our focus is this puzzling issue of meaning rather than an investigation into the history and laws of the tractate.[1] Num. 6:1–21 characterizes the Nazir as a holy person, man or woman, who separates himself to the Lord, accepting three areas of prohibition: drinking wine, cutting of the hair, and uncleanness as a result of contact with a corpse. Scripture also describes the Nazir's exit or cleansing ritual, which was dependent upon the Temple. M. Naz. 5:4 accordingly notes that, after the destruction of the Temple, Nazir was not a relevant or contemporary practice:

> E. When Nazirites came up from the Exile and found that the Temple had been destroyed, Nahum the Mede said to them, "Now if you had known that the Temple was destroyed, would you have taken vows to be Nazirs?"
> F. They said to him, "No."
> G. Nahum the Mede declared them unbound [by the Nazirite vow].
> H. But, when the matter came to the sages, they said to him, "Whoever took a Nazirite vow before the Temple was destroyed is a Nazir.
> I. "And whoever did so after the Temple was destroyed is not a Nazir."

Nahum holds that the destruction of the Temple released individuals from prior vows to be a Nazir. While sages declare those prior vows binding, they hold that, once the Temple was destroyed, any new Nazirite vows were ineffectual. In both views, then, the destruction of the Temple diminished the category Nazir, rendering it a status that no new individuals could take on.

---

[1] See Neusner, 1999, pp. 104–119, in which the problem of using the Mishnah as a source for history is discussed at length. For the history of Mishnah law, Nazir and the Division Women, see Neusner, 1980.

Although sages declared the vow to be a Nazir ineffectual, the Mishnah's preservation of the laws of the Nazir helps us understand the structure of the Mishnah and the society its framers wished to create.[2] Redacted around 200 C.E., the Mishnah simultaneously presents and represents a Temple society long destroyed within a defeated and finished society. What was the Mishnah's response to this devastating situation? A people must be made holy, just as the Temple was holy. Within this book—and through it—the rabbis who redacted the Mishnah built a social structure intended to replace a world destroyed with one that was ideal, orderly, and stabile.[3] Though on the surface the topics and discussions in the Mishnah reflected an ideal and virtually utopian society, the presenters of these rulings and discourses were vitally interested in conveying real messages.

In his *The Halakhah—Encyclopaedia of the Law of Judaism* (pp. 384–385), Jacob Neusner opens his section on Tractate Nazir with a lengthy presentation that is vital as background to this essay:

> For the special vow of the Nazirite, like the vow in general, draws in its wake consequences for the life of the family of which that individual that takes the vow is (by definition) a key member: the householder, his wife, and slaves. Not drinking wine, not shaving the head, not contracting corpse-uncleanness are matters that are personal and impinge upon the household; they do not pertain in any weighty way to public life, on the one side, or to relations between the people, Israel, and God, on the other. The Nazirite cannot attend to the deceased, cannot drink wine with the family, and subjects himself to his own rule when it comes to his appearance. As is a priest to the family of Israel, so is the Nazirite to the household of Israel, a particular classification of persons, distinguished in consequential and practical ways as to nourishment and comportment.
>
> Nor should we miss the negative case. The vow does not encumber all Israel in relationship to God. It is not an obligatory act of service, as an offering is, but a votive one. And while other votive acts of service, e.g., the thank-offering or the peace offering, engage the priesthood in the Temple, the vow does not, and the Nazirite vow brings about offerings given to the priest at the door of the tent of meeting, in the manner of the offering of the person afflicted with the skin ailment described in Leviticus Chapters 13 and 14; and there he stays.

---

[2] Nazir can be compared to Sotah. As Destro points out (1989, p. 7), Sotah "finds a justification in the fact that the rite itself would have no meaning in a cultural world which did not apply it, and it would have no meaning in a cultural world which did not apply it, and it would have been really 'lost' only if an absolute silence had been maintained about its destiny. When the silence is broken, everything takes on a different meaning. That is because the rite becomes important because it deeply analyzed and is made to 're-enter' into the cultural basis through the event of its elimination."

[3] For a more extensive discussion of this topic see Neusner, 1992.

While this essay is designed to explore the structure of Mishnah Nazir, emphasis here will be on the implicit message of the tractate as related to the Division Women. The topic falls into three themes: 1. Mishnah Nazir's place in the Order of Women; 2. the Mishnah's relationship to scripture; 3. the rituals of the Nazir.

Mishnah Nazir's Place in the Order of Women

Traditional commentaries explain the placement of Nazir in the Division of Women on the basis of a statement in B. Sot. 2a:

> Now, the *Tana* has just completed Nazir. Why did he teach Sotah [immediately thereafter]? [The answer] is as Rabbi [taught]. For it was taught in a *baraita*: Rabbi says: "Why is the tractate of Nazir juxtaposed to the tractate of Sotah? To teach you that anyone who sees a *sotah* in her [state] of disgrace should separate himself from wine [by vowing to become a nazir]." But [if that is so], let the *Tana* [first] teach Sotah and then Nazir!? [The Talmud explains the sequence as we have it:] Once [the *Tana*] taught Ketubot and, [in it], the [chapter] *Hamadir* ("One Who Vows"), he taught Nedarim [immediately afterwards]. And once he taught Nedarim he taught Nazir, which is [thematically] similar to Nedarim.

In his introduction to the Mishnah Maimonides also supports this perception, adding; "After Ketubot, Nedarim, since the whole [Torah's] chapter on vows discusses the oath of women. For scripture writes: [Num. 30:16] 'between a man and his wife and between a father and his daughter.' When they have concluded the marriage, and enter under the canopy he [the husband] can null and void her vow. Thus Nedarim is adjacent to Ketubot. After Nedarim comes Nezirut. This is because [becoming a] Nazirite is encompassed by vows. For if a woman vows to be a Nazirite, there is a husband to nullify and void [the vow]." Maimonides thus accentuates the Torah's emphasis on the woman who makes the vows. Hence Tractate Nedarim, and Nazir's place in the Mishnah's Division of Women.

Jacob Neusner[4] offers a different approach to this query.[5]

> I may propose that it is justified to call the seven tractates [of the Mishnaic Division Women] a system chiefly because the Mishnah presents them as a division. For they do not present a common theme, women and their

---

[4] Neusner, 1980, p. 14.

[5] In Neusner, 2000, p. 385, the author chooses to present the traditional explanation, writing: "The Nazirite vow forms a subdivision of the category, vows, and is

affairs, as indicated by the presence of Nedarim and Nazir.... So from our present perspective the division neither presents a system though, as indicated, it does contain a system, nor even centers its interest on a single theme.... Still, in a moment I shall argue that before us there is a clearly defined and neatly conceived system of laws, not about women in general, but concerning what is important about women to the framers of the Mishnah. This is the transfer of women and property associated with that same transfer from one domain, the father's, to another, the husband's, and back. And as I said, the whole constitutes a significant part of the Mishnah's encompassing system of sanctification, for the simple reason that Heaven confirms what men do on earth.... That is indeed very much part of a larger system, which says the same thing over and over again.[6]

While Neusner's approach emerges in the subsequent analysis of Tractate Nazir, his clarification that "it does contain a system" calls for elaboration. Close examination reveals that the Mishnah redactors presented an integral and systematic structure, which created the vision of an ideal society, centered on the destroyed Temple. They stated their concept of this situation, and their preferences. After the destruction of the Temple they created—or recreated—a social structure which did not hesitate to make use of heaven to establish their authority, in particular through the use of scripture.[7] Within the bounds of this system they were extremely wary of anomalies[8] that might endanger the boundaries and hierarchy they envisioned as necessary to maintain this society.[9] And it is clear that all writers, including the Mishnah framers, consciously or unconsciously inserted their cultural biases into their creations. Though during Temple times the Nazir were of no concern to the priests, and were considered to be as holy as they were, once the

---

treated as a continuous with the exposition of that topic. That is because the right of the husband to annul his wife's vow extends to the Nazirite vow that she may take. That is surely the formal reason that justifies situating the tractate where it is."

[6] In his later volume (1999, p. 82), Neusner employs the traditional approach and writes that Nazir is modeled after Nedarim; they are "true continuities, which make the two tractates into a single continuous statement." Though I have offered additional considerations, my proposals are primarily based on the principles put forward in Neusner's analysis of Mishnah.

[7] Neusner, 1980, p. 16, phrases this correctly when he writes, "Mishnah's is a system of sanctification through the will and word of God in heaven and through that which on earth corresponds to God's word, which is the will and word of man."

[8] Destro, 1989, p. 34, writes, "Every liminality is a possible opening to chaos, if not destruction; it is the most deceitful antinomy of the structure." Quoting Douglas, 1969, p. 102, he writes: "Inarticulate, unstructured areas emanate unconscious powers which provoke others to demand that ambiguity be reduced."

[9] See Douglas, 1978, whose grid group structure would be comparable to the social structure elected by the Mishnah's rabbis.

Nazir were defined as a potential threat the Mishnah redactor's view and implicit message was that they were obviously nonconformists, who disagreed with the accepted interpretation.[10]

The Division Women is one of six divisions in which a few rabbis conveyed their conceptual understanding of their entire world, one in which they were at the center.[11] In this world the locus was men—and men who were Torah scholars, whose emphasis was Torah study. In this world women represent both an "anomaly and a threat,"[12] especially when they are moving from one setting or status to another."[13] "That is why, as with other anomalies or threats, the Mishnah is obliged to devote considerable attention to the formation of a system regarding women—a system of law to regulate the irregular."[14] The Nazir does not just represent a few additional chapters in Tractate Nedarim. rather, it is an independent Tractate, providing its own message to the Mishnah's system and world.

As we shall see, the redactors of the Mishnah felt that the Nazir, like women, represented an anomaly and a threat to its view of the ideal society. Once woman is viewed as "abnormal," in a society where only men are considered "normal," it devolves on the Mishnah to restore normality and to build a well-regulated world. And it must do so with the Nazir. Scripture has already described how, like women, the Nazir moves from one setting and boundary to another, thus upsetting the balance between heaven and earth created by the priests and rabbis in the time of the Temple. Those individuals who decide to cross these boundaries are therefore weakening the social structure.[15]

To establish the order and balance of the world of the Mishnah, the Rabbinic (or priestly) hierarchy must be restored. Since the Nazir is abnormal, deviant and threatening to Rabbinical authority, the process described and discussed in the Mishnah is that of the restoration of normal Rabbinic male society. This, therefore, required a "system of law to regulate the irregular." If the Nazirites could be regulated during all stages of their journey, they would become part of the system. It was Heaven that had given to the rabbis the power to legislate the Nazir.

---

[10] Rubin, 1995, p. 29, also supports this view concerning priests in his analysis of the Nazir.
[11] See Neusner, 1993, pp. 40–43.
[12] See also Wegner, 1988, pp. 5–19.
[13] Ibid., p. 46.
[14] Ibid., p. 43.
[15] See Douglas, 1978, p. 8.

Clear classifications would stabilize Rabbinical power—and thus their society. An explicit set of institutional classifications based on scripture therefore had to be defined, for these rules would be part of the entire system of the Mishnah, adhering to the literary pattern as well as the legal system. All the additions or changes to scripture which were inserted but which were based upon scriptural requirements followed the principles found throughout Tractate Nazir, which instructed the Israelites on how to become a Nazir. These included precepts as to what could or could not be done during this period, with whom they could or could not be in contact, how long they were required to behave in this fashion, and how they could return to normative social male society.

We have seen that the Nazir, a liminal personality in the world of the rabbis, find a natural place in the Mishnah's Order of Women. It was therefore not fortuitous that the Mishnah's redactors selected only three parables to present in Tractate Nazir, all of which describe women.

1. In M. 2:3 while discussing the prohibition of drinking wine for the Nazir the Mishnah tells the following story: "M'SH B: A woman was drunk, and they filled her cup for her, and she said, 'Lo, I am a Nazirite from it.'"
2. In M. 3:6 there is discussion of a person who, while out of the land of Israel, takes the vow of Nazir: "M'SH B: Helene the Queen—her son went off to war, and she said, 'If my son comes home from war whole and in one piece, I shall be a Nazir for seven years.' Then at the end of the seven years she went up to the Land."
3. While discussing the bringing of the offerings at the completion of the Nazir period, M. 611 relates the following story:
   D. They said to him, "M'SH B: 'On behalf of Miriam of Tadmor [Palmyra] one of the drops of blood was properly tossed, and they came and told her that her daughter was dying, and she found her dead."
   E. And the sages said, "Let her bring the rest of her offerings when she will be clean."

Hence the place of these writings in the Division (or Order) of Women.[16]

---

[16] The same can be argued but on a lesser scale for the last two chapters in Tractate Sotah. The community in this case is confused, out of order, and requires ritual to reenter a normal routine. I thank Professor Nissan Rubin for his comments on this issue and for other anthropological insights into the understanding of Nazir.

For the framers of the Mishnah the Nazir posed an additional problem. Neusner (1993, pp. 83–124) identifies the concept of *zekhut*, which can be loosely translated as merit or virtue. The Rabbinic literature, primarily in the Babylonian and Land of Israel Talmud, informs us that both men and women can attain *zekhut* through a simple act of renunciation and self-abnegation. A person thus did not have to spend countless hours in Torah study to reach the level of spirituality required for Heaven to bestow on him the privileges of *zekhut*. One single remarkable deed, one uncoerced act of grace not required by heaven would enable him to achieve the same goal as Torah study.[17] The rabbis, however, seemed to be willing to make this statement accepting the merits of *zekhut* only when they did not feel their authority or social structure threatened by those few individuals likely to attain this *zekhut* level. The earlier sages, however, such as the framers of Mishnah redacted in approximately 200 C.E. could not afford this luxury, for after the destruction of the Temple which was the locus of Judaism they were simultaneously engaged in acts of scholarly creation and were fighting for the survival of their people.[18] That devastating destruction of the Temple also shattered and eroded two groups of authentic regulators within Temple society: the sages and their disciples, and the priestly caste. Since these teachers of Mishnah had to replace both groups, they could not afford any threat to the establishment of their authority. For them only Torah could be *zekhut*, as clearly stated in M. Peah 1:1. After listing those deeds, performances and acts which benefit the individual both in this world and the next, the Mishnah declares, "But the study of Torah is as important as all of them [other *mitzvot*] together."[19] It is therefore only through the study of Torah that he— and not she—attains the privileges awarded by heaven.

The framers of the Mishnah therefore ended up by replacing these regulators, in particular the priests. By recreating a system based on their traditional conception of the Temple, this small group of teachers and students attempted to overcome chaos. With scripture, names and earlier traditions as their authority, they set out to present their view of how society should be ordered. Clearly, this small group of

---

[17] Neusner, 1993, pp. 83–124, cites numerous examples from Rabbinic literature to prove this point.

[18] The issue of the crisis for Israel during this period is discussed by J. Neusner, *Turning Points* (Oxford, 2002).

[19] Additional sources in the Mishnah stressing the importance and priority allotted to Torah study are M. Hor. 3:8, M. B.M. 2:11, and M. Ket. 4:14.

teachers could not allow any threat to its authority or to the social structure it envisioned. The Nazir was precisely such a threat, for simply by uttering a few words a Nazir could achieve that status, that *zekhut* which the rabbis attained through the zealous study of Torah. It is because here Nazirs were as much of a liability as women that they appeared along with them in the Division entitled "Women."

To understand the rabbis' status during the times of the Temple it is important to grasp fully their concerns regarding the Nazir, for in those days specific laws of scripture equated the Nazir status to that of the priests. In his introduction to Mishnah Tractate Nazir, Albeck (1957, pp. 189–190) elaborates on this proposition and discusses various non-Rabbinic sources such as Philo, who equates the holiness of the Nazir with that of the priest, and even of the high priest. Both the priest and the Nazir, he writes, are prohibited from drinking any alcoholic beverage, and for practical purposes can drink only water. Josephus asserts the same opinion. Following Philo, Albeck suggests that during the period of the Second Temple becoming a Nazir was considered commendable, since one who dedicates himself to the Lord reveals thereby his great love and awe of his Maker. While the prophet Amos (2:11) equated the status of the Nazir with that of prophet, at the end of the period of the prophets, the Nazir's status was paralleled with that of the priests. And this was so although, as J. Licht (1985, p. 83) argues, the great majority of the Nazarites most probably never served in the Temple.

One might suggest that, within its normative halakhic discourse, the Mishnah implicitly conveys the message that the priest and Nazir are not on the same level. M. 7:1, the sole instance in Tractate Nazir in which a Nazir and priest are explicitly discussed and compared,[20] states:

7:1A. A high priest and a Nazir do not contract corpse uncleanness on account of [burying even] their close relatives.
    B. But they do contract corpse uncleanness on account of a neglected corpse.
    C. [If] they were going along the way and found a neglected corpse—
    D. R. Eliezer says, "Let a high priest contrast corpse uncleanness, but let a Nazir not contract corpse uncleanness."
    E. And sages say, "Let a Nazir contract corpse uncleanness, but let a high priest not contract corpse uncleanness."

---

[20] In M. Mak. 3:9, the Nazir and priest are also presented together, but these are not relevant to our discussion.

> F. Said to them R. Eliezer, "Let a priest contract corpse uncleanness, for he does not have to bring an offering on account of his uncleanness.
> "But let a Nazir not contract corpse uncleanness.
> "For he does have to bring an offering on account of his uncleanness."
> G. They said to him. "Let a Nazir contract corpse uncleanness, for his sanctification is not a permanent sanctification,
> "but let a priest not contract corpse uncleanness,
> "for his sanctification is a permanent sanctification."

The message is clear. The sages have informed us that, even upon entering the "holy" space the Nazir cannot reach the status of the high priest—or even of the common priest. He remains in his pseudo-holy or liminal status.[21]

In his discussion of vows and Nazir, Neusner (2000, p. 421) accurately describes the rabbis' attitude towards the Nazir; "Sages do not treat respectfully the person who takes vows. Vow takers yield to the undisciplined will, to emotion unguided by rational considerations.... A *distaste* for vowing and a disdain for people who make vows then characterize the law." The Mishnah Tractate Nedarim preceding Tractate Nazir *clearly* conveys this outspoken disapproval, for even when regulated, the Nazir's existence *can* still prove a threat. Discussing substitute language equivalent to vows, M. 1:1 states:

> 1:1G. [He who says] "As the vows of the evil folk...," has made a binding vow of a Nazir, or in the case of [bringing] an offering, or in the case of an oath.
> H. [He who says,] "As the vows (*neder*) of the suitable folk" has said nothing whatsoever.
> I. "As their [suitable folks'] free will offerings (*nedavah*)"... he has made a binding vow in the case of a Nazir or in the case of [bringing] an offering.

Since, as specified by scripture in Num. 6:2, the acceptance of Nazirite restrictions is primarily through vows (*neder*) rather than through free will offerings (*nedavah*), the Mishnah informs its readers that those who choose to make the vow of the Nazir are placed in the category of evil[22] persons.

---

[21] See Rubin, 1995, p. 25.
[22] Even a cursory examination of the term *rasha* (evil person) in the Mishnah shows that the word literally refers to an evil person.

THE STRUCTURE AND IMPLICIT MESSAGE OF TRACTATE NAZIR   119

The stage is thus set for further discussions of the Nazir. Here the point of departure is that the category of persons who make the vow of the Nazir is evil, and that taking the Nazir vow is wrong.[23] The rabbis chose not to ignore or discard the Nazir both because this was part of the Temple society which they were recreating, and because this was an explicit Torah ruling. But what they *could* do—as we shall see—was to package the Nazir to fit their utopian society.

The Mishnah and Scripture

The Mishnah tractate Nazir, the fourth book of division Nashim (Women) rests upon the deep foundation set forth and written down in the Torah,[24] Num. 6:1–21. These passages can be divided into three subjects: 6:1–6:8 discusses the behavior obligations of the Nazir.

6:1	And the Lord said to Moses.
6:2	say to the people of Israel, when either a man or a woman makes a special vow, the vow of a Nazarite, to separate himself to the Lord.
6:3	He shall separate himself from wine and strong drink; he shall drink no vinegar made from wine or strong drink; and shall not drink any juice or grapes, fresh or dried.
6:4	All the days of his separation he shall eat nothing that is produced by the grapevine, not even the seeds or the skins.
6:5	All the days of his vow of separation no razor shall come upon his head; until the time is completed for which he separates himself to the Lord, he shall be holy; he shall let the locks of hair grow long.
6:6	All the days he separates himself to the Lord he shall not go near a dead body.
6:7	neither for his father nor his mother, nor for his brother or his sister, if they die, shall he make himself unclean; because his separation to God is upon his head.
6:8	All the days of his separation he is holy to the Lord.

Num. 6:9–6:12 discusses the termination of the *niziros* as a result of *tumah* and the required sacrifices.

---

[23] It is interesting that Tosefta only includes the statement on suitable folks and ignores the evil folks.
[24] All Bible translations are from *The New Oxford Annotated Bible*.

6:9	And if any man dies very suddenly beside him, and he defiles his consecrated head, then he shall shave his head on the day of his cleansing; on the seventh day he shall shave it.
6:10	On the eighth day he shall bring two turtledoves or two young pigeons to the priest to the door of the tent of meeting.
6:11	And the priest shall offer one for a sin offering and the other for a burnt offering, and make atonement for him, because he sinned by reason of the dead body. And he shall consecrate his head that same day.
6:12	And separate himself to the Lord for the days of his separation, and bring a male lamb a year old for a guilt offering; but the former time shall be void, because his separation was defiled.

Num. 6:13–6:21 presents the concluding ritual for the nazir and the required sacrifices.

6:13	And this is the law for the Nazirite, when the time of his separation has been completed: he shall be brought to the door of the tent of meeting.
6:14	And he shall offer his gift to the Lord, one male lamb a year old without blemish for the burnt offering, and one ewe lamb a year old without blemish as a peace offering.
6:15	And a basket of unleavened bread, cakes of fine flour mixed with oil, and their cereal offering and their drink offerings.
6:16	And the priest shall present them before the Lord and offer his sin offering and his burnt offering.
6:17	And he shall offer the ram as a sacrifice of peace to the Lord, with the basket of unleavened bread; the priest shall offer also its cereal offering and its drink offering.
6:18	And the Nazirite shall shave his consecrated head at the door of the tent meeting, and shall take the hair from his consecrated head and put it on the fire, which is under the sacrifice of the peace offering.
6:19	And the priest shall take the shoulder of the ram, when it is boiled, and one unleavened cake out of the basket, and one unleavened wafer, and shall put them upon his hands of the Nazirite, after he has shaven the hair of his consecration.

6:20 And the priest shall wave them for a wave offering before the Lord; they are a holy portion for the priest, together with the breast that is waved and the thigh that is offered; and after that the Nazirite may drink the wine.

6:21 This is the law for the Nazirite who takes a vow. His offering to the Lord shall be according to his vow as a Nazirite, apart from what else he can afford; in accordance with the vow which he takes, so shall he do according to the law for his separation as a Nazirite.

Simply by uttering a few words the holy Israelite is separated from his class, or from the caste of holy Israel, and crosses the border into the caste of the "super holy," the priests. Like the priests, "he separates himself to the Lord." Only at the termination of this separation, after Temple rituals, does he or she regain original status, once again crossing the imaginary caste boundary.

The laws of the Nazirite in the Mishnah clearly amplify what we have found in Numbers. The Mishnah law integrates the biblical law. While the Mishnah does not find a need to modify these laws, in some instances it offers clarification and additional facts.

Neusner (1989, p. 4) identifies three types of relationships between Scripture and Mishnah. Tractate Nazir falls into the second category: "Second, Scripture sets forth a topic but does not then dictate the inner logic by which the topic will be worked out in a series of illustrative cases, as is the fact in the first relationship. Therefore the subject-matter is scriptural, but the treatment of the subject entirely autonomous of Scripture." Regarding specifically Tractate Nazir, he elaborates (ibid., p. 38):

> The facts of Scripture—Numbers 6:1ff.—are reworked by the framers of this tractate into an essay on problems of classification, e.g., the application of taxic indicators, the issue of when many things are one thing and one many, and the resolution of doubt. Overall, the tractate works out Scripture's facts in a manner entirely autonomous of Scripture's elaborate treatment of those same facts.

And he goes on to clarify this (Neusner 1999, p. 77): Scripture has contributed facts. The halakhah has provided the insight and dynamics to translate the insight into detailed forms. . . . Building on these foundations, the Mishnah would articulate the halakah of the Oral Torah—finding its own voice to do so." Neusner also reminds us (1981, p. 199) "that on the whole, the direct relevance of Scripture on the formation of the Mishnah is limited, even though its authority is undeniable. The Mishnah in general does not quote it, and rarely links its own ideas to those of Scripture."

At first glance, Tractate Nazir seems to be highly dependent on Scripture. Chapter 1 of Tractate Nazir reflects Scriptures' opening statement, Num. 6:2, "when a man or a woman makes a special vow, the vow of a Nazarite." It then develops and reworks scripture (similar to Mishnah Nedarim), word forms and euphemisms as well as the formulary for the vow. But the framers of the Mishnah also had their own agenda, for their genius lies also in the creation of a document presenting a uniform formalization of the whole. Both received authority from heaven via Scripture and the uniformity of the document therefore lent credibility to realistic and non-realistic issues. The fact (as discussed by Destro, 1989, p. 7) that non-realistic materials are intensively analyzed by the Mishnah causes the issue to "re-enter" the cultural basis: it comes alive. Furthermore, the discussion of issues which were part of a world destroyed, such as Nazir, is part of the social defense used to overcome crises in a time of great difficulty (ibid., p. 12). The sages were tolerant in dealing with these themes in order to stabilize these issues within their normal juridical framework.[25] They wished to defend and reinforce Scripture's laws relating to the priests within a situation very different from its original environment, thereby strengthening the authority of those who analyzed and presented the materials.

The framers were careful to follow the formularies stated in the opening of Tractate Nedarim.

> 1:1A. All euphemisms for [the form of words for] vows are equivalent to vows: and for bans (*ḥerem*) are equivalent to bans, and for oaths are equivalent to oaths, and for Nazirite vows are equivalent to Nazirite vows.

Thus we find the opening statement in Tractate Nazir.

> 1:1A. All euphemisms for [the form of words for] a Nazirite vows are equivalent to Nazirite vows [and binding].

Only then does Tractate Nazir begin to offer its own interpretation of the Nazir's vow, offering diverse formulations in invoking it. The Mishnah then continues with the stipulations imposed upon the vow.

---

[25] Destro, 1989, p. 146, discusses this issue and calls this action of the rabbis "tolerance—strengthening."

The Mishnah is concerned with a third component of the vow—its duration, and this interest is based upon Scripture's statement (Num. 6:4–6): "All the days of separation." While Scripture does not identify any specific minimum period during which one is a Nazir, the framers of the Mishnah introduce a thirty-day time period.[26]

Scripture left open the generative question that the Mishnah takes as the center of its program, the standard duration for the Nazir's vow. This concept becomes the basis for much of the discussion throughout tractate Nazir. By introducing this time framework as a basic point of departure for the basic framework of the Nazir the rabbis have reworked and redirected the Scriptural theme of Nazir to agree with their interpretation.

The effects of language are clearly manifested in Tractate Nazir (as well as Tractate Nedarim).[27] Heaven pays attention when a person utters certain formularies that obligate, restrict or prohibit him (or her) from specific objects, activities or persons. A person's intent must be facilitated and made clear. Only when the intent conveyed by the language is clear and unmistakable has the language fulfilled its responsibility of embodying intent. When such intent is clarified, the words uttered by the potential Nazir take effect and his period of being a Nazir commences.

The rabbis' detailed definitions of the Nazir vow would seem to be more than a halakhic issue. The dependency upon the rabbis' decision linking the process of becoming a Nazir to controllability, in the words of Eilberg-Schwartz, "represents a symbolic reversal of the priestly system" (1990, p. 195). By reversing the ascribed authority of the priests to their own acquired authority, the rabbis achieved great control.

The rabbis, as we have noted, were the heirs of the priests. The priestly role of defining the boundaries of the community declined along with the group's genealogy, descent and status. The rabbis, the framers of the Mishnah took on this role. This symbolic transformation took shape and was manifested through the interpretation of the Scripture laws in the Mishnah.[28] In his discussion of impurity and contamination in early Rabbinic Judaism Elberg-Schwartz (1988, pp. 196–215) identifies and discusses the differences between the priests and the rabbis from

---

[26] Maimonides explains the concept of thirty days to be from early tradition (*halakhah mepi kabalah*).

[27] See Neusner, 1999a, pp. 79–94, and Neusner, 2000, pp. 410–425, for a discussion at length of the issue of language.

[28] Elberg-Schwartz, 1988, p. 196, lists different sociological and anthropological sources which link symbolic transformation to changes in the nature of the religious community.

the perspective of ascribed and achieved status. The priest's status was ascribed to him through his genealogy (an outside control) while the rabbi's acquired status was attributed to Torah knowledge—an inside control. Elberg-Schwartz's understanding of the development of the Mishnah is to be understood not only within the framework of contamination but as applicable to the world of Mishnah as a whole and hence to our clarification of Nazir. Since the laws of Nazir were incorporated into Scripture, the rabbis could not discard them. In fact Scripture—the divine sanction—served as a source for basing and reinforcing their authority.

What the rabbis do is to redefine, elaborate and even reverse the symbolism of the priestly system (or Scripture) as much as possible without actually repudiating it. While Scripture devotes a few lines to the topic of Nazir, an entire tractate is assigned to and bears the title of this theme. An examination of the tractate and the discussions of the rabbis, especially in the first chapters which discuss how one becomes a Nazir, reveals that the laws of Nazir become a function of how an individual uses or conceives a given issue. What Scripture states does not obligate an in-depth analysis. In contrast a large portion of the Mishnah's halakhah is devoted to the theme of the vow; euphemisms that invoke the vow of Nazir, the duration of the vow and the sacrifices that are related to the vow.[29] This definition and employment of the Nazir vow emphasizes the vower's intent rather than an ascribed mindless, unthinking formula. This enhancement of Scripture through the language of the vow is part of the rabbis' reverse process from outside to inside control, that very control which strengthens the rabbis' acquired status. As in the case of the Mishnah's rabbis, in which achievement is relevant to the determination of status, individuals feel that they are exercising more control over who they are and ultimately over who they want to be. For the less outside factors such as genealogy (e.g., acquired status in the case of priests) affect the individual, the greater the person's control over his life and achieved status. In the words of

---

[29] Neusner, 1999, pp. 86–87, offers a more detailed insight, presenting the program of vows in the Mishnah as follows:
    i. The Special Vow of the Nazirite
  A. The Language of the Vow to Be a Nazirite
  B. Stipulations and the Nazirite Vow
  C. The Duration of the Vow
  D. Annulling the Vow
    ii. The Special Offering of the Nazirite
  A. Designation and Disposition of the Nazirite's Offering

Elberg-Schwartz (1988, p. 197), these are now actors and not objects. In this light we can understand the result of the Mishnah's extensive discussions of Scripture. Knowingly or unknowingly, through the power of language these individuals greatly enhanced their achieved status and authority in their developing social organization, structure and community.

The Rituals of Nazir

The Three Prohibitions

As part of the Mishnah's mnemonic program, and[30] in its redactor's intent to encourage public discourse, the three prohibitions or taboos (as stated in Scripture: wine, hair cutting, and corpse-uncleanness) evoked by the vow are repeated twice in 6:1 and 6:5. M. 6:1 states: "Three things are prohibited to a Nazir: [corpse] uncleanness, cutting the hair, and anything which goes forth from the grapevine." This is followed by a discussion that deals primarily is concerned with the details of the wine prohibition. In 6:5 the statement is repeated; "Three things are prohibited to a Nazir: [corpse] uncleanness, cutting the hair, and anything which goes forth from the grapevine." This is followed by a discussion of hair cutting and corpse uncleanness.

Interestingly enough, the redactors of the Mishnah do not voice a favorable view of the Nazir. *Kesherim* (suitable folk) do not make vows. Vow takers are often not rational and undisciplined[31] as are many of the cases cited in Mishnah Nazir.[32] As stated above, the rabbis were also apprehensive about paralleling the Nazir with the priest. Yet once the vow was taken he or she was considered to have crossed over the boundary and to have entered into a state of holiness. The three prohibitions of the Nazir, in fact, are also prohibited to the priest during his service in the Temple, as stated in M. Ta. 2:6G: "The members of the priestly watch are permitted to drink wine by night but not by day."

---

[30] See Neusner, 1999, p. 100, for a discussion of this theme.

[31] See ibid., p. 92, and my above discussion citing Neusner, 2000, p. 421, for analysis of the Mishnah's negative approach to the Nazir.

[32] See, for example, among the many cases found in M. Nazir: 2:2: "[If] one said, This cow says, Lo, I am a Nazir if I stand up;" 2:5: [If one said] Lo, I am Nazir, and I take it upon myself to bring the hair offering of [another] Nazir and his friend heard and said, So am I, and I take upon myself to bring the hair offering of another] Nazir."

2:7: "A. and the members of the father's house[33] [are] not [permitted to drink wine] either by day or night. B. Members of the priestly watch and members of the public delegation are prohibited to get a haircut[34] and wash their clothes." The prohibition of corpse contamination is specific not to the Temple service but is in force at all times. Though the reasons given by the later rabbis for the prohibitions might differ from Nazir, the taboo is the same. A priest while performing his service in the Temple—a physical bordered area of holiness—in order to remain in a state of holiness cannot drink wine, cut his hair, or be contaminated by a corpse. And the same holds true for the Nazir, though these three prohibitions now cover non-physical bounds and borders of holiness.

A discussion of the rituals of Nazir calls for at least a brief definition of ritual. In his two papers on the meaning of ritual (1979 and 1995), F. Bird offers the following understanding of this concept (1995, pp. 23–24):

> I define rituals as symbolic acts that are intrinsically valued and repeated, ritual actors trying to behave in keeping with expected characters and roles by using stylized gestures and words. Whenever we act ritually, we use prepared oral or written scripts that, in varying detail, spell out how we should speak, gesture and place our selves. Rather than acting discursively to choose our own words and movements, we follow guides that prescribe precisely what words we ought to say and what movement we ought to make ... In ritual, people play the roles of characters required by their scripts. These characters may vary according to the type of ritual.

Bird goes on to suggest that in order to express their identification the ritual actors use various techniques such as wearing special costumes or identifying marks (1995, p. 24).[35] Thus in a sense ritual involves make-believe, for the actors are following a script and identify with its characters. The symbols they employ are heavily weighted with commonly accepted/shared meanings, and they esteem both behavior and words which honor oral or written scripts. Ritual is not only a means

---

[33] These are the priests who are actually doing most of the sacrificial work in the Temple.

[34] Although M. Kel. 1:9 states a priest whose hair is loosed or long (wild) can not enter certain inner areas of the Temple, that does not affect the fact that while serving in the Temple he cannot cut his hair.

[35] Bird bases his works on a large variety of sociological and anthropological theories of ritual. The interested reader may wish to examine Bird's comprehensive work for details regarding the sources.

of social interaction and of reinforcement of social boundaries;[36] as Bird demonstrates, it is also a way for people to channel and facilitate communication among the actual participants. The latter communicate with themselves and with each other by the concurrent transmission of diversified means of communication. Bird thus seems to agree with M. Douglas (1970, pp. 67–73), who perceives bodily functions as a medium of expression, limited, however, by controls exerted by the social system. Bodily control is thus a direct expression of social control. The success of imposing entire or partial bodily control is directly connected to social forms, for "when the correspondence between bodily and social controls is traced, the basis will be laid for considering covarying attitudes in political thought and ideology" (p. 71).

Rituals are multi-dimensional and serve to simultaneously facilitate several forms of communication. Bird (1995) identifies five forms of communication associated with ritual; (1) constitutive, which reconstitute the world view envisioned by their scripts, (2) self-representative, in which through the ritual people represent themselves to themselves and others, (3) expressive, which provide for the actor to express feelings, often of a highly charged nature, (4) regulative, a means of communicating beliefs and moral codes, and (5) invocative, designed to bring on desired states by invoking the deity or deities. Our discussion of Nazir will clarify and illustrate these forms as well as serve as a structural framework for understanding the Nazir's rituals as presented in the Mishnah.

The Exit or Reentry Ritual

The concluding ritual would seem to center on the cutting of the hair. Scripture's prohibition for the Nazir to cut his hair receives little attention in the Mishnah. It states in 6:3:

> B. [If] he cut his hair or thugs forcibly cut his hair, he looses thirty days.
> C. A Nazir who cut his hair, whether with scissors or with razor, or who pulled out any hair whatsoever is liable.
> D. A Nazir shampoos and parts his hair [with his fingers]. But does not comb his hair.
> E. R. Ishmael says, "He should not shampoo his head in the dirt.
> F. because it makes the hair fall out.

---

[36] See Mary Douglas' (1966) presentation of this concept.

All additional discussions of hair in Mishnah Nazir relate to contiguous issues pertaining to Nazir such as cutting the hair as a result of contracting corpse uncleanness, sacrifices, the exit ritual, etc.

Hair is one of the few visible corporal manifestations which is controllable. It is the only human organ which can be acted on without doing physical harm to the body. The variety of ways in which hair can be manipulated—cut, trimmed in various patterns and shapes, allowed to grow, colored, and styled enables it to function as a "silent language" transmitting public and private messages to a given society (Hull, 1959, p. 1). An essay by Trau, Rubin and Vargon (1988) analyzes three major works concerned with the symbolic significance of hair written by a psychologist, Berg (1951), and by two anthropologists, Leach (1958) and Hallpike (1969). The authors of the essay correctly, in my view, support Hallpike's criticism of Berg's and Leach's argument that while hair implies connotations of growth, cutting and shaving smack of phallic or castration symbolism. They agree with Hallpike's contention that the growth of long hair tends to place the "hairy individual" outside of society, while the cutting of hair represents social control symbolizing re-entry into the community, or agreement to abide by a specific regime of discipline within society (1988, p. 175). Our case of Nazir serves to buttress the evidence for their argument. The Nazir identified by his hair growth is both symbolically separated and personally detached from the community, placed into a type of "liminal state." Only after ritual of cutting of the hair does he symbolically re-enter the community.

Other cases in the Mishnah would seem to support this view of hair. M. M.Q. 3:1 states:

A. These cut their hair on the intermediate days of a festival:
B. (1) he who comes from overseas or from captivity;
C. (2) and he goes forth from prison.
D. (3) and he whose excommunication has been lifted by sages.
E. (4) and so too: he who sought absolution from a sage [for release from a vow not to get a haircut] and was released.
F. And a Nazarite or mesora[37] who emerges from his state of uncleanness to his state of cleanness.

---

[37] A state of uncleanness parallel to the uncleanness of the corpse. See Leviticus 14. This state is traditionally attributed to the sinning of the unclean person. See Leviticus Rabbah 14.

While it is not feasible in this essay to examine the specifics of each element of the Mishnah's case, it is clear that each of the examples asserting that it is permitted to cut one's hair even at a time when this should be prohibited represents a case of re-entry into the community. These illustrations, all sharing the same common denominator, are presented alongside Nazir.

M. Naz. 6:7 summarizes Nazirs who have successfully completed their vow in ritual obligations of cleanliness.

A. The cutting of the hair in the case of [completing the vow in a state of] cleanliness: How is it done?
B. One would bring three beasts, a sin offering, a burnt offering, and a peace offering (Num. 6:14).
C. And he would slaughter the peace offering and cut off his hair after their [slaughter], the words of R. Judah.
D. R. Eleazar says, He would cut his hair only after the sin offering.
E. For the sin offering takes precedence under all circumstances.
F. For if he cut his hair after any one of the three of them, he has carried out his obligation.

During the period of abstinence the Nazir views and presents himself, and is viewed by the community symbolically, in the same way as the priest who during his Temple service is separate from the laymen in a liminal stage of holiness. The exit ritual or reentry into society would seem to be symbolically identified with the laws governing the priest who is prohibited from serving in the Temple. For example, M. Bek. 7:2 writes that a bald-headed priest can not serve in the Temple. The Nazir is now bald, and hence unworthy for consideration as part of the holy group. An additional parallel is made between the Nazir and the *mesora* [leper]. It is one of the two Temple period rituals for which the Mishnah requires shaving of the hair (see M. Neg. 14:4). Also aware of this similarity, Mishnah Nazir (6:6) shows the need to differentiate between Nazir and Mesora. The emphasis in the comparison to *mesora* is on the state of uncleanness. The concluding rituals of the Nazir are therefore activated in two instances, when the Nazir completes his period of the vow without becoming unclean, or when he is becoming unclean. In the latter case the Nazir is required to perform the exit rituals and recommence his Nazirite period. This symbolic identification, especially in the case of exit from uncleanness, can be viewed as a *mesora* who, in the minds of the Rabbinical Jew, is a sinner.

M. Mid. 2:5 informs us of an office in the southeastern corner of the Temple mount that was dedicated to the Nazir for the performance of his exit ritual, "in which the Nazirites cook their peace offerings, shave off their hair, which they burn under the pot." This is the only time the Nazir is required to be on Temple grounds, and there he shaves his hair, burning it under the cauldron cooking the peace offering sacrifice (M. Naz. 6:8). The Nazir's symbolically holy hair, which had identified him within a different group, is now burned in the Temple under the pot of the sacrifice eaten by the layman, a reminder he is no longer in a holy status, and is no longer compared to the priest. The additional peace offering portions received by the priest which exceed the customary smaller portion[38] in the standard sacrifice, as well as the dedicated office in the Temple mount where the exit ritual is performed serve to emphasize this distinction.[39] M. Naz. 6:9 informs the reader of this ritual.

A. He would cook the peace offering or seethe it.
B. The priest takes the cooked shoulder of the ram and one unleavened cake out of the basket and one unleavened wafer and puts them in the hand of the Nazir (Num. 6:19).
C. And he waves them.
D. And afterward the Nazir was permitted to drink wine and to contract corpse uncleanness.
E. R. Simeon says, Once the blood of any one of the sacrifices has been tossed in his behalf, the Nazir was permitted to drink wine and to contract corpse uncleanness.

The fact that as part of the exit ritual the Nazir is also obligated to bring a sin offering would suggest that the Nazir has committed a sin. The traditional explanation[40] of what constitutes the Nazir's sin derives from the vow of abstention taken, resulting in abstention from the

---

[38] There are a variety of differences between the Nazir's peace offerings and that of other Jews. General peace offering are eaten two days and one night. The Nazir's sacrifice is eaten one day and one night. A standard peace offering includes unleavened cake mingled with oil and unleavened wafers spread with oil and cakes mingled with oil, of soaked fine flour and cakes of leavened bread (Lev. 7:12–113). The Nazir, by contrast, brings only two types rather than four. And while from the standard peace offering the priest receives breast and thigh portions, from Nazir he also receives shoulder pieces.

[39] The only other group to receive a dedicated office to perform their ritual is the *mesora*.

[40] See B. Ta. 11a and Maimomides Mishneh Torah *Deot* 3:1.

enjoyment of wine. Our understanding of Mishnah Nazir would suggest an additional elucidation. Scripture presents the vow of Nazir as a life-long commitment, while the Mishnah modifies this vow to permit the establishment of a time-frame.[41] Alternatively, however, the Mishnah accepts Scripture's view of the responsibility of the Nazir to the "holiness" of Israel. If you enter these borders, you do not voluntarily disregard them, for doing so is sinful. The Nazir has chosen to forsake his vow of holiness. He is abandoning identification and representation with the holy world of Israel. This is the sin: forsaking the Nazirite vow.[42] And, like other transgressions, this sin requires a sin offering.

The Prohibition of Drinking Wine and Corpse Uncleanness

The Mishnah in essence restates and elaborates on Scripture's prohibition (Num. 6:3) for the Nazir to drink wine as well as all derivatives of the grape. In M. 6:2 the redactors summarize the prohibition:

A. And he is liable (1) for wine itself, (2) for grapes by themselves, (3) for grape pits and (4) for grape skins by themselves.
B. R. Eleazar b. Azariah says, He is liable [in the case of (3) and (4)] only if he will eat two pits and their skin [that covers it].
C. What are grape pits and what are grape skins?
D. *Zaggim* are what is outside and *harsanim* are what is inside, the words of Rabbi Judah.
E. R. Yose says, "That you not err:
F. "It is like the bell of cattle.
G. "What is outside is the hood and what is inside is the clapper."

It is interesting to note that the Mishnah ignores Scripture's term *sechar* [strong drink], and simply includes it in the wine category. Only once does the word *sechar* appear in the Mishnah, at M. Pes. 3:1 where it is a Median beer [*shechar hamidi*]. In this case strong drink is specifically identified as a grain liquid and not as a product of the grape. By excluding *sechar*, the redactors of Mishnah pursue a similar pattern regarding the Nazir's wine prohibition in the case of the priest. In Leviticus

---

[41] See, for example, M. Naz. 1:3 as discussed above.
[42] Nachmanides (Num. 6:13) suggests this interpretation of the Nazir's sin.

10:9 Scripture states: "Drink no wine nor strong drink, you nor your sons with you, when you go into the tent of meeting, lest you die; it shall be a statute forever throughout your generations." The Mishnah in its discussions of the priests Temple service in M. Ker. 3:3 and M. Ta. 2:6 deletes the term "strong wine" and speaks only of "wine." As in the case of the Nazir, strong drink is most probably understood as being included in wine and grape derivatives. This would seem to be consistent with the parallel made by the Mishnah between the Nazir's holiness and the symbolic representation of the priest during his Temple service.

As in Greco-Roman world of late antiquity,[43] wine was a popular commodity in the world of the Mishnah, used in all areas of life. In the Mishnah it served in a multi-functional capacity. A cursory examination of the Mishnah reveals its use in business transactions, trade, payments, religious rituals and for other religious purposes, and as a social drink. Wine seems to have been considered so essential that even on the Sabbath, if a fire were to break out in a one's house, a jug of wine is among the limited number of articles it is permitted to save (M. Shab. 16:3).[44] The dangers of wine as a social drink were accented. For example, M. San. 8:5 IIE–F states: "Wine and sleep for the wicked are a benefit for them and a benefit for the world.[45] But for the righteous, they are bad for them and bad for the world."[46] And especially for one serving in the Temple or, as in the case of the Nazir, enclosed within the inner symbolic boundaries of holiness, the effects of wine could be embarrassing and even offensive. While the effect of wine on the function of the priest during his Temple service and the Nazir during his vow might differ, the stated prohibition is the same, for both are within the inner boundaries of holiness—the priest is physically located within the borders of the Temple, and the Nazir is symbolically placed within the boundaries of the vow.

Just as hair is an external symbol of separation of the Nazir from the Israelite community, wine serves as a sign of social separation from the lay community. The inability to sit and socialize at a meal over a

---

[43] Goodenough, 1956, presents an encompassing study of wine in this period, showing the sexual or phallic symbolism of wine in the Greco-Roman world; I feel this has no bearing on the Mishnah's presentation of wine.

[44] Removing items from a burning house might entail issues of Sabbath desecration.

[45] While intoxicated or sleeping they cause no problem to others.

[46] Other examples in the Mishnah include M. Ab. 3:10: "drinking wine at noon... drives a man out of the world."

glass of wine raised obvious limitations to interaction with fellow Jews. The drinking of alcoholic beverages, in this case wine, was a symbolic means for facilitating social relations among people, and social ties were often established in this way.[47] Not drinking was tantamount to withdrawing from many opportunities for social life.[48] Being in a state of holiness required separation and therefore withdrawal.

For the world of the Mishnah, whose center of focus is the Temple society, what is clean is holy and what is unclean is abnormal. As M. Douglas elucidates, "Holiness and impurity are at opposites poles... among the restrictions some are intended to protect divinity from profanation and others to protect the profane from the dangerous intrusion of divinity" (1966, pp. 7–8).[49] For the Mishnah, in seeking holiness for its cult and world, the unclean must be avoided and kept away, especially among those who represent the "holy." The Nazir, who is in a state of "super" holiness, must therefore remain holy—and clean or pure. Since contact with a corpse, as Scripture informs us (Lev. 21:1–3), represents uncleanness, it is therefore not holy, and impure. It is interesting to note that corpse uncleanness, even to one's closest relatives, is a prohibition not symbolically identified with the priest[50] during his Temple service as are the prohibitions of hair and wine, but rather is comparable to the prohibitions imposed on the High Priest. This requires the High Priest to avoid corpse contact, even to his parents, in any place inside and outside of the Temple, both during services and at all other times. Maintaining the state of cleanliness is an issue that transcends borders and boundaries. It would therefore seem that the parallelism to the High Priest even beyond the walls of the Temple was needed to supplement the comparison to the priest within the physical Temple boundaries. In discussing the differences between the Nazir and the High Priest in the case of corpse uncleanness, M. Naz. 7:1 (quoted above) makes this interrelationship clear.

---

[47] M. Adler, 1991, discusses the issue of alcoholic drinking in pre-industrial societies. Although little information is available on the social realities of the Mishnah redactors' social world one can assume that these similarities did exist.

[48] This issue is discussed in Garsney, 1999, and Harnik, 1994, who also present a survey of studies covering this topic.

[49] See also Neusner (1993a, p. 1) for an intensive discussion of this issue. Neusner also elucidates the philosophical issue of why a corpse should be considered unclean.

[50] A priest is permitted to become unclean to a corpse only in the case of his closest relatives, his parents. The High Priest is prohibited even from leaving the Temple grounds to follow the burial procedure of his parents (so as not to be in direct contact). See M. San. 2:1.

The unique language of the Mishnah and its rules contains, expresses and presents a message to its readers that goes beyond a specific place, society, reality and time.[51] It presents its own culture, its own world which has the power to form its own authority. It achieves order and balance to ward off and counter the threat of chaos.[52] In our case this is the threat of the Nazir, who is liminal to his society, problematic for the rabbis, and is controlled by rules laid down by Scripture which have been developed and reworked by the framers of the Mishnah. The three taboos of cutting the hair, wine and corpse uncleanness convey this message to the Nazir and his society, a message regarding the expectations concerning holiness which derive from this adopted status and role, and a holiness viewed in parallel to that of the priest serving in the Temple. Only after the performance of an exit ritual in a designated office within the Temple grounds does the Nazir, who has been perceived as a sinner escaping the world of the holy, leave this status and return to the cult. Only then, as M. Naz. 6:9 informs us, was the Nazir permitted to drink wine and contract corpse uncleanness. For then this message has been successfully conveyed to—and grasped—by the Nazir and by his fellow cult members.[53]

Bibliography

Adler, Marianna, "From Symbolic Exchange to Commodity Consumption: Anthropological Notes on Drinking as a Symbolic Practice" in *Drinking: Behavior and Belief in Modern History* edited by Susanna Barrows and Robin Room, Berkeley, Los Angeles, Oxford, 1991.

Albek, Hanokh, *Shisah Sidre Mishnah Mefurashim Biyedei Chanoch Albek Seder Nashim*. Israel, 1957.

Berg, C., *The Unconscious Significance of Hair*. London: George Allen and Unwin, 1959.

Bird, Frederick, "The Nature and Function of Ritual Forms: A Sociological Discussion." *Studies in Religion*. Volume 9, Number 4, 1979.

---

[51] Neusner, 2000, p. 422, explains how language acts as the message of Nazir: "So, sages' statement through the Halakhah of Nedarim-Nazir is clear. Vows are means used on earth by weak or subordinated person to coerce the more powerful person by invoking the power of Heaven." While not disagreeing with this suggestion, I offer an additional approach.

[52] See Neusner, 1999b, pp. 211–245, for a detailed discussion of the issue and the ramifications of Mishnah's language.

[53] My special gratitude goes to the following colleagues whose assistance in developing this essay has been invaluable: Dr. Nissan Rubin, Dr. Meir Bar Ilan, and Dr. Lynn Visson.

———, "Ritual as a Communicative Action," in J. Lightstone and F. Bird, eds., *Ritual and Ethnic Identity: A Comparative Study of the Social Meaning of Liturgical Ritual in Synagogues*. Waterloo, 1995.
Destro, Adrina, *The Law of Jealousy: Anthropology of Sotah*. Atlanta, 1989.
Douglas, Mary, *Cultural Bias*. London, 1978.
———, *Natural Symbols*. New York, 1970.
———, Mary, *Purity and Danger. An Analysis of Concepts of Pollution and Taboo*. Harmondsworth, 1969.
Eilberg-Schwartz, Howard, *The Savage in Judaism*. Bloomington and Indianapolis, 1988.
Garnsey, Peter, *Food and Society in Classical Antiquity*. Cambridge, 1999.
Goodenough, Erwin, *Jewish Symbols in the Greco-Roman Period*. Volume 6. New York, 1956.
Hall, E. T., *The Silent Language*. Garden City, 1959.
Hallpike, C. R., "Social Hair," in Lessa and Vogt, *Reader in Comparative Religion*. New York, 1979, pp. 99–104.
Harnik-Feely, Gillian, *The Lord's Table; The Meaning of Food in Early Judaism and Christianity*. Washington, 1994.
Leach, E. R., "Magical Hair," in the *Journal of the Anthropological Institute* 88: pp. 147–164, 1958.
Licht, Jacob, *A Commentary on the Book of Numbers*. Jerusalem, 1985.
Neusner, Jacob, translator and editor, *The Mishnah: A New Translation*. New Haven and London, 1988.
———, *The Four Stages of Rabbinic Judaism*. London and New York, 1999.
———, *Androgynous Judaism*. Macon, Georgia, 1993.
———, *Purity in Rabbinic Judaism. A Systematic Account of the Sources, Media Effects and Removal of Uncleanness*. Atlanta, 1993a.
———, *Turning Points: Five Transformations in the History of Judaism*. Oxford, 2002.
———, *A History of the Mishnaic Law of Women* part five. Leiden, 1980.
———, *Method and Meaning in Ancient Judaism*. Atlanta, 1989.
———, *Method and Meaning in Ancient Judaism*. Chico, 1981.
———, *Scripture and the Generative Premises of the Halakah: A Systematic Inquiry*. Volume Two, Binghamton, New York, 1999a.
———, *The Mishnah: Religious Perspective*. Leiden, 1999b.
———, *The Halakhah, An Encyclopedia of the Law of Judaism*. Volume IV, Leiden, 2000.
Rubin, Nissan, *The Beginning of Life—Rites of Birth, Circumcision, and Redemption of the First Born in the Talmud and Midrash*. (Hebrew). Hakibutz Hameuchad, Israel, 1995.
Trau, H., Rubin, N., Vargon, S., "Symbolic Significance of Hair," in *Koroth*. Special Issue, 1988, pp. 173–179.
Wegner, Judith Romney, *Chattel or Person, The Status of Women in the Mishnah*. New York and Oxford, 1988.
Weisman, Zev, "Hanizirut Bamikrah—Tifuseha vShorasheha," in *Tarbitz*, 36, 1957, pp. 207–220.

ARCHAEOLOGY AND THE MISHNAH'S HALAKHIC TRADITION: THE CASE OF STONE VESSELS AND RITUAL BATHS

Eyal Regev
Bar-Ilan University

Scholars of Rabbinic texts rarely use archaeological evidence as a tool in addition to their historical-philological study. Indeed, the juxtaposition of the material culture and the Rabbinic sources was dealt with by several scholars, such as Kreuss, Brand and, more recently, Sperber and Adan-Bayewitz. But although such studies provide an essential contribution to our understanding of the material culture and the way the rabbis lived, these scholars usually used the archaeological evidence in order to identify certain vessels or to illustrate the objects to which the rabbis were referring.[1] Thus, the archaeological artifacts were used as an interpretive tool, illuminating the original meaning of the text. However, the archaeological research rarely had a notable methodological effect on Rabbinic studies.[2] In this article I suggest examples for the use of stone vessels and ritual baths (*miqva'ot*) in dating several halakhic traditions in the Mishnah.

There is an additional possible contribution of the archaeological findings to the understanding of Rabbinic culture. Examination of some stone vessels and ritual baths in light of certain written sources (some of them non-Rabbinic) may suggest the existence of regulations, practices, and a social reality that are not explicitly mentioned in Rabbinic literature or elsewhere.[3] In this category are special ritual baths with a

---

[1] See S. Krauss, *Talmudische Archäologie* (Leipzig, 1910–1912); Y. Brand, *Ceramics in Talmudic Literature* (Jerusalem, 1953); D. Sperber, *Material Culture in the Land of Israel during the Talmudic Period* (Ramat Gan, 1993); idem, *Nautica Talmudica* (Ramat Gan and Leiden, 1986); D. Adan-Bayewitz, *Common Pottery in Roman Galilee: A Study of Local Trade* (Ramat Gan, 1993).

[2] For a similar direction to the one suggested here, see D. Adan-Bayewitz and M. Aviam, "Iotapata, Josephus, and the Siege of 67: Preliminary Report on the 1992–1994 Seasons," in *Journal of Roman Archaeology* 10, 1997, pp. 131–165, who suggest dating the Tannaitic traditions of "Walled Cities" (e.g., M. Arak. 9:6) according to the findings in Yodfat and Gamala.

[3] Z. Safrai, *The Economy of Roman Palestine* (London and New York, 1994).

partition for purification at higher (priestly) levels of purity and the use of stone vessels in order to observe another, more common, level of purity—non-priestly purity. These will be demonstrated below.

Stone Vessels[4] and the Red Heifer Ritual

According to Rabbinic law, stone vessels are not susceptible to impurity, probably because they are made from organic material. Thus, the use of stone vessels made life easier for those who scrupulously refrained from contact with impure objects and liquids.[5] Rabbinic sources frequently mention the use of stone vessels, though most of them allude to such vessels only in passing. One case, however, is different: At M. Par. 3:2 and 3:11, stone vessels' use is strangely emphasized as an intrinsic aspect of the ritual of the red heifer. According to the biblical commandment (Num. 19), in order to be cleansed of corpse impurity, the priestly establishment should slaughter a red heifer, grind its ashes, mix it in water, and then sprinkle the "water of *ḥattat*" on the impure people and objects. The biblical law does not mention the specific kind of vessels or instruments that should be used in this procedure. It is the Mishnah (as well as the parallel laws at T. Par. 3:3–4) that requires the use of a variety of stone vessels in the ritual of the ashes of the red heifer.

The Mishnah's very detailed description of this ritual leads to an interesting question: Is the intention to describe the Temple cult precisely as it actually existed, or is this a mythologization of the ancient ritual ("a myth about ritual"), without historical credibility? Although I do not intend to decisively determine which possibility is correct, it is interesting to compare the literary description with the archaeological findings of stone vessels from the Temple Mount excavations.

---

[4] For the collection of Rabbinic passages and the archaeological evidence see R. Deines, *Jüdische Steinefasse und pharisäische Frummigkeit. Ein archäologisch-historischer Beitrag zum Verständis von Joh 2, 6 und der jüdischen Reinheitshalacha zur Zeit Jesu* (Tübingen, 1993).

[5] Deines, ibid.; E. Regev, "The Use of Stone Vessels at the End of the Second Temple Period," in Y. Eshel, ed., *Judea and Samaria Research Studies, Proceedings of the 5th Annual Meeting* (Ariel, 1997), p. 83. This was probably accepted also by non-Pharisaic or Rabbinic Jews and also among the Qumran sectarians, since many stone vessels were excavated in Qumran. See ibid., pp. 89–91, and H. Eshel, "CD XII:15–17 and the Stone Vessels Found at Qumran," in E. Hazon and M. E. Stone, eds., *The Damascus Document: A Centennial Discovery, The Third Orion International Symposium* (Leiden, 2000), pp. 45–52.

M. Par. 3:2–3

> 3:2A. There were courtyards in Jerusalem, built on rock, and under them was a hollow, [which served as a protection] against a grave in the depths.
>
> B. And they bring pregnant women, who give birth there, and who raise their sons there.
>
> C. And they bring oxen, and on them are doors, and the youngsters sit on top of them, with stone cups (כוסות של אבן) in their hands.
>
> D. [When] they reached the Siloam, they descended and filled them, and mounted and sat on top of them.
>
> E. R. Yose says, "From his place did he let down and fill [the cup, without descending]."
>
> 3.3A. They came to the Temple mount and dismounted.
>
> (B. The Temple mount and the courtyards—under them is a hollow against a grave in the depth.)
>
> C. And at the door of the courtyard was a set up a flask of [ashes of] purification [rites done in the past].
>
> D. And they bring a male sheep and tie a string between its horns, and they tie a stick or a bushy twig on the head of the rope, and one throws it into the flask.
>
> E. And one hits the male, and it starts backwards.
>
> F. And one takes [the ashes spilled onto the stick] and mixes as much of it as could be visible on the surface of the water.
>
> G. R. Yose says, "Do not give the Sadducees an opportunity to cavil. But he takes it and mixes it.[6]

According to the Mishnah, all these measures were taken to prevent defilement. The water for the red heifer ritual was poured by the children into stone cups. When the children arrived at the Temple[7] with

---

[6] English translations of the Mishnah and Tosefta follow Neusner. The parallels in the Tosefta (3:2–3) contain additional details, e.g.: "They said before R. Aqiba in the name of R. Ishmael, "Stone cups were suspended from the horns of the oxen. When the oxen kneeled down to drink, the cups were filled up." He said to them, "Do not give the Minim a chance to cavil after you." The Minim were probably not Sadducees, but pagans. Cf. E. Regev, "The Sadducean Halakhah and the Influence of the Sadducees on Social and Religious Life," unpublished doctoral dissertation (Bar-Ilan University, 1999), p. 178.

[7] M. Par. 3:3 states פתח העזרה, but according to T. Par. 3:4 it was the gate of the women's court near the חיל.

the cups filled with water, the ritual continued by using a special jar, referred as "a flask of (ashes of) purification." Although the Mishnah does not explicitly say so, it seems that this was a vessel made of stone, probably a big jar.[8] Thus, both the "water of ḥattat" and the "ashes of ḥattat" were stored and mixed in stone vessels.

The Rabbinic description of the ritual may seem legendary or fictional to a critical observer. But it would be surprising if the later rabbis created a myth about a priestly ritual and the scrupulous demands of purity. After all, according to Rabbinic tradition, their forerunners, especially Yohanan b. Zakkai, pursued the reduction of the purity boundaries of the making of the ashes by insisting that the level of purity of a *tebul yom* (in contrast to the higher purity level of *meʿoravei shemesh*) suffices, and thus they paid relatively less attention to purity boundaries. Moreover, as Jacob Neusner has already shown, the Rabbinic attitude towards the Temple cult was generally very far from mythologization. Instead, the rabbis cherished the technical study of the cultic regulations. Mythologization of the ritual of the Day of Atonement rarely exists in the Mishnah, Talmuds, and halakhic midrashim, and it is characteristic of later poetic prayers.[9] Is it possible, then, that the Rabbinic description was not "a myth about ritual" but based on reality?

Here, archaeological considerations may contribute to the literary-historical examination. In the Temple Mount excavations in the late 1960s, B. Mazar discovered an enormous number of stone vessels south and south-west of the Temple Mount's walls. Some of them surely fell

---

[8] Other sources attest the use of stone vessels and tools for producing and storing the ashes. In M. Par. 3:11, Ishmael stresses that "When it was burned up, they beat the cinders with rods and sifted the ashes with sieves." R. Ishmael says: "They used stone hammers and stoneware sieves." This view probably derives form a previous understanding that stone vessels were in use throughout the procedure. Moreover, according to T. Par. 3:4, "stone flasks (קליליות של אבן) were set up along the wall of the stairs of the women's court, and [with] their covers of stone visible to the rampart, and in them were ashes of every cow they had burned." If such scrupulousness characterized their storage, it is more than reasonable that stone vessels were used to sprinkle the ashes.

[9] For the controversy with the Sadducees and the Qumran sectarians concerning the making of the ashes of the red heifer in tebul yom, see M. Par. 3:7–8; T. Par. 3:6, and 3:8; Neusner, *A Life of Rabban Yohanan ben Zakkai* (Leiden, 1962), p. 52; J. M. Baumgarten, "The Pharisaic-Sadducean Controversies about Purity and the Qumran Texts," in *Journal of Jewish Studies* 31, 1980, pp. 157–170. For the mythologization of the priestly ritual of the day of atonement in the later piyyutim, see M. D. Swartz, "Ritual about Myth about Ritual: Towards an Understanding of the 'Avodah' in the Rabbinic Period," in *Journal of Jewish Thought and Philosophy* 6, 1997, pp. 135–155. For other signs of Temple myths cf. R. Petai, *Man and Temple* (New York, 1967).

or were thrown down from the Temple itself, probably by the Romans. Additional vessels were discovered in recent excavations in the same areas. Two types of vessels are especially common. The first is the Calyx krater, usually referred to by archaeologists as Kallal. This is a large jar that was used for storing food and liquids. The complicated production technology of the Kallal, its large dimensions, and the decorative motifs that often graced the rims of the jar all point to the conclusion that it was an expensive vessel. The fact that many Kallal vessels were found in the Temple Mount excavations testifies to its use in facilitating observance of purity restrictions.[10] The other type is the small cup, usually referred to by archaeologists as a "measuring cup." These are faceted, barrel-shaped, generally handmade vessels.[11]

Hence, both types of vessels made of stone that are mentioned in Mishnah and Tosefta Parah are found in the Temple Mount excavations, and there is every reason to believe they were used in the Temple cult. Although there is no archaeological indication that the Kallal and the measuring cup actually served in the red heifer ritual, I find it more than reasonable. There is no doubt that such vessels make it possible to prevent contamination and were used in the daily Temple cult, and it would be only natural to use them in relation to the "product" that was manufactured and kept in the highest level of purity. Indeed, if some other product, person, or place in the Temple were contaminated with corpse impurity, they were purified by the ashes of the red heifer. But if the ashes themselves were contaminated, then the purity of the Temple and the cult were in danger.

The conclusion that, as Rabbinic sources insist, Kallal vessels and cups made of stone were used in the ritual of the red heifer still does not prove the authenticity of the Mishnah's description, although it is now clear that it is not completely fictional. At least some reality lies

---

[10] On the Kallal see B. Mazar, "The Excavations in the Old City of Jerusalem near the Temple Mount—Second Preliminary Report, 1969–1970 Seasons," in *Eretz-Israel* 10, 1971, pp. 18f. (in Hebrew); N. Avigad, *Discovering Jerusalem* (Jerusalem, 1980), pp. 127f., 173ff.; Y. Magen, *The Stone Vessel Industry in Jerusalem during the Second Temple Period* (Tel Aviv, 1988) (in Hebrew); E. Mazar and B. Mazar, "Excavations on the Slope of the Temple Mount," in *Qedem* 29, 1989, pp. 86–87, nos. 26–27, and pp. 98–99, nos. 13–16), and cf. pp. 53–55; Regev, "The Use of Stone Vessels," pp. 81f., 87–89.

[11] For their character and distribution in Jerusalem, see Avigad, *Discovering*, pp. 127ff.; Magen, *The Stone Vessel Industry*; J. M. Cahill, "The Chalk Assemblages of the Persian/Hellenistic and Early Roman Periods," in A. de Groot and D. T. Ariel, eds., *Excavations at the City of David 1978–1985, III, Stratigraphical, Environmental, and Other Reports* (Jerusalem, 1992), pp. 210f.; Regev, "The Use of Stone Vessels," pp. 79–81.

behind it. The most legendary part of the description is the use of children and male sheep in order to prevent impurity. Indeed, a somewhat different tradition of three children who sprinkle the ashes is attested to in the Epistle of Barnabas,[12] and thus there might be some historical basis for the Rabbinic description of children's involvement in the ritual. Interestingly, this pattern can be found in other Rabbinic passages: According to M. Sheq. 8.5, virgins who had not reached sexual maturity wove the Temple curtain, probably since they were not suspected of menstrual impurity. Similar phenomena occur in the cult of Athena, where the goddess' dress (Pepelos) was woven by young girls.[13] One may wonder whether these two examples are historical facts or only attest to other cultic myths. True, parallelism does not point to authenticity, but it shows that even if the use of children and sheep in the red heifer ritual is not historical, the idea derives from a popular pattern of exaggeration in the description of the scrupulous adherence to purity and ritual in the cult. If one does accept the authenticity of the examples of the weaving of the curtain and the dress, then it will be possible to stress that the components of the tradition about the red heifer ritual have a background not only in the material culture of Herodian Jerusalem but also in the description of other ritualistic acts among Jews and Greeks.

My impression is that the Tannaim were not responsible for this glorification of this ritual, since the Mishnah's description is not a standard work of the rabbis in the days of Ushah. Jacob Neusner concluded that M. Par. 3:2–3 is the work of the Ushan generation, since two pericopae are attributed to Yose.[14] But it is now possible to confine this conclusion to Yose's comments on an earlier tradition. I suggest that it is a reworking of earlier (perhaps even oral) traditions that contain authentic details and perhaps also some mythic exaggerations.

---

[12] Cf. J. Neusner, *A History of the Mishnaic Law of Purities, X, Parah, Literary and Historical Problems* (Leiden, 1976), p. 218, who emphasized the differences between this tradition and the Rabbinic description. One also might conclude that this text only testifies to a common Jewish legendary tradition regarding the making of the ashes.

[13] See S. Lieberman, *Hellenism in Jewish Palestine* (New York, 1902), pp. 167–168.

[14] See Neusner, *Purities X*, pp. 94, 96, 120, 148–150. In T. Par. 3:3, the use of stone cups is attributed to Aqiba and Ishmael, namely to the end of the Yavnean generation, (ibid., pp. 128f.). Neusner comments: "While the historical narratives of M. 3:1–11 are heavily glossed by Ushans...which suggests that a quite different narrative will have been produced by the glossators, it is clear that the fundamental issues of the narratives are Yavnean" (ibid., p. 150, cf. also pp. 173, 177, 204). I therefore suggest that some of the details in the narrative are pre-Yavnean.

I am not sure that the later rabbis could preserve in such detail a description of an infrequent ritual without basing it on detailed sources. Thus, in this case, the findings of stone vessels near the Temple Mount, along with other historical considerations, may lead to a new perspective on an outstanding chapter in Rabbinic literature.

Stone Vessels as Attesting to Hullin ("Non-Priestly") Purity

One of the most basic postulates of the Mishnah's (and Tosefta's) Order of Purities is that people should live and eat in a state of purity. This applies to the consumption not only of sacred ("priestly") food (viz., priestly dues and sacrifices and also second tithe) but also to non-sacred food. This basic level of purity is called Hullin (the higher levels are Terumah, Qodesh, and Ḥattat). According to the Rabbinic system, in order to be pure in the level of Hullin it is sufficient to immerse in a ritual bath, that is, to be a Tebul Yom, there being no need to wait until sundown, as in the case of the higher, "priestly" purity.[15] In previous studies I have tried to show that the observance of Hullin purity is attested in the archaeological findings of many stone vessels, and especially measuring cups, in many areas and sites in the land of Israel: the Judean Hills, the Judean Desert, south and west Samaria, Galilee, the Golan Heights and Transjordan, and even in the Negev.[16] It is significant that such adherence to purity laws took place not only in the urban centers (especially in Jerusalem) but also in rural settlements. But in what way do these vessels attest to "non-priestly" purity and not to the biblical "priestly" purity?

The relatively large number of vessels, and the fact that they were found in almost every known Jewish settlement in the land of Israel, even the smallest, leads to the conclusion that they were not used for only eating and handling priestly dues (viz., heave-offerings) and second tithe. Thus, for example, in Iotapata (Iodphat), the Galilean town that Josephus claimed to fortify against Vespasian in 67 B.C.E., at least

---

[15] Cf. Neusner, *Purities X*, pp. 91ff.; J. Neusner, *A History of the Mishnaic Law of Purities, XXII, The Mishnaic System of Uncleanness* (Leiden, 1977), p. 252; E. Regev, "Pure Individualism: The Idea of Non-Priestly Purity in Ancient Judaism," in *Journal for the Study of Judaism in the Persian, Hellenistic and Roman Periods* 31, 2000, p. 189.

[16] For a bibliographical survey of the findings and discussion, see Deines, pp. 115–165.

one hundred and twenty fragments of stone vessels were found.[17] Moreover, a typological examination shows that most of the stone vessels discovered outside Jerusalem were not used for storage. Most of them are small domestic mugs, pitchers, and bowls that contained drinks and food for daily meals. One probably would have needed much larger vessels to store in purity his annual heave-offering of his crop after the harvest. The priest who collected much greater amounts of heave-offering would also have preferred larger storage vessels.

It seems to me that there is also a chronological correlation between the first attribution to the observance of Hullin impurity and the emergence of the "Jewish" industry of stone vessels. The earliest references to Hullin purity/impurity in Rabbinic sources allude to controversies between the Houses of Hillel and Shammai, and it thus seems that, at least according to Rabbinic tradition, this phenomenon emerged during the days of their masters, Hillel and Shammai, that is, in the late Herodian period (a decade or two before the turn of the era). This is precisely the widely held dating of the emergence of the stone vessels in Jerusalem.[18]

However, it would be wrong to see the common observance of Hullin impurity as an exclusively Pharisaic-Rabbinic phenomenon. It would also not be correct to explain it as characteristic only of a certain elite of Rabbinic sages.[19] Adherence to purity in daily life outside the realm of the Temple, sacrifices, and priestly dues, especially in relation to prayer and the study of Torah (and of course, non-sacred meals), appears in Josephus, the Apocrypha, and among the Qumran sectarians. It is also reflected in ritual baths near synagogues (e.g., in Herodion and Gamla).[20]

---

[17] Adan-Bayewitz and Aviam, "Iotapata, Josephus, and the Siege of 67," p. 164.

[18] B. Mazar, "The Excavations in the Old City of Jerusalem." For more details see Regev, "Pure Individualism," pp. 183f., with further conclusions regarding the end of the use of stone vessels around 200 C.E. (although there are no archaeological finds later than the period of the Bar Kokhba revolt).

[19] This impression is partly derived from the Gospels' reference to the Pharisaic purity laws and social exclusion of sinners and estrangement of those who did not observe Hullin impurity. Cf. Regev, "Pure Individualism," pp. 199–201. For the rabbis as an elite, cf. Oppenheimer 1977 and Levine 1989. However, several purity regulations do bear a pattern of behavior of an elite. See Regev, "Pure Individualism," pp. 192–202.

[20] For the historical sources, additional archaeological attestations relating to ritual baths, and the religious and social of the observance of such purity in the daily life, see Regev, "Non-priestly Purity" and "Pure Individualism."

RITUAL BATHS WITH A PARTITION AS A CHRONOLOGICAL
INDICTOR OF THE MISHNAIC TRADITION

From the Hasmonean period onwards, the most common method of purification was immersion in a ritual bath, a small plastered pool carved in rock with steps leading into it. Our understanding of the reality of Mishnah and Tosefta Tractate Miqvaot (and other relevant halakhot) was substantially improved by the discovery of more than three hundred ritual baths dating from the Hasmonean to the Byzantine periods (most of them from the Second Temple period). Most of the laws in tractate Miqvaot discuss the problem of drawn water, which render the bath invalid, since it must consist at least forty seahs (between 500 to 1000 liters; later Rabbinic calculations estimate it as about 750 liters) of undrawn water that derives directly from a spring or rainfall. Several methods of rendering invalid water usable by mingling it with valid water are described, but some of them are abstract and unclear without a visual illustration, which now emerges from many archaeological excavations.[21]

For example, M. Miq. 6:8 discusses the mingling the water of two ritual baths from a higher bath, containing drawn and invalid water, to a lower bath, containing undrawn and valid water:

A. They clean immersion pools:
B. A higher pool by the lower pool,
C. And a distant by a nearby [pool].
D. How so?
E. One brings a pipe of earthenware or lead,
F. and puts his hand under it until it is filled with water,
G. and draws it along and makes it touch.
H. Even by as much as a hair's breadth suffices.
I. [If] the upper one contains forty seahs [of fit water]
J. and in the lower pool there is nothing—
K. one draws [water and carries it] on the shoulder and puts it into the upper one,
L. until there will descend into the lower one forty seahs.

---

[21] See R. Reich, "Miqwa'ot (Jewish Ritual Immersion Baths) in Eretz-Israel in the Second Temple and the Mishnah and Talmud Periods," Ph.D. diss. (Hebrew University, Jerusalem, 1990) (in Hebrew), for a comparison of the archaeological evidence with Rabbinic sources and an extensive description of the ritual baths excavated by the late 1980s. Several more baths were discovered in the last ten years. For the different ways of making the bath's water valid according to Rabbinic halakhot, see ibid., pp. 12–33.

T. Miq. 5:5 dictates a similar approach, joining two adjacent baths with a pipe: the slightest touch between them makes them virtually one valid bath of more than forty seahs of undrawn water (of the valid bath), and when one separates between them after few seconds the invalid bath becomes valid:[22]

A. They clean the immersion-pools,
B. the upper by the lower,
C. and the distant by that which is near—
D. how so?
E. One brings a pipe of wood, bone, or glass
F. and places his hand(s) [under] the lower [end of the pipe]
G. until it will be filled with water
H. and conveys it, and touches it [the water of the pool to the water of the pipe].
I. Even if it is [touching] by as little as a hair's breadth, it suffices.
J. And if the pipe is bent in any measure at all, it is unfit.
K. Under what circumstances?
L. When they were on top of the other.
M. But if they were side by side,
N. He brings a knee-shaped pipe on one side, and a knee-shaped pipe on the other side, and a pipe on the middle—
O. and he touches [the water of the one to that of the other]
P. and descends and immerses.

Ritual baths that correspond to the Mishnah's description were identified by Yadin at Masada, where in the south slope of the fortress two baths were revealed. One of the pools had no steps and a short pipe connected them. Yadin identified the bath that had no steps as a "treasury" that contained undrawn water and was used for rendering the other bath's water valid by a slight touch between the two bodies of water through the pipe, as the Mishnah prescribes.[23]

More than ten ritual baths with a "treasury" were also found in the Hasmonean and Herodian palaces in Jericho, several were excavated south of the Temple Mount, one in the Herodian quarter in Jerusalem,

---

[22] See ibid., pp. 22–24, for the connecting of two ritual bath through a pipe. For the literary relationship between M. Miq. 6:8 and T. Miq. 5:5, see J. Neusner, *A History of the Mishnaic Law of Purities, XIV, Miqvaot, Literary and Historical Problems* (Atlanta, 1995), pp. 68, 73, 76.

[23] Cf. Reich, "Miqwa'ot," pp. 292–301; E. Netzer, *Masada IV: The Buildings, Stratigraphy and Architecture* (Jerusalem, 1991), pp. 127–131. On the "treasury" in general, see Reich, "Miqwa'ot," pp. 24–27.

one in Herodion, but this type is quite rare in comparison to more than three hundred other baths without a "treasury." Other pairs of stepped baths that could be easily joined by an external pipe, as the Tosefta depicts, were also excavated, such as in the villa in the Herodian quarter in Jerusalem, but they were also not common. However, the most relevant fact for the present discussion is that no treasuries were found from the period later than 70 C.E. The technique described above seems to have vanished after the destruction of the Second Temple (in spite of the extensive excavations in Jewish settlements all around Judaea, the Galilee and the coastal plain).[24]

This lacuna in the archaeological evidence leads me to conclude that M. Miq. 6:8//T. Miq. 5:5 were composed before 70 C.E., or at least were based on pre-70 C.E. tradition. It is indeed curious why this technique, that had a practical advantage, was not continued. Such a conclusion about the early roots of M. Miq. 6:8//T. Miq. 5:5 differs from Neusner's observation that these pericopes are from the time of Yavneh or Ushah. Neusner based his conclusion on Eleazar b. Azaria's comment regarding the practice of making the upper water clean by the lower water, which actually means mingling of water by a "treasury" or pipe (M. Miq. 3:2).[25] However, since Eleazar was not introducing the practice but only commenting on an already existing halakhah, I think the archaeological evidence leads to the conclusion that he was referring to a pre-70 C.E. practice, and thus the pericope in M. Miq. 3:2 (and consequently the basic parts of M. Miq. 3:1 on which the discussion in the following pericope is built) is later than M. Miq. 6:8//T. Miq. 5:5. When Eleazar discussed his practice, it was probably merely a theoretical issue.

I now turn to the case of a ritual bath with a partition described in M. Sheq. 8:2:

A. "All utensils found in Jerusalem,
B. "on the path down to an immersion pool, are assumed to be unclean.
C. "[If they are found] on the path up from the immersion pool, they are assumed to be clean.

---

[24] On the distribution of ritual baths with a "treasury," see Reich, "Miqwa'ot," especially the descriptions of the sites, pp. 270–278, 221, 202f., and 284, respectively. A few years ago I noticed a "treasury" in the excavations of Archelais (near the Jordan river). On baths that could be easily joined by a pipe, cf. Reich, pp. 174–179.

[25] Neusner, *Purities XIV*, pp. 101, 105, 158f.

D. "For the way down is different from the way up," the words of R. Meir.
E. R. Yose says, "All of them are clean,
F. "except for a basket, shovel, or pick, [which are] particularly used for digging graves."

The Mishnah distinguishes between the path down to and the path up from the immersion pool. Utensils of an unknown status of cleanness found on the path down must be deemed unclean; but when they are found on the path up from the ritual bath, they may be deemed clean, since it is probable that the one who lost them already immersed, so that both the person and the utensils are pure.[26] It is noteworthy that such a ritual bath is not mentioned in its natural contexts, Miqvaot, but in Sheqalim, in relation to the special arrangements and daily life that pertain to the pilgrimage to Jerusalem. Interestingly, ritual baths with a partition between the paths were discovered in archaeological excavations, most of them in Jerusalem, but also in its surroundings from Pisgat Ze'ev in the north, to the North Mountain of Hebron in the south, as well as in Gezer, Jericho, and Qumran.[27] The architectural character of the partition between the paths up and down the staircase varies. In most of the baths it is a short (5–10 cm.) plaster belt all along the staircase, in others there are different doorways to each path (that is, a wall, which is actually uncarved rock, divides them), and in a few cases there is a combination of plaster partition as well as separate doorways.

Most of the ritual baths of this type were found at Jerusalem in sites from the Herodian period (37 B.C.E.–70 C.E.) and ceased to exist after the destruction of the Second Temple. This fact is not surprising, since the Jewish population in the city almost vanished during the middle

---

[26] The only possible explanation I can raise for Yose's contrary attitude is that he refers to the time of the pilgrimage to Jerusalem, when everyone was considered pure (cf. T. Bik. 2.8).

[27] For the correspondence between M. Shek. 8:2 and the archaeological evidence, see R. Reich, "Mishnah Shekalim 8:2 and the Archaeological Evidence," in A. Oppenheimer, et al., eds., *Jerusalem in the Second Temple Period, Abraham Shalit Memorial Volume* (Jerusalem, 1980), pp. 225–256 (in Hebrew). For the different ritual baths, see Reich, "Miqwa'ot," pp. 34ff.; D. Amit, "Ritual Baths (Mikva'ot) from the Second Temple Period in the Hebron Mountains," in Y. Eshel, ed., *Judea and Samaria Research Studies, Proceeding of the 3d Annual Meeting* (Kedumim-Ariel, 1993), pp. 157–189 (in Hebrew); Z. Greenhut, "Village Settlements in the Periphery of Jerusalem from the Early Roman to the Byzantine Period," in S. Dar and Z. Safrai, eds., *The Village in Ancient Israel* (Tel Aviv, 1997), pp. 147–150 (in Hebrew).

and late Roman period. In Jericho and Qumran as well there are no ritual baths after 70, for the very same reason. The ritual baths that consist of partitions in the rural outskirts of Jerusalem, especially in the North Hebron Mountains (near Gush Ezion) ceased to exist no later than after the Bar Kokhba revolt, when the rural settlement in Judaea was destroyed.[28] There are no such ritual bath in the Galilee, either before or after 70 C.E. To the best of my knowledge, there is no single ritual bath with a partition dated after 135 C.E., and most of them were abandoned after 70 C.E. Thus, it should be concluded that M. Sheq. 8:2 reflects pre-70 reality in Jerusalem, and perhaps the practice that still continued in its outskirts until the Bar Kokhba revolt.[29]

Although the pericope of the Mishnah is attributed to Meir (and Yose adds his own reservations), it is almost impossible that it appeared in the Ushan generation, and it is even doubtful that it emerged in Yavneh. I think that the archeological findings lead to the conclusion that the source of this passage, or at least its halakhic tradition, goes back to a pre-70 C.E. Jerusalem Rabbinic school.

Ritual Baths with Partitions and "Priestly" Purity

About fifteen percent of the ritual baths from the Second Temple period had a partition. The question is the purpose of this special installation and why it was characteristic of only a small number of the baths? From M. Sheq. 8:2 it appears that the partition separated the impure who go down to immerse from the pure who go up from immersion. But in the archaeological remains, the partition is too short and too low to prevent physical contact between the two. Thus, it only signified a division. Such a separation between the entrance and exit is attested in other texts, all of them pertaining to the Temple cult: the rulings

---

[28] Amit, "Ritual Baths."

[29] J. Neusner, *A History of The Mishnaic Law of Appointed Times, III, Sheqlim, Yoma, Sukkah* (Leiden, 1982), avoids any suggestion regarding the chronological provenance of this passage. J. N. Epstein, *Introduction to Tannaitic Literature* (Jerusalem and Tel-Aviv, 1957), pp. 162, 235f., noted the connection between Yose's comment and another halakhah attributed to Abba Shaul in the Yerushalmi. Abba Shaul lived in the last generation before the destruction (cf. T. Y.T. 3:8) and handed down several traditions in Yavneh In general, Epstein (pp. 25–27) believed tractate Sheqalim is one of the oldest documents in Rabbinic literature. For a foundation of a pre-70 dating of Sheqalim, see M. Sheq. 8:5 (Simeon b. Gamaliel in the name of Simeon the Segan).

regarding the ramp that led to the altar, as well as the entrance to the Temple in Rabbinic sources, and also the switching of the priestly courses in the Temple according to the Temple Scroll.[30] Consequently, it seems that these ritual baths had some connection to the Temple cult. But how can this be the case when the ritual baths were located dozens of kilometers from the Temple (e.g., Jericho, Gezer, etc.)? This question leads me to turn to the archaeological evidence.

One possible solution is that these were priests' ritual baths. Indeed, most of these ritual baths were found in areas and sites with priestly populations, such as in Jerusalem itself, Jericho, Qumran, and the outskirts of Jerusalem.[31] Several baths of this particular type were found on farms that specialized in intensive oil manufacture, both south (Kh. Hillal) and north (Pisgat Ze'ev) of Jerusalem. It is possible that these farms provided oil and other products for the Temple,[32] and those who provided it intended their manufacture to suit the demands of those who immersed in similar ritual baths with a partition. But why did the priestly population need separate ritual baths? The biblical commandments distinguish the special purity restrictions of heave-offerings, and in Rabbinic sources this became the basis of the purity system: The grades of purity pertaining to heave-offering and Qodesh are higher.[33] This illustrates that there may have been distinguished purity levels also in the ritual baths. I suggest that those who immersed in these baths were either priests on their way to serve at the Temple and eat priestly dues or even non-priests who manufactured items for the Temple and priests that required this special level of purity.

Baths with a "Treasury" or Mixing Baths as an Indication of Pharisaic Halakhah

The ritual baths with a "treasury" or pairs of baths that could be easily connected by a pipe are quite rare. I suggest that they correspond

---

[30] M. Zeb. 6:3; M. Mid. 2:2, Temple Scroll 45:3–7, respectively. For details and bibliography see E. Regev, "Ritual Baths of Jewish Groups," in *Cathedra* 82, 1996, pp. 6f (in Hebrew). For similar phenomenon in Greek cultic traditions, cf. Liberman 1984, pp. 273f.

[31] See Regev, "Ritual Baths of Jewish Groups," pp. 8–11; E. Regev, "More on Ritual Baths of Jewish Groups and Sects: On Research Methods and Archaeological Evidence—A Reply to A. Grosberg," in *Cathedra* 83, 1997, pp. 170–172 (in Hebrew).

[32] See Amit, "Ritual Baths," pp. 157–189; Greenhut, "Village Settlements," pp. 147–150.

[33] Cf. M. Hag. 2:6–7; M. Par. 8:7; M. Zab. 5:12; M. T.Y. 2:1, 4:1–3.

only to the Pharisaic-Rabbinic halakhah[34] and not with those of the Sadducees and the Qumran sectarians. As noted above, by connecting a ritual bath that contained drawn water to another bath that contained undrawn water, it was possible to make the first valid for immersion. But such a mixture of liquids might have been unacceptable and inappropriate according to the Sadducean and Qumranic halakhic systems.

A quite similar act of pouring an impure liquid into a vessel containing a pure liquid is described in M. Yad. 4:7 as a dispute between the Pharisees and Sadducees. The Sadducees complained that the Pharisees declared that the "unbroken stream of liquid" was pure. This peculiar halakhic issue is also mentioned in 4QMMT, where the authors (probably the Qumran sectarians in their early stage of formation) opposed the Pharisaic view that the stream is pure.[35] This controversy has no direct relationship to the laws pertaining to ritual baths, but it seems that the problem of connecting two bodies of liquids, one pure or valid, and the other not, is indeed common to M. Yad. 4:7 and M. Miq. 6:8//T. Miq. 5:5. The Pharisees held a lenient view in the two cases. Thus, I presume that those who declare that when pure liquid falls from an upper vessel into a lower vessel containing impure liquid, the upper liquid is contaminated—that is, impurity "climbs" up the stream—would not accept the technique in which contact of drawn water in one ritual bath with undrawn water in the other renders the first valid. According to this interpretation, the Mishnah's Sadducees and the authors of MMT did not agree with the practice of mingling the water of the ritual baths. Indeed, the line of reasoning in M. Yad. 4:7 can be applied to the question of mingling of ritual baths' water, since it concerns the connection between two liquids. Those who held a stricter view regarding the connection between liquids in the case of an unbroken stream of water may have held the same line of thinking regarding the contact between drawn and undrawn water.[36]

---

[34] Although the question of the relationship between the Pharisees and the later rabbis is complex, in this case it is impossible to ignore the two groups' pre-70 C.E. common halakhic heritage, since the ritual baths with a "treasury" were found only from the period before 70 C.E.

[35] See J. M. Baumgarten, "The Pharisaic-Sadducean Controversies about Purity and the Qumran Texts," in *Journal of Jewish Studies* 31, 1980, pp. 157–170.

[36] See Regev, "Ritual Baths of Jewish Groups," pp. 12–15; Regev, "More on Ritual Baths." For the Sadducean and Qumranic line of thinking, also referring to M. Yad. 4:7, see D. R. Schwartz, "Law and Truth: On Qumran-Sadducean and Rabbinic Views of Law," in D. Dimant and U. Rappaport, eds., *The Dead Sea Scrolls, Forty Years of Research* (Jerusalem, 1992), pp. 229–240.

Support for this suggestion can be found in the excavations at Qumran. Ten ritual baths were excavated there, but none of them seemed to use a "treasury" or mingling water by a pipe. This fact corresponds with my interpretation of the controversy regarding the stream in 4QMMT. If my suggestion is correct, then the ritual baths with treasuries in the sites mention above—south of the Temple Mount, in the Herodian quarter in Jerusalem, in Jericho, Masada, Herodion and elsewhere—all attest to their inhabitants' tendency to bathe according to the Pharisaic halakhah. This conclusion may contribute to the understanding of the use of Rabbinic laws in the daily life before 70 C.E.

Bibliography

Adan-Bayewitz, D., *Common Pottery in Roman Galilee: A Study of Local Trade* (Ramat Gan, 1993).
——, and M. Aviam, "Iotapata, Josephus, and the Siege of 67: Preliminary Report on the 1992–1994 Seasons," in *Journal of Roman Archaeology* 10, 1997, pp. 131–165.
——, "The Tannaitic List of 'Walled Cities' and the Archaeological-Historical Evidence from Iotapata and Gamala," in *Tarbiz* 66, 1997, pp. 449–470.
Amit, D., "Ritual Baths (Mikva'ot) from the Second Temple Period in the Hebron Mountains," in Y. Eshel, ed., *Judea and Samaria Research Studies, Proceeding of the 3d Annual Meeting* (Kedumim-Ariel, 1993), pp. 157–189 (in Hebrew).
Avigad, N., *Discovering Jerusalem* (Jerusalem, 1980).
Baumgarten, J. M., "The Pharisaic-Sadducean Controversies about Purity and the Qumran Texts," in *Journal of Jewish Studies* 31, 1980, pp. 157–170.
Brand, Y., *Ceramics in Talmudic Literature* (Jerusalem, 1953).
Cahill, J. M., "The Chalk Assemblages of the Persian/Hellenistic and Early Roman Periods", in de Groot, A., and D. T. Ariel, eds., *Excavations at the City of David 1978–1985, III, Stratigraphical, Environmental, and Other Reports* (Jerusalem, 1992), pp. 190–274.
Deines, R., *Jüdische Steinefasse und pharisäische Frummigkeit. Ein archäologisch-historischer Beitrag zum Verständis von Joh 2, 6 und der jüdischen Reinheitshalacha zur Zeit Jesu* (Tübingen, 1993).
Eshel, H., "CD XII:15–17 and the Stone Vessels Found at Qumran," in Hazon, E., and M. E. Stone, eds., *The Damascus Document: A Centennial Discovery, The Third Orion International Symposium* (Leiden, 2000), pp. 45–52.
Greenhut, Z., "Village Settlements in the Periphery of Jerusalem from the Early Roman to the Byzantine Period," in Dar, S., and Z. Safrai, eds., *The Village in Ancient Israel* (Tel Aviv, 1997), pp. 147–159 (in Hebrew).
Lieberman, S., *Hellenism in Jewish Palestine* (New York, 1902).
Magen, Y., *The Stone Vessels Industry in Jerusalem During the Second Temple Period* (Tel Aviv, 1988) (in Hebrew).
Mazar, B., "The Excavations in the Old City of Jerusalem near the Temple Mount—Second Preliminary Report, 1969–1970 Seasons," in *Eretz-Israel* 10, 1971, pp. 1–34 (in Hebrew).
Mazar, E., and B. Mazar, *Excavations in the Slope of the Temple Mount* (Jerusalem, 1989).
Netzer, E., *Masada IV: The Buildings, Stratigraphy and Architecture* (Jerusalem, 1991).
Neusner, J., *A Life of Rabban Yohanan ben Zakkai* (Leiden, 1962).
——, *A History of The Mishnaic Law of Purities* (Leiden, 1976–1977).
——, *A History of The Mishnaic Law of Appointed Times, III, Sheqlim, Yoma, Sukkah* (Leiden, 1982).

Petai, R., *Man and Temple* (New York, 1967).
Safrai, Z., *The Economy of Roman Palestine* (London and New York, 1994).
Regev, E., "Ritual Baths of Jewish Groups and Sects in the Second Temple Period," in *Cathedra* 82, 1996, pp. 3–21 (in Hebrew).
——, "More on Ritual Baths of Jewish Groups and Sects: On Research Methods and Archaeological Evidence—A Reply to A. Grosberg," in *Cathedra* 83, 1997, pp. 169–176.
——, "The Use of Stone Vessels at the End of the Second Temple Period," in Y. Eshel, ed., *Judea and Samaria Research Studies, Proceedings of the 5th Annual Meeting* (Kedumim-Ariel, 1997), pp. 79–95.
——, "The Sadducean Halakhah and the Influence of the Sadducees on Social and Religious Life," unpublished doctoral dissertation (Bar-Ilan University, 1999) (in Hebrew).
——, "Non-priestly Purity and Its Religious Perspectives according to Historical Sources and Archeological Findings," in Poorthuis, M. J. H. M., and J. Schwartz, eds., *Purity and Holiness: The Heritage of Leviticus* (Leiden, 2000), pp. 223–244.
——, "Pure Individualism: The Idea of Non-Priestly Purity in Ancient Judaism," in *Journal for the Study of Judaism in the Persian, Hellenistic and Roman Period* 31, 2000, pp. 176–202.
Reich, R., "Mishnah Shekalim 8:2 and the Archaeological Evidence," in Oppenheimer, A., et al., eds., *Jerusalem in the Second Temple Period, Abraham Shalit Memorial Volume* (Jerusalem, 1980), pp. 225–256.
——, "Miqwa'ot (Jewish Ritual Immersion Baths) in Eretz-Israel in the Second Temple and the Mishnah and Talmud Periods," Ph.D. diss. (Hebrew University, Jerusalem, 1990) (in Hebrew).
Schwartz, D. R., "Law and Truth: On Qumran-Sadducean and Rabbinic Views of Law," in Dimant, D., and U. Rappaport, eds., *The Dead Sea Scrolls, Forty Years of Research* (Jerusalem, 1992), pp. 229–240.
Sperber, D., *Material Culture in Eretz-Israel during the Talmudic Period* (Ramat Gan, 1993) (in Hebrew).
——, *Nautica Talmudica* (Ramat Gan and Leiden, 1986).
Swartz, M. D., "Ritual about Myth about Ritual: Towards an Understanding of the 'Avodah' in the Rabbinic Period," in *Journal of Jewish Thought and Philosophy* 6, 1997, pp. 135–155.

THE POETICS OF THE MISHNAH

Avraham Walfish
Herzog Teachers Academy

Problems in Understanding Mishnaic Redaction

Over the past hundred and fifty years, scholars have invested much effort in attempting to understand the principles that govern the redaction of the Mishnah. While the "presentation of vast amounts of information in a systematic and orderly way"[1] is undoubtedly the governing principle underlying Mishnaic redaction, few tractates *consistently* follow a clear and logical pattern, and many tractates fail to display any discernible thematic development at all. Two examples will illustrate the point.

(1) Tractate Shabbat might logically have been expected to open with a presentation of its "central pivot,"[2] the list of thirty-nine fundamental categories of work on which the entire system of activities forbidden or permitted on the Sabbath is founded. However, this pericope instead appears almost inconspicuously at M. Shab. 7:2, while the Mishnah's redactor devotes most of the first six chapters to two major topics: a chronological presentation of laws governing pre-Sabbath preparations (chaps. 1–4)[3] and laws relating to carrying from private to public domains on the Sabbath (chaps. 5–6). A convincing reason for the juxtaposition of these two themes in the six opening chapters

---

[1] Jacob Neusner, *Judaism—The Evidence of the Mishnah* (Chicago and London, 1981), p. 241.
[2] Abraham Goldberg, *Commentary to Mishnah Shabbat—Critically Edited and Provided with Introduction, Commentary and Notes* (Jerusalem, 1976), p. xiv (Hebrew). Y. D. Gilat, "On the Development of the Categories of Work Forbidden on the Sabbath," in *PAAJR* XLIX (1982), p. 10, comments that any modern redactor asked to arrange the laws of tractate Shabbat would open with this pericope. It should be noted, however, that Maimonides, whose principles of arrangement and presentation usually conform fairly well to modern ways of thinking, also defers the list of thirty-nine kinds of work until the seventh chapter of his Laws of the Sabbath in his Code of Jewish Law.
[3] Goldberg, *Shabbat*, p. xiv, who notes that chap. 1 progresses from "close to the time of the afternoon prayer" (M. Shab. 1:2) to "close to dark" (M. 1:3 *et seq*) and finally "as dark descends" (M. Shab. 1:11). He further notes that chap. 4 deals with covering food, which is permitted during twilight (M. 2:7), while chap. 2 and 3 deal with activities that may be performed only during daylight hours. On p. 37, n. 1, he

is based on associative, rather than logical, concerns: chaps. 2, 4, 5, and 6 all open with the question *bamah*[4]—with what? Starting with M. Shab. 7:2, the Mishnah shifts to a logical arrangement, continuing through chap. 15, based on the thirty-nine categories of work. We thus see in the first fifteen chapters of Tractate Shabbat at least three different principles of organization: chronological, associative, and logical.

The opening pericope of the tractate doesn't seem to conform to any of these principles of organization. While it could serve to introduce the laws of the forbidden activity of carrying an object from one domain to another, this topic is not addressed further until chap. 5.[5] Several theories have been advanced to explain why this pericope was chosen to open the tractate, all of which are based on considerations that differ from the three organizing principles listed above.[6] Finally, it should be noted that the different organizing principles do not coexist harmoniously. The complications caused by shifting from one ordering principle to another may be illustrated by noting that the laws of carrying in chaps. 5 and 6 (connected to previous chapters by associative arrangement) and in M. Shab. 7:3–11:5 (logical arrangement) are separated from one another by M. 7:1–2, which present the fundamental halakhic principles underlying *all* forbidden work on the Sabbath.

(2) Tractate Gittin opens in a most puzzling fashion: "He who delivers a writ of divorce from overseas must state, 'In my presence it was

---

notes, however, that chronologically chap. 2 (lighting candles) should follow chap. 3 (see the *baraitot* on B. Shab. 35b and discussion by Lieberman, *Tosefta Ki-Fshutah* [New York, 1962, vol. 4, pp. 895–896], and suggests an associative reason for following the end of chap. 1 (kindling a fire prior to the Sabbath) with chap. 2.

[4] I have followed the vowel-pointing of MS Kaufman rather than the more popular reading: *bameh*, followed by Hanokh Yalon in the Albeck edition of the Mishnah and by standard prayer-books. Throughout this paper, I will follow the Mishnah text of the Kaufman manuscript, unless otherwise indicated.

[5] It is touched on briefly in M. 1:3; however, the categories established in M. 1:1 are not required in order to understand this pericope. In truth, even chaps. 5 and 6 can be readily understood without the categories of M. 1:1, and the analysis of "carrying" underlying M. 1:1 is not carried forward until chaps. 10 and 11.

[6] Goldberg, *Shabbat*, pp. 2–4, and Yehudah Shaviv, "Why does Tractate Shabbat Open with the Work of Taking Out," in *Sinai* 105 (1990), pp. 220–230 (Hebrew), summarize the several approaches suggested in classical commentaries to Mishnah and Talmud and suggest some novel approaches of his own. Goldberg, *Shabbat*, p. xv, and Neusner, *Judaism*, pp. 183–184, have noted that the division between domains and the laws of transporting objects from one domain to another is the most extensively discussed topic in the tractate (see further discussion in Neusner, *The Halakhah—An Encyclopedia of the Law of Judaism* [Leiden, 2000], vol. IV, pp. 1–2, 52–56. This insight can shed further light on the redactor's way of opening the tractate, but this does not resolve all the difficulties discussed above.

written and in my presence it was signed.'" This pericope deals with the final stage of the divorce proceedings—the delivery—and focuses on a rather extraordinary instance thereof. Logically one might have expected the discussion to open with the final pericope of the tractate, which discusses the circumstances under which a husband is permitted to divorce his wife. Were we to continue re-arranging the contents of the tractate in a logical fashion, something like the following order would emerge:[7] the husband's charge to write (or write and deliver) a bill of divorce (M. 6:5–7:2), the requirements for writing and signing a bill of divorce (M. 2:2–2:5, 3:1–2, 8:5, 9:3–8, 1:5), presentation of a bill of divorce to the wife (M. 8:1–3), conditional divorce (M. 9:1–2, 7:3–9), circumstances which disqualify a bill of divorce (M. 8:4, 8:8–9), agency for delivery (M. 3:3, 3:5–6, 4:1–2, 1:1–3, 2:1) and reception (M. 6:1–4) of a bill of divorce, the status of a divorced woman (M. 9:9, 4:7–8). Much of the material in Gittin—most saliently, chap. 5 and most of chap. 4, which constitute an associatively arranged "improving the world" section[8]—would not appear in this logically-reconstituted tractate.

These examples illustrate that the Mishnah's redactor often: (a) does not open a tractate at the logical beginning point;[9] (b) does not continue a tractate in accordance with a clearly perceptible logical guideline; (c) shifts back and forth among different systems of arranging the material. Even tractates that display a clear and logical arrangement frequently interject smaller or larger units that diverge from the topical structure. Thus, for example:

(1) Tractate Rosh Hashanah interrupts the discussion of the New Moon witnesses (M. 1:4–2:6) with a digression (M. 2:2–5) about the bonfires. This logically should appear at the end of the discussion of the New Moon.

---

[7] Neusner, *Halakhah*, vol. IV, p. 499, explains: "The Halakhah takes as its principal problem the delivery of the writ of divorce to the wife." This assertion, if true, still stands in need of justification. Maimonides, by contrast, in his Laws of Divorce, follows an arrangement similar to the one we have suggested both in the list of ten fundamental requirements of the divorce procedure that opens his presentation and in the subsequent chapters of this section.

[8] See Hanokh Albeck, *Six Orders of Mishnah—Commentary* (Jerusalem and Tel-Aviv, 1959) (Hebrew), *Nashim*, pp. 269–270. Neusner, *Halakhah*, vol. IV, p. 480, calls this a "good order of the world" section.

[9] The Babylonian Talmud notes this point on several occasions, querying: "*tanna' heikha' ka'i*—in what context was this pericope said (literally: where was the *tanna* standing)?" (B. Ber. 2a, B. Ta. 2a) or similar formulations (B. Naz. 2a, B. Sot. 2a; cf. B. Mak. 2a).

(2) Several tractates interrupt a topical discussion by inserting a lengthy collection of material connected to a particular pericope by form rather than content. Examples: the laws of reading the Scroll of Esther in Tractate Megillah are interrupted by a collection of pericopae (M. 1:5–11) that open with the formula *ein bein... ela* ("there is no difference between [A and B] except for..."); the laws of a menstruant woman in Tractate Niddah are interrupted by a sequence of pericopae of the form, "all A is B, but some B is not A" (M. 6:2–10); Kelim Chapter 17 digresses from the topic of disqualification by breakage of a receptacle with a list of measures calculated either by intermediate, large, or small exemplars of the measuring unit (M. 17:6–12).[10]

It is therefore no wonder that many modern scholars have had difficulty subscribing either to Zacharias Frankel's characterization of the Mishnah's redaction—that "each unit is in its proper place and all parts of the structure are interconnected"[11]—or to Solomon Schechter's extreme, contrary view, which characterizes the Mishnah as "an ill-arranged transcript of one version of the Oral Law."[12] Rather, several scholars have attempted to grapple with the many problems posed by Mishnaic redaction. Most such attempts, notably those of J. N. Epstein and Hanokh Albeck, have been grounded in the philological methods of "higher criticism."[13] Others, such as Abraham Goldberg, have focused on educational goals and mnemotechnical stratagems assumed to underlay the Mishnaic redactor's compositional technique. Still, despite the efforts of such scholars, many difficulties remain, and the following remarks may safely be taken to represent the discomfort felt by many scholars:

> [The Mishnah's redactor] did not... endeavour to iron out his material into a standard style and form but was content to enclose it within the bounds of a minimum of general uniformity and impart to it a common

---

[10] These and other examples, are listed in Zacharias Frankel, *The Ways of the Mishnah* (Leipzig, 1867), p. 314 (Hebrew), and Albeck, *Commentary*, pp. 88–89. Neusner, *Halakha*, usually skips this material, since it does not fit the logical arrangement presented in his study; see vol. II, p. 413; vol. V, p. 315. He does bring the extraneous material in Kelim 17 (vol. V, pp. 58–59), without explaining why it is germane to the topic.

[11] Frankel, *Ways*, p. 282. Translations in this article from sources or research published in Hebrew are mine unless otherwise indicated. In my English translations of Mishnah, I have consulted the translations in Neusner, *Halakhah*, but have modified them when I thought necessary.

[12] Solomon Schechter, *Studies in Rabbinical Theology*, third series, p. 145.

[13] Some scholars have found fault with the regnant "higher critical" approach, most notably Y. Y. Weinberg, *Collected Writings of Rabbi Yehiel Ya'akov Weinberg* (Scranton, 1998), vol. 1, p. 201 (Hebrew); Abraham Goldberg, "The Order of Halakhot in the Mishnah and the Tosefta," in *World Congress of Jewish Studies* 5, 3 (1972), p. 81.

direction and purpose. His object was to construct an edifice free from chaos and confusion rather than one of impeccable architecture.

Thus the composition of materials in Mishnah, which to the modern reader seems unsystematic, is due to various structuring principles in use at the time. Complete coherence and uniformity are on principle not to be expected in the system of the rabbis.[14]

Poetic Phenomena in the Mishnah

In order to uncover a more coherent and uniform system of arrangement in the Mishnah, it will be necessary to utilize different tools of analysis than have been employed to date. Some "poetic" phenomena have been noted intermittently in the Mishnah by previous scholars, including the following:

a. Alliteration and rhyme
   M. Shev. 8:5:[15]
   ein notnin lo la-bayyar v'lo la-ballan, lo la-sappar v'lo lasappan
b. Paranomasia
   M. A.Z. 5:4:[16]
   She-yishtom v'yistom
c. Inclusio

---

[14] Guenter Stemberger, *Introduction to the Talmud and Midrash* (Edinburgh, 1991), p. 138. In a similar vein E. E. Urbach, "Mishnah," in *Encyclopedia Judaica* (Jerusalem, 1971), vol. 12, p. 104, notes: "The state of the extant sources does not enable us to decide whether, in redacting the Mishnah, Rabbi applied a single, uniform, and comprehensive principle." David Daube, *Collected Works of David Daube* (Berkeley, 1992), p. 277, ascribes difficulties in understanding the redaction of tractate Baba Qamma to "the limits of Rabbinic systematization, the line beyond which the Rabbis are incapable of re-modeling their Biblical material." Compare also David Weiss Halivni, "The Reception Accorded to Rabbi Judah's Mishnah," in E. P. Sanders, ed., *Jewish and Christian Self-Definition* (Philadelphia, 1981), vol. 2, p. 212.

[15] This and other examples are cited by L. A. Rosenthal and N. Braverman. See L. A. Rosenthal, *Die Mischna—Aufbau und Quellenscheidung* (Strassburg, 1903), p. 112; idem, *Ueber den Zusammenhang der Mischna* (Berlin, 1918), pp. 117f.; N. Braverman, "Soundplay and Rhythm in Mishnah and Tosefta," in *World Congress of Jewish Studies* 10, 4, 1, 1990, pp. 72–73 (Hebrew).

[16] Saul Lieberman, *Siphre Zutta—The Midrash of Lydda* (New York, 1968), pp. 118–120 (Hebrew), who cites further examples from elsewhere in Tannaitic literature. Other examples are found in Saul Lieberman, *Studies in Palestinian Talmudic Literature* (Jerusalem, 1991), p. 58 (Hebrew); Goldberg, *Shabbat*, p. 91, n. 4; Haim Moshe Klein, "All Parts of the Structure are Interconnected," in *'Alei Sefer* 14 (1987), pp. 5–28; Jonah Fraenkel, *The Ways of the 'Aggadah and Midrash* (Givatayim, 1991), p. 675, n. 24 (Hebrew). A striking wordplay at the beginning of Baba Qamma was noted by Rashbam (Tosefot Rabbeinu Peretz to B. B.Q. 2a, s.v. *ha-shor*): *ha-shor v'ha-bor ha-mav'eh v'ha-hev'er*.

"... Tractates Shabbat and Eruvin together are as one tractate, and perhaps they once indeed were one tractate, which was separated due to its excessive length. It is possible to see a connection between the beginning of Tractate Shabbat and the end of Tractate Eruvin, insofar as the redactor opens Shabbat with matters of transporting from one domain to another and the last chapter of Eruvin deals chiefly with transporting an object in a public domain and with transporting from one domain to another."[17]

d. Anaphora
   M. Shab. Chapters 2, 4, 5, 6:[18]
   ba-mah madliqin / tomnin / b'heimah yotza / isha yotza

Close reading of the entire Mishnaic corpus reveals that these, as well as other, literary phenomena appear quite frequently, suggesting that their role in Mishnaic redaction is far more significant than has previously been suspected.[19] In many instances, the literary use of language appears in the Mishnah precisely at those points at which the departure from the logical or thematic order is most blatant. This suggests that attention to the literary component of Mishnaic redaction may enable us to take full account both of the composite, non-uniform character of the materials utilized by the redactor and of the coherent structure the redactor imposed upon them.

This discussion focuses on several poetic phenomena in the Mishnah, noting their impact on how the Mishnah's redactor arranges—and

---

[17] Abraham Goldberg, *The Mishnah Treatise Eruvin—Critically Edited and Provided with Introduction, Commentary, and Notes* (Jerusalem, 1986), pp. 266–267 (Hebrew). Further examples in the Mishnah and other Tannaitic documents are found in Moshe Weiss, *The Order of the Mishnah in Tractate Pe'ah and Its Relationship to the Tosefta*, Dissertation, Bar-Ilan University, Ramat-Gan, 1978, p. 165 (Hebrew); Benjamin De Vries, *Studies in Talmudic Literature* (Hebrew) (Jerusalem, 1968), p. 106; Marc Hirshman, "Mitzvah and Its Reward in the Mishnah and Tosefta: Toward Understanding the Philosophy of the Sages," in *World Congress of Jewish Studies* 10, 3, 1 (1990), p. 55 (Hebrew).

[18] J. N. Epstein, *Introduction to Tannaitic Literature* (Jerusalem, 1957) (henceforth: *ITL*), p. 283 (Hebrew); Goldberg, *Shabbat*, p. 123. Epstein notes a further example in *Introduction to the Text of the Mishnah* (Jerusalem, 1948) (henceforth: *ITM*), p. 671 (Hebrew).

[19] A few recent writers have also noted the centrality of literary phenomena in Mishnaic redaction, most notably H. M. Klein (article cited above, n. 16, as well as other articles listed in the bibliography to my dissertation, *The Literary Method of Redaction in Mishnah based on Tractate Rosh Hashanah*, Hebrew University, February, 2001, pp. 412–413) (Hebrew) and Natan Margalit, "Gender in Mishnah Kettubot, Chapter 1," in *Prooftexts* 20, 2000, pp. 61–86. Both writers have noted important literary points in the Mishnah chapters they have analyzed, but neither writer has done enough, in my view, to justify their methodological assumptions and to establish criteria for what qualifies as a literary phenomenon or as a valid interpretation.

sometimes refashions—his materials. I begin by setting forth the premises and methodological principles on which these analyses and interpretations are based. This requires attention to the following issues: (1) What is a literary phenomenon and how may it be identified? (2) Does the presence of literary phenomena justify interpreting the Mishnah as a literary text? (3) What criteria, if any, may be suggested for evaluating the validity of a suggested interpretation?

Defining and Identifying Literary Phenomena

At first blush, it would seem counter-intuitive to relate to the Mishnah as a literary text. The Mishnah's language is prosaic, for the most part, and does not have obvious aesthetic purposes. Inasmuch as the Mishnah is a legal text, we would not be inclined to treat it as a literary one. However, our intuition here is unreliable. "Literature" is a notoriously difficult term to define, but leading literary scholars have suggested definitions that relate to the employment of language. Roman Jakobson[20] has suggested that the literary use of language is equated with "the principle of parallelism," in which

> equivalence in sound, projected into the sequence as its constitutive principle, inevitably involves semantic equivalence, and on any linguistic level any constituent of such a sequence prompts one of the two correlative experiences which Hopkins neatly defines as "comparison for likeness' sake" and "comparison for unlikeness' sake."

Rene Wellek and Austin Warren, in their classic work, *Theory of Literature* (1963), after considering several possible definitions of literature, suggest that (pp. 22–23):

> The simplest way of solving the question is by distinguishing the particular use made of language in literature.... The ideal scientific language is purely "denotative:" it aims at a one-to-one correspondence between sign and referent. The sign is completely arbitrary, hence it can be replaced by equivalent signs. The sign is also transparent; that is, without drawing attention to itself, it directs us unequivocally to its referent....
>
> In [literary language], the sign itself, the sound symbolism of the word, is stressed. All kinds of techniques have been invented to draw attention to it, such as metre, alliteration, and patterns of sound.

---

[20] Roman Jakobson, "Linguistics and Poetics," in R. DeGeorge and F. DeGeorge, eds., *The Structuralists from Marx to Levi-Strauss* (New York, 1972), pp. 108–109. Ruth Finnegan, *Oral Literature in Africa* (Oxford, 1977), p. 131, also regards parallelism—more generally repetition—as the foundation of all poetry (oral and written), and see the citation in Walfish, *The Literary Method*, p. 380 (near n. 72).

If we accept that the literary quality of a literary text is determined by linguistic patterns, including "parallelism" (in Jakobson's sense) and "sound symbolism," then the frequent appearance in the Mishnah of the kinds of phenomena noted above provides adequate justification for treating it as a literary text.

No doubt this characterization of the Mishnah will intuitively strike many readers as a solecism, but I would caution the reader to treat this intuition with a measure of mistrust. Our contemporary intuitions are conditioned by our experience of modern texts, which divide (more or less) neatly into "denotative" and "literary" texts.[21] In the pre-modern world it was common for texts of a scientific, analytic, philosophical, or legal character to be cast in literary form.[22] Many recent scholars have noted that the legal portions of the Pentateuch are carefully crafted from a literary point of view.[23] The literary acumen of the rabbis may be clearly perceived both in the many astute observations in the Midrash regarding scriptural literary techniques and in the fine literary craftsmanship characteristic of aggadic texts. Hence it is not surprising to find many of the same literary techniques in Rabbinic legal texts, and there is nothing improbable in viewing these techniques as an inherent and essential feature of those texts.

While many of the examples of literary phenomena found in the Mishnah are intuitively obvious, many other possible instances are

---

[21] Contemporary writers have protested this division. See, for example, Eric Donald Hirsch, Jr., *Validity in Interpretation* (Cambridge, MA, and London, 1967), pp. vii–viii; idem, *The Aims of Interpretation* (Chicago and London, 1976), pp. 130ff.

[22] Ellis Havelock, *Preface to Plato* (Cambridge, MA, 1963) demonstrates that Homeric verse served as an encyclopedic compendium of knowledge of all kinds in the early Greek oral culture, arguing that (pp. 42–43): "The only possible verbal technology available to guarantee the preservation and fixity of transmission was that of the rhythmic word organized cunningly in verbal and metrical patterns which were unique enough to retain their shape." Specifically regarding legal texts, scholars have demonstrated the literary craftsmanship that characterizes such works as the Codex Hammurabi (Stephen Kaufman, "The Second Table of the Decalogue and the Implicit Categories of the Ancient Near Eastern Law," in J. H. Marks and R. M. Good, eds., *Love and Death in the Ancient Near East* [Guilford, 1987], pp. 112ff.), ancient Aramaic legal documents (B. Porten, "Structure and Chiasm in Aramaic Contracts and Letters," in J. Welch, ed., *Chiasmus in Antiquity* [Hildesheim, 1981], pp. 169–182), and law codes of medieval Germanic tribes (H. J. Berman, *Law and Revolution—The Formation of the Western Legal Tradition* [Cambridge, MA, and London, 1983], pp. 58–59).

[23] Among the most prominent studies, I would include Meir Paran, *Forms of the Priestly Style in the Pentateuch* (Jerusalem, 1989); J. Milgrom, *Leviticus 1–16: The Anchor Bible* (New York, London, Toronto, Sydney, and Auckland, 1991), pp. 38ff.; J. M. Sprinkle, *The Book of the Covenant* (Sheffield, 1994); Mary Douglas, *Leviticus as Literature* (Oxford, 1999).

doubtful. Repetitions of words or sound patterns often occur naturally in ordinary language usage, thus raising the question how we may distinguish significant repetitions, indicative of literarily aware design, from the trivial prosaic repetitions that abound in everyday speech and prosaic writing. Following the lead of those who have investigated the use of literary artistry in biblical texts,[24] I would suggest that literary repetitions be identified on the basis of the following criteria: (1) the degree of similarity of the words to one another, in sound and/or meaning; (2) the frequency with which a word appears in the corpus as a whole and in the specific text in question; (3) the proximity of the instances of the repeated word to one another; (4) the prominence of the repeated word within the text; (5) the structural function of the repeated word (e.g., parallelism, chiasmus, envelope structures, anadiplosis, anaphora, epiphora); (6) conceptual links between the instances of the repeated word.

While the employment of these criteria is not mechanical, depending unavoidably on the intuitive judgment of the interpreter, nonetheless adherence to these criteria can substantially narrow areas of disagreement. In this article I limit myself (for the most part) to instances of literary phenomena that clearly pass the test of these criteria, namely, repetitions in which the similarity between the words examined is apparent and the literary design underlying the repetition is made apparent by the following factors: the word appears rarely in the immediate and/or general context of the Mishnah and the word plays a prominent role in the meaning and/or literary structure of the unit in which it appears.

The Appropriateness of Literary Interpretation

Several arguments may be raised against interpreting literary phenomena in the Mishnah as we characteristically do in literary texts. First, it may be doubted whether the literary phenomena found in the Mishnah were produced intentionally, and, second, it might be suggested that even if produced intentionally these phenomena might serve different, non-literary purposes. Both of these arguments might be supported by ascribing the production of the Mishnah to "organic thinking" of the

---

[24] The work of Shimon Bar-Efrat, *Narrative Art in the Bible* (Sheffield, 1989), p. 212, is particularly important in this regard, because he has suggested clear criteria for identifying literary phenomena in the Bible. My criteria are largely, though somewhat loosely, based on his.

sort posited by Max Kadushin and I. Heinemann or by explaining the Mishnah's literary features as a natural corollary of its oral provenance.[25] It may be further argued that the Mishnah is a composite text, whose final redaction reflects a loose compilation of disparate documents rather than a tightly integrated text.

I find it difficult to believe that the extensive and sophisticated literary framework found in the Mishnah may be attributed to automatic or subconscious mental processes. But even if we dismiss this intuition as being insufficiently alive to the kinds of associative thinking that characterize pre-modern cultures, the conclusion that we ought not apply literary modes of interpretation to the Mishnah is still unwarranted. Literary scholars—including those who found meaning on "authorial intention"—routinely operate on the assumption that the features and meanings of a literary text far transcend those of which the author (or redactor) was consciously aware.[26] Scholars have noted that the techniques commonly assumed to characterize oral literature are found in abundance in written literature as well,[27] and some have suggested persuasively that modern written literature represents the continuing human ability to preserve within modern technological culture some of the cadences of humanity's ancient oral roots.[28]

Several scholars have suggested that the literary repetitions and parallelisms in the Mishnah are indeed intended, but that their purpose

---

[25] Some recent scholars have questioned whether the Mishnah was composed orally. See Martin Jaffee, "Writing and Rabbinic Oral Tradition: On Mishnaic Narrative, Lists, and Mnemonics," in *The Journal of Jewish Thought and Philosophy* 4, 1994, pp. 142ff.; Harry Fox, Introduction to H. Fox and T. Meacham, eds., *Introducing Tosefta—Textual, Intratextual and Intertextual Studies* (1999), pp. 21ff. In my view, this question has little bearing on the character, purpose, and meaning of literary features in the Mishnah. See arguments and sources presented in Walfish, *The Literary Method*, p. 370.

[26] See J. Cheryl Exum, "'Whom Will He Teach Knowledge?' A Literary Approach to Isaiah 28," in D. J. A. Clines, D. M. Gunn, and A. J. Hauser, eds., *Art and Meaning: Rhetoric in Biblical Literature* (Sheffield, 1982), pp. 108–109, citing E. D. Hirsch, Jr.—the foremost proponent of the "authorial intent" theory of meaning—and Cleanth Brooks as noting that interpretation is not limited to "the possible amount of pen-biting which the interrelations may have cost the author" (Brooks). See E. D. Hirsch, *Validity*, pp. 21ff., and compare observations of two other critics who incline towards authorial intent but include within it "divinatory activity:" Frank Kermode, *An Appetite for Poetry* (London, 1989), p. 169; Rober Alter, *The World of Biblical Literature* (London, 1992), p. 104.

[27] Ruth Finnegan, *Oral Poetry—Its Nature, Significance, and Social Context* (Cambridge, 1977), p. 131.

[28] See Matt Calinescu, "Orality in Literacy: Some Historical Paradoxes of Reading," in *The Yale Journal of Criticism* 6, 2, 1993, pp. 185–186; Robert Pinsky, *The Sounds of Poetry—A Brief Guide* (New York, 1998), pp. 115–116.

is mnemotechnical rather than literary-conceptual.[29] I find this argument unconvincing, both because many of the literary repetitions and parallels in the Mishnah are of questionable mnemotechnical value[30] and because the bifurcation between mnemotechnical value and conceptual meaning reflects modern modes of thought and ought not to be ascribed to pre-modern texts. Quite to the contrary: in pre-modern texts, and particularly in oral compositions, the mnemotechnical value of a literary technique was intimately bound up with the conceptual associations with which it was linked.[31] Hence it may be presumed that word repetitions, wordplays, and literary patterns found in the Mishnah, alongside whatever mnemotechnical value they may possess, were designed to create conceptual associations and patterns, in much the same way as they do in more overtly literary works.

Validity in Interpreting the Mishnah

Whereas the identification of a literary repetition or literary pattern may be done with a high degree of objective certainty, its interpretation must be grounded in a creative reconstruction that necessarily involves a high degree of subjectivity. Many contemporary literary scholars accept, or even revel in, the subjectivity and indeterminacy of the interpretative enterprise; however, the field of Jewish studies—particularly in Israel—continues to be largely dominated by scholars who insist on more rigorous standards for evaluating the validity of suggested textual interpretations.[32] If Mishnah interpretation employs literary tools, as I believe it should, then the demand for rigor should be accordingly relaxed, but this need not mean the surrender of all

---

[29] See sources cited in Walfish, *The Literary Method*, pp. 367, 371, and especially Jose Faur, "Oral Recitation and Its Influence on the Style of the Mishnah and Its Terminology," in *Assufot* 4, 1990, pp. 27–34. Jacob Neusner, *Method and Meaning in Ancient Judaism* (Missoula, 1979), p. 158, also stresses the mnemotechnical purpose of Mishnaic style, but he focuses on different aspects and cadences of the redaction than those treated in this article.

[30] For example words that are repeated at great distance from one another (such as envelope structures) are very unlikely to aid a Mishnah reciter's memory. Moreover, the lack of a predictable pattern in repetitions and wordplays would severely impair their effectiveness as a mnemotechnical technique, as is demonstrated at length in Walfish, *The Literary Method*, pp. 372ff.

[31] See Walfish, *The Literary Method*, pp. 380ff.

[32] There are some notable exceptions to this rule. Several scholars in recent decades have done biblical interpretation within deconstructive, feminist, and other poststructuralist modes. In the field of Rabbinic literature, a few scholars have begun to

yardsticks of validity. While literary theory has moved beyond the framework of the New Criticism and has cast serious doubts on many of their philosophical assumptions, leading literary theorists have noted that in practice the "close reading" methods advocated by the New Criticism continue to enjoy wide recognition as the most reliable foundation for interpretative practice.[33]

While the validity of a proposed interpretation may be never be determined with certainty, it may be evaluated relative to other possible understandings by examining the number and centrality of aspects of the text for which it provides a plausible explanation. I call this gauge of interpretative validity the criterion of "coherence:" does the proposed interpretation of a given literary phenomenon "cohere" with other aspects of the text? In addition to coherence, interpretations may be subjected to a criterion I call "correspondence:" does the proposed interpretation "correspond" to ideas familiar to us from the cultural milieu in which the Mishnah was composed, or might it reasonably be expected to be part of that milieu?[34] In evaluating "correspondence," we would search for similar ideas in progressively widening cultural circles to which Mishnaic thinking might be related. We may support a proposed interpretation by adducing similar concepts elsewhere in the Mishnah, in other tannaitic or in later talmudic sources, in sources belonging to cultures with which Jews of the Mishnaic period had contact, or in general human culture.

---

utilize similar methods of interpretation, including Daniel Boyarin, Jose Faur, Aryeh Cohen, and David Kraemer. An application of post-structuralist reading to the Mishnah can be found in Margalit, *Gender*.

[33] See Catherine Burgass, *Challenging Theory* (Aldershot, Brookfield, Singapore, and Sydney, 1999), pp. 80–82 (cf. pp. 87–89); Joseph Carroll, *Evolution and Literary Theory* (Columbia and London, 1995), pp. 222–223; E. D. Hirsch, *Aims*, pp. 124, 127ff. Burgass, pp. 74–80, also argues that many of the insights of New Criticism actually correspond to important elements of post-modern theory.

[34] This "diachronic" criterion has sometimes been seen as contradicting the "synchronic" criterion I have labeled "coherence." The synchronically-minded New Criticism was designed in large measure as a reaction against the historicist criticism, which sought to interpret literary works in light of authorial biography and *Geistesgeschichte*. However, there is no inherent contradiction between the New Critical stress on the coherence of the text and the need to interpret the text in light of meanings that were available to the author and original audience of the text. Several New Critics recognized this, as documented in Meir Weiss, *The Bible from Within* (Jerusalem, 1984), pp. 8–17, and the balance between textual and historical contextual criteria of interpretation is central to the work of theorists from other schools, such as E. D. Hirsch and J. J. McGann. The combination of synchronic and diachronic factors in interpretation is also apparent in the work of such modern scholars of Judaica as Robert Alter, Jonah Fraenkel, David Stern, Jeffrey Rubenstein, and others.

The criteria of correspondence and coherence are neither necessary nor sufficient to establish the validity of a proposed interpretation. An interpretation that appears inherently plausible may convince without resorting to these measures, whereas an inherently implausible suggestion may fail to convince even if it satisfies both criteria. Moreover there are instances in which one or another of these criteria are unavailable. Nevertheless judicious employment of these tools may serve as a (more or less) objective yardstick against which subjective proposals may be measured, enabling the interpreter to satisfy himself that the interpretative process has not strayed far from the path of plausibility.

Poetic Phenomena in the Mishnah—Examples

Having outlined the grounds of our interpretative methodology, we may now examine several passages that demonstrate the literary phenomena embedded in the Mishnah's redaction and exemplify the ways in which such features may be interpreted. All the phenomena we examine in this section are found in dozens—in some cases, hundreds—of examples throughout the Mishnaic corpus, as I have demonstrated elsewhere.[35]

Envelope Structures (Inclusio)

This literary device, in which words from the opening of a literary unit are repeated in the closing of the unit, is highly common in the Mishnah, framing units of different sizes: pericopae, collections,[36] chapters, and tractates. We will examine one *inclusio* of a tractate and a few instances of *inclusio* of a chapter.

Inclusio *of a Tractate*

An instructive example of a tractate framed by an *inclusio* is Berakhot. This tractate opens with the laws governing recitation of the *Shema* (chaps. 1–3), continues with the laws regarding the Prayer (eighteen

---

[35] See appendices to Walfish, *The Literary Method*.
[36] I use the term "collection" to refer to a group of several pericopae that form a literary unit, based on content and/or form. The Hebrew term widely used for such units is *qovetz*.

benedictions—chaps. 4–5) and benedictions recited over eating (chaps. 6–8),[37] and concludes with a list of blessings recited on exceptional occasions (chap. 9). Unlike the first eight chapters, which deal with daily recitations, the ninth chapter deals with benedictions occasioned by events that occur only from time-to-time.[38] Although the subject matter of the Mishnah varies significantly from the opening of the tractate to its conclusion, the final pericope of chap. 9 closes the circle:[39]

> One is obligated to say a blessing on evil just as one says a blessing over good, as is said: "And you shall love the Lord your God with all you heart and all your soul and all your *m'od*" (Deut. 6:5) . . . "All your *m'od*"—over each measure (*middah*) which He measures out to you, thank (*modeh*) Him with all your might (*bekhol m'od*).

The midrashic interpretation of *m'od* as simultaneously containing three distinct meanings[40] leads the Mishnah to read the verse as mandating equally profuse thanks to God for bad occurrences as for good ones. This central verse of the *Shema* thus serves as the prooftext for the Mishnah's exhortation to bless God for evil with the same heartfelt

---

[37] In my presentation of the subjects treated in this tractate, I have combined two of Neusner's sections (iii–iv: blessings on enjoying benefits of creation and protocols of communal meals) into one. See Neusner, *Halakha*, vol. I, pp. 54–61.

[38] Regarding one of these occasions, M. Ber. 9:2 specifically notes that the blessing for seeing the great ocean may be recited only if the individual sees it "occasionally" (*lifraqim*), which the Talmud interprets as meaning not more than once every thirty days. Later authorities cogently apply this principle to other occasions and benedictions listed in this chapter.

[39] The parallel between the opening and closing of the tractate is noted briefly by Tzvee Zahavy, *The Mishnaic Law of Blessings and Prayers: Tractate Berakhot* (Atlanta, 1987), p. 125. The literary closure of the tractate indicates that the arrangement of laws is governed by a guiding theoretical theme (although perhaps not a clearly formulated theoretical question), underlying the laws and providing them with a conceptual-spiritual structure and focus. Thus the literary use of language employed by tractate Berakhot can help satisfy our quest for such themes and structures, whose apparent lack was termed "disappointing" by Neusner, *Halakha*, vol. I, p. 65. For examples of how specific Mishnah units in Berakhot work out the tractate's conceptual concerns in concrete halakhic (and aggadic) detail, see my articles "Wordplays in the Mishnah," in *Netuim* 2, 1995, pp. 77–78 (Hebrew); "Parallelism in the Mishnah," in *Netuim* 3, 1996, pp. 63–66 (Hebrew); "'The Flowing Prayer' (M. Ber. 4:3, 5:5)—On the Boundary between Inspiration and Ecstasy," in *Tarbitz* 65, 1996, pp. 301–314 (Hebrew); "Good and Bad and that which Separates Them—Teaching a Chapter of Mishnah," in D. Gutenmacher, ed., *Lifnim* (Jerusalem, 2000), pp. 117–128 (Hebrew).

[40] Midrashic interpretations frequently read a scriptural word as though it were written repeatedly and ascribe different meanings to each occurrence. See further examples in Jonah Fraenkel, *The Ways of the Aggadah and the Midrash* (Givatayim, 1991), pp. 113, 149ff.

sincerity with which one blesses Him for good.[41] This pericope, which serves as an appropriate conclusion to chap. 9,[42] demonstrates how the first passage of the *Shema* serves not merely as a formal daily recitation but as a source of spiritual instruction that informs one's outlook upon and reactions to all events that befall him. The *Shema* passage frames the tractate conceptually as well as literarily.[43]

Our interpretation of the *inclusio* that frames Tractate Berakhot coheres with themes that recur throughout the tractate. The interaction between halakhic form and spiritual meaning underlies many passages, including:

1. Said R. Joshua b. Qorha: Why does the *Shema* passage precede, "And if you shall hear"? So that he should accept upon himself the kingdom of Heaven first ... (M. Ber. 2:2)
2. ... They said to him [= Rabban Gamaliel]: Did you not teach us that a bridegroom is exempt from recitation of the *Shema* on the first night? He said to them: I will not listen to you to put the kingdom of Heaven away from myself even one moment (M. Ber. 2:5)
3. R. Eliezer said: He who makes his prayer [a] fixed [rule]—his prayer is not [regarded as] supplication (M. Ber. 4:4)
4. The original pious ones would tarry for one hour and pray in order to direct their hears to God (M. Ber. 5:1)
5. R. Judah said: Whatever is produced by means of a curse—one does not recite a blessing over it (M. Ber. 6:3)

---

[41] This reading of the Mishnah as an aggadic exhortation rather than as a halakhic ruling is supported by the language (*keshem* = just as) and the prooftext, as well as by the fact that pericopae cited earlier in the chapter (M. Ber. 9:2 and 3) have already mandated the recitation of different blessings for good and bad occurrences. This reading follows the talmudic discussion (B. Ber. 60b) and the classical Mishnah commentators).

[42] This point is developed in greater detail in my article, "Good and Bad."

[43] A further literary parallel between the opening and closing pericopae of the tractate is the following repetition:
... from the time the priests *enter* to eat of their heave-offering (M. Ber. 1:1)—
One should not *enter* the Temple Mount with his walking stick ... (M. Ber. 9:5) The entire discussion regarding the Temple Mount in M. 9:5 seems out of place, and the term *enter* (*k-n-s*), which seems strikingly inappropriate in the context of M. Ber. 1:1, has attracted much scholarly attention—see commentaries of *Tiferet Yisrael* and H. Albeck, *Commentary*, ad loc.; L. Ginzberg, *Perushim Vehiddushim Bayerushalmi*, New York 1981, part 1, pp. 3–4 (Hebrew). Albeck, *Commentary* plausibly suggests a reading of the term that correlates the "entry" of the priests with the Temple service, thus heightening the connection between these two pericopae. The redactor presumably intended this *inclusio* to suggest that the reading of *Shema* serves, after the destruction of the Temple, as a commemoration of and replacement for the Temple service. See M. Perkins, "The Evening *Shema*: A Study in Rabbinic Consolation," in *Judaism* 43, 1994,

Moreover, there are passages that illustrate how the system of faith and beliefs that a Jew daily reaffirms in the *Shem'* recitation serves as the foundation for the prayers and blessings discussed elsewhere in the tractate. This theme emerges most starkly in the three passages (M. Ber. 5:3, the end of M. Ber. 8:8, and the next to last section of M. Ber. 9:5) that deny legitimacy to prayers that reflect heretical beliefs. These themes cohere well with our interpretation of the tractate's *inclusio*, as an indicator that the formal *Shema* recitation is designed to foster the beliefs and attitudes that ought to inform all of one's daily prayers and activities.

Both of these themes—connection of outer form with inner meaning and insistence on the importance of the Rabbinic structure of faith and beliefs—recur frequently in the Mishnah and in other Rabbinic texts. In particular we may note the discussion of M. Ber. 9:5 in both Talmuds, which includes the story of Aqiba's execution at the hands of the Romans. Both the Palestinian (Y. Ber. 9:3, 14b) and the Babylonian (B. Ber. 61b) versions of this story emphasize that Aqiba's impressive affirmation of his love for God amid the horrible pain of his execution took place at the time for reciting the *Shema*. Clearly the storytellers of the Talmud wanted to stress the interaction between *Shema* as a halakhic performance and as a dramatic personal affirmation of faith,[44] thus confirming that the idea suggested by the Mishnah's *inclusio* was not foreign to the Rabbinic mind. Having satisfied the criteria of coherence and correspondence, our proposed interpretation of Berakhot's *inclusio* may be regarded as a well-grounded and highly plausible understanding of the meaning of the tractate's literary shape.

---

pp. 27–36, and my critical comments in "Survey of Publications in the Field of Mishnah," in *Netuim* 4, 1998, pp. 108–109, and see my articles, "Literary Considerations in the Redaction off the Mishnah and Their Meanings," in *Netuim* 1, 1994, pp. 38–39; "Methodology of Learning Mishnah," in *Alei Etzion* 7, 1998, pp. 48–51. The word *k-n-s* also links these two pericopes with m. 4:2 and m. 9:4. The idea that the daily prayers serve as replacement for the Temple service is a leitmotif of tractate Berakhot (see Zahavy, *Blessings*, pp. 22, 56, 78; this satisfies the criterion of coherence) and is well-attested in many other places in Rabbinic literature (correspondence).

[44] The appearance of this idea in the talmudic discussion of M. Ber. 9:5 suggests that the talmudic redactors noted the *inclusio* in the Mishnah and gave this phenomenon literary expression in the form of stories that combine the "with all your soul and with all your *m'od*" motif from the end of the tractate with the "time of reciting *Shema*" motif from its opening. Further evidence that talmudic redactors reacted to literary phenomena in the Mishnah may be found in my article, "The Mishnah Viewed Intertextually—A Study of Three Pericopae in Light of Aggadic Discussions in Tannaitic and Amoraic Literature," in A. Bazak, ed., *On the Way of the Fathers* (Alon Shevut, 2001), pp. 259–267 (Hebrew).

Inclusio *of a Chapter*

M. Ta. Chapter 1

"is not a sign of blessing" (M. Ta. 1:1)[45]—"is a sign of curse" (M. Ta. 1:7)

This *inclusio* contributes greatly to understanding how the redactor has structured this chapter. The chapter is composed of two pre-existent collections: M. Ta. 1:1–3, which I will call A, and M. Ta. 1:4–7, which I will call B.[46] Each collection deals with a different topic: A deals with prayers for rain, which take place every year, and seems to be unnecessary in Tractate Taanit.[47] B opens the topic of the tractate, describing the series of fast days designed to bring rain during a year of drought. A and B differ from one another in terms of diction as well as topic. The pericopae in A repeatedly utilize the word-pairs "mention-ask" (*mazkirin-sho'alin*) and "first-last" (*rishon-aharon*). These words play no role in B, which is characterized by words such as: individuals-community (*yehidim-zibbur*), eating-drinking, fasting (*ta'anit, mit'anim*). The reason for opening tractate with the extraneous material of A, rather than proceeding immediately to B, is not readily apparent.

The appearance of nearly identical phrases, not found anywhere else in tannaitic literature at the beginning of the first collection and at the end of the second collection suggests why the redactor juxtaposed these units. Besides serving the structural-redactional function of weaving

---

[45] Printed versions of the Mishnah read "sign of curse" in M. Ta. 1:1 as well as in 1:7, but the Kaufman manuscript reading is well-attested in other authoritative textual witnesses, as documented by E. S. Rosenthal, "Regarding the Interpretation of Mishnah Ta'anit 1:1–2," in *Yad Re'em*, 1975, p. 261, n. 1 (Hebrew). The context of M. Ta. 1:1 indicates clearly that the phrase employed by there is a euphemism the import of which is identical to the phrase used in M. Ta. 1:7—and to the reading of the printed versions. The inconsistency between these two pericopae regarding the use of euphemism may reflect the different sources of collections A and B, but it is unclear why the redactor did not iron out this difference.

[46] Z. Frankel, *Ways*, p. 312 notes the division between a "sort of introduction" to the chapter in M. 1:1–3 and the main body of the chapter in M. 1:4–7. He does not explain why this "sort of introduction" is necessary. Epstein, *ITL*, p. 46 divides the chapter between M. Ta. 1:1–2 and 2:3–7, utilizing diachronic criteria. I have preferred here, as elsewhere, to rely on synchronic criteria in analyzing the structure and meaning of Mishnaic redaction.

[47] This is underscored by the opening of the chapter *in medias res* with "*me'eimatai* (from when)?" B. Ta. 2a suggests that this pericope seems to be either a continuation of M. Ber. 5:2, which describes the two additions to the *amidah* that relate to rain, or of M. R.H. 1:2, which notes that Sukkot is when God judges the world with regard to its annual rainfall.

together collections A and B, this *inclusio* serves a conceptual function as well. The chapter opens with the idea that prayers for rain are inappropriate during the Sukkot festival,[48] because rain is not a "sign of blessing." It closes with the idea that after the month of Nisan, rain is "a sign of curse." Earlier, M. Ta. 1:2 noted that after the month of Nisan all agree that there are no prayers for rain.[49] The *inclusio* of the chapter thus creates an equation: one prays for rain only when rain is a "sign of blessing." Moreover, "sign of blessing" has theological overtones, as indicated clearly by the conclusion of the chapter: rain after Nisan is not characterized as a "sign of curse" because of its negative side effects, such as causing the harvested grain to rot, but because it serves in the narrative of 1 Sam. 12:17 as a sign of divine displeasure. This idea applies to the festival of Sukkot as well, as illustrated by the famous Mishnaic parable, comparing rainfall while sitting in the *sukkah* to a servant pouring water for his master, who promptly throws the water in the servant's face. By placing the "sign of blessing/curse" at the beginning and end of the chapter, the redactor indicates a connection between the prayer for rain and rain's function as a barometer of divine pleasure and displeasure.

This connection may be understood as follows: the times appointed by Mishnaic halakhah for reciting the prayers for rain are not governed by the climatic and agricultural benefits that accrue from seasonal rain as much as by its theological implications. We pray for seasonal rain, between the end of Sukkot and the end of Nisan, because it conveys divine blessing; we don't pray for unseasonal rain, because it expresses divine displeasure. Utilizing this literary frame for a chapter of the Mishnah that describes fasts for rain would suggest that these fasts are motivated by the theological ramifications of drought rather than by its hydrological and agricultural ramifications alone. This idea, indeed, is echoed in several other features of this chapter as well as in other chapters in this tractate. Space permits us only to note briefly the following points: (a) M. Ta. 1:4–5 both open with the formula:

---

[48] Both Eliezer and Joshua agree on this point, although they disagree regarding its practical ramifications.

[49] The similar language at the conclusion of M. Ta. 1:2 and the conclusion of M. 1:7 ("until the end of Nisan, as it says, 'And he brought down the rain for you...'" [M. 1:2]—"If Nisan has ended and it rains..." [M. 1:7]) may also be regarded as an *inclusio*, because it can be demonstrated that frequently the redactor creates a transposed *inclusio* by moving one of the instances of the parallel language to a pericope adjacent to one of the poles of the chapter. See instances in Walfish, *The Literary Method*, pp. 350–351.

"date X arrived and rain did not fall," whereas in M. Ta. 1:6–7 we have three repetitions of: "these [fasts] passed and they were not answered." This indicates that the initial fasts are motivated by the lack of rainfall, but the later fasts focus on theological rather than climatic phenomena: the cause for concern is now the lack of divine response. (b) The concluding phase of the series of fasts is the despairing adoption in M. Ta. 1:7 of practices of mourning, one of which is explained as being rooted in the sense that the people are "ostracized by God" (*menudim lamaqom*). (c) Chapter 2 describes the prayer service of fast days, including several practices that relate the fast to symbols of exile and the destruction of the Temple (see especially M. Ta. 2:1). (d) The story of Honi in M. Ta. 3:8 presents a kind of dialogue between Honi and God, in which Honi presents his demands before God and God responds with forms of rainfall that seem designed to express His unwilling accedence to the demands.

These as well as other features of Tractate Taanit corroborate the conception of rainfall as a dialogue between God and Israel, as indicated by the *inclusio* of chapter 1.

Sanhedrin Chapter 3

| M. 3:1 | ... When (*bizeman*) he brings evidence about them that they are relatives (*qerobim*) or invalid.... | M. 3:8 | So long as (*kol zeman*) he brings evidence he reverses the ruling.... Come forth (*qirbu*), so-and-so and so-and-so.... |

This chapter deals with litigation of property cases. The opening and closing pericopae use similar wording to describe two very different stages of the legal proceedings. The first pericope describes the court as an ad-hoc body, in which judges are selected by the litigants themselves. Three disputes are recorded between Meir and sages regarding the degree to which the litigants control the proceedings. Meir, who apparently regards the ad-hoc court as a kind of arbitration procedure,[50]

---

[50] See Asher Gulack, *Foundations of Jewish Law* (Tel-Aviv, 1967), part 4, p. 30 (Hebrew); Mordechai Sabato, "Court of Arbitrators (M. San. 3:1–3)," in M. Bar-Asher, ed., *Rabbi Mordechai Breuer Festschrift* (Jerusalem, 1992), pp. 469–470 (Hebrew). Commentators have debated whether the Mishnah regards this as the normative way of dealing with property cases or as an alternative procedure to judgment by an established court. See discussion in Moshe Benovitz, "Property Witnesses," in D. Boyarin, et al., eds., ʿ*Atarah L'Haim* (Jerusalem, 2000), p. 30, especially nn. 8–10 (Hebrew).

requires cooperation and consent of both litigants with regard to all stages of the proceedings: after each party has appointed a judge, both parties together appoint the third judge; each party may disqualify the judge appointed by the other side; and each party may disqualify witnesses appointed by the other side.[51] Sages, who apparently regard the court as an authoritative body despite its ad-hoc origins, insist that the litigants' control over its operations be limited: the third judge must be appointed by the other two judges and neither judge nor witness may be disqualified unless proof is brought that he is either a relative of one of the parties (detailed in M. San. 3:4) or has been disqualified by improper conduct (detailed in M. San. 3:3). The phrases in M. San. 3:1 that are highlighted by their repetition at the end of the chapter are taken from the Mishnah's presentation of sages' view.

The chapter ends with two sections about the ability of the court to restrict the presentation of evidence by the litigants. In the first section, sages allow the court to set a time limit for presenting new evidence after a ruling has been established, and Simeon b. Gamaliel disagrees, arguing: "What is he supposed to do, when he didn't know that he had witnesses and found witnesses, or when he didn't know that he had proof and he found proof?" In the second section, concluding the chapter, a litigant, having asserted that he has no further evidence, suddenly produces evidence when he realizes that he is about to lose the case. In this case, the Mishnah rules, without dissent, that the evidence is disallowed, presumably because the behavior of the litigant casts serious prima facia doubt on its reliability.

The two words, *zeman* and *q-r-b*, that link the beginning and end of the chapter appear together in two of Meir's disputes with sages in

---

[51] Meir's claims struck interpreters of the Mishnah as far-reaching, and commentators were especially puzzled by the ability to disqualify witnesses, which would seem effectively to paralyze the court's ability to hear and decide the case. Both Talmuds offer an array of understandings of Meir's position, and contemporary scholars have continued to debate the issue. Gulack and Sabato understand Meir as advocating the view that this court of arbitration is an instrument utilized and controlled by the parties to achieve a settlement rather than an authoritative body with power of coercion. Benovitz, "Property Witnesses," pp. 39–42, suggests that the ability to disqualify witnesses is rooted in the nature of the case this court is authorized to adjudicate (in his view), in which—he argues—only witnesses authorized in advance by the parties are qualified to testify. It is also possible that Meir does not intend to allow the parties to disqualify judges and witnesses unless they advance a claim to justify the disqualification. This suggestion is based on reading the word *posel* as meaning "finds a disqualifying factor," rather than as meaning "vetoes." This reading of *posel* apparently underlies some of the talmudic suggestions, and Benovitz's claim (p. 33) that this is not the simple meaning of the term is unsupported.

M. San. 3:1, and each term appears in one of the two sections in M. San. 3:8: *zeman* in the first section and *q-r-b* in the second. The meaning of the terms is different in the two pericopes (see Wordplays, *infra*): *zeman* means "occasion" in M. San. 3:1 and "time frame" in M. 3:8, and *q-r-b* means "relative" in M. San. 3:1 and "to approach" in M. 3:8. The parallel terms also play different roles in the respective sections in which they occur: *zeman* is the focal point of the dispute recorded in M. San. 3:8, but in M. 3:1 it appears only as part of a stock formula: "*Eimatai? Bizman...*" (When is this said? When...). *Q-r-b* is central to sages' argument in M. San. 3:1, because kinship is one of the two claims that may be advanced to disqualify witnesses (or judges), both here and in M. San. 3–4 ("And these are those who are invalid... And these are relatives"); but in M. San. 3:8, *qirbu* (come forth) is a stock phrase for summoning witnesses—perhaps utilized here to emphasize the point that the witnesses have been available to the litigant all along and do not need to be subpoenaed.[52] The fact that the terms appear together in M. San. 3:1, but separately in the two sections of M. 3:8, along with the differences in meaning and centrality in the two parts of the chapter, highlights the careful attention to language necessary for the redactor to produce the linguistic echo of M. San. 3:1. Each word appears twice more in all of Tractate Sanhedrin (*zeman* in M. 5:2 and 10:6; *q-r-b* in M. 6:6 and M. 10:4), increasing the probability that the appearance of these terms at the beginning and end of our chapter is calculated rather than accidental.

The idea underlying this *inclusio* is not difficult to decipher. M. San. 3:1 and 3:8 mirror one another in their content and language. The dispute between Meir and sages in M. San. 3:1 concerns the nature of the relationship between the litigants and the ad hoc court they have established. According to Meir, the court is an instrument employed by the litigants, who retain strict control over the court's operations: selection of all judges and even of witnesses depends upon the continuing acquiescence of each of the litigants to the proceedings. Sages maintain that the court, although established initially by the litigants, can function only as an autonomous body that assumes authority as soon as the first two judges—each representing the choice of one of the two litigants—have been selected. The question of the court's

---

[52] The Mishnah thus alludes in its language to the qualification of this law in T. 6:4, which rules that the evidence is accepted if the litigant can establish that it was unknown to him at the time when he denied having evidence to present.

authority vis-à-vis the litigants in the initial stages of the trial is mirrored by the discussion in M. San. 3:8 that raises similar questions regarding the trial's concluding stages. Simeon b. Gamaliel, like Meir in M. San. 3:1, safeguards the rights of the litigants. Sages, however, maintain that the viability of the judicial process demands that the judges be allowed to set a limit, even arbitrarily, for producing evidence. In their view, if no time limit is set on the litigants' ability to overturn a verdict, then no case may ever be declared closed and the judicial function of settling disputes would be seriously impaired.[53] Both sages and Simeon b. Gamaliel agree that the judges may peremptorily dismiss evidence brought by a litigant whose behavior casts serious doubt on the reliability of that evidence.

The similar language employed by the Mishnah at the beginning and the end of the chapter thus underscores the conceptual similarity between the two discussions and presents this similarity as a guiding motif of the chapter as a whole. The ad hoc composition of the court described in M. San. 3:1 contains an inherent tension between the subjugation of the judges to the voluntary submission of the litigants and the authority needed for any court to fulfill its function. Meir and Simeon b. Gamaliel weight the scales in favor of the litigants, whereas sages in both cases favor the authority of the judges.

The literary and conceptual integrity achieved by the Mishnah's redactor may be seen in bold relief against the backdrop of the parallel material found in the Tosefta. The dispute between Meir and sages appears at the beginning of Tosefta Sanhedrin Chapter 4, which roughly parallels M. San. 3:1–5. The two laws that close the Mishnaic chapter appear at T. San. 6:4, which parallels M. San. 3:6–8, and they are followed by additional laws regarding the ability of witnesses to renege on their testimony (T. San. 6:5) and the determination that witnesses have committed perjury (T. San. 6:6). The division of the Mishnaic chapter into two separate chapters and the placement of the laws of M. San. 3:8 in the middle, rather than the end, of the second Toseftan chapter undo any literary connection between the dispute of Meir and sages and the two laws of M. San. 3:8. It is thus not surprising that the language of T. San. 5:1 contains no literary allusions to that of T. San. 6:4: neither the word *zeman* nor the word *q-r-b* appear in T. 5:1, and the word *q-r-b* is absent from T. San. 6:4 as well. The comparison of the redaction of similar material in the Mishnah and Tosefta

---

[53] See Eliav Shohatman, *Civil Procedure in Jewish Law* (1988), p. 426 (Hebrew).

thus reveals the kinds of conscious redactorial decisions that create the Mishnah's literary patterns.[54]

Surprisingly, however, the Toseftan parallel to the Mishnah indicates a connection between the disputes at the beginning and the end of chap. 3 that the Mishnah has elided. The sages' opinion of M. San. 3:8 is attributed in the Tosefta to Meir, and Simeon b. Gamaliel's opinion is attributed there to "sages." Had the Mishnah's redactor followed the attributions found in the Tosefta, this would have strengthened the connection between M. San. 3:1 and 3:8. Why didn't he avail himself of this method of clinching the literary connection between the two discussions?[55]

The answer to this question will again reveal the conceptual thinking underlying the Mishnah's redactional strategy. The Toseftan attribution of both disputes to Meir and sages reveals a paradoxical situation: Meir, who accords sweeping powers to the litigants throughout the conduct of the trial (M. San. 3:1), accords authoritative standing to the judges at the end of the trial. Sages, who disagree with Meir, also seem to shift their positions. They accord autonomous standing to the judges during the conduct of the trial but insist on the rights of the litigants after the decision has been rendered.

The reversal of positions might be explained in different ways. Perhaps the rabbis felt the necessity to strike a balance between granting the court the ability to decide and persuading the litigants to accept the court's decision. Hence the proponent of allowing judges to set a time limit on overturning their verdict balanced this ruling by according the litigants the power to control the proceedings prior to the issuing of a verdict; at the same time the proponent of granting the judges the

---

[54] The term "conscious" is employed with full awareness of the philosophical and philological assumptions involved. Philologically I am assuming that the material assembled by the Tosefta's redactor around the middle of the third century (or material similar to it) was available to the Mishnah's redactor. Philosophically I am assuming that the existence and meaning of a literary pattern cannot be entirely divorced from the conscious design imposed upon the text by authorial intention. Both assumptions can be supported, in my view, and see my discussion in *The Literary Method*, pp. 21–26. Above and beyond the merits of the philological and philosophical arguments, I believe it to be intuitively highly plausible that neither did the Mishnah redactor happen upon material susceptible to literary redaction, nor did the literary patterns he produced occur by happenstance. As I have argued above, even if we do not impute to the Mishnah's redactor conscious intention, this will not materially affect our conclusions.

[55] I am again assuming that the different traditions regarding the attribution of the opinions is not an accident of historical transmission but reflects conscious redactional activity.

power to run the trial felt this could work only if the litigants knew that there could be no time limitation on their right to appeal the verdict by presenting new evidence. I believe, however, that the positions of Meir and sages as presented in the Tosefta can be explained more persuasively by examining their positions from a different vantage point. The two issues disputed by Meir and sages may both hinge on the same fundamental question: is the main purpose of the court to arrive at a just verdict or to achieve settlement of the dispute?[56] Adoption of the former view would bear two consequences, which correspond to the two rulings of sages: in order to arrive at a truly just verdict, the court should be as autonomous as possible, and there should be no limitation placed on producing evidence. Meir, on the other hand, felt that the court's chief goal is to settle the dispute; therefore the litigants should be given control over the composition of the court and the conduct of the trial, so that they have confidence in the court's verdict. On the other hand, once a decision is rendered, the need to achieve closure takes precedence over the need to reexamine the correctness of the verdict.

The Tosefta's presentation of the disputes between Meir and sages, while *enabling* us to note and analyze the seemingly paradoxical shift of opinion on the part of both disputants, does not *invite* us to examine these disputes in light of one another. The Mishnah's presentation differs from that of the Tosefta in both respects. The *inclusio* invites us to relate the two disputes to one another, but the attribution of opinions masks the paradoxical crossover of opinions. On the contrary, the Mishnah indicates that in both places the anonymous majority opinion holds that the authority is accorded to the judges, while the opinion which enhances the power of the litigants is only maintained by a

---

[56] Shohatman, *Civil Procedure*, p. 426, roots the controversy in the conflict between justice/truth and the public welfare. A similar issue is central to T. 1:2–9, which considers the respective merits of adjudication and arbitration as well as several other issues rooted in the tension between the formal demands of the law and the moral demands of social justice. Our issue also emerges from the talmudic discussion of M. San. 3:1, at B. San. 23a, which culminates with the statement by Zeira that the process in which the litigants select the first two judges and the judges select the third judge ensures that "the verdict will come out truthful." Rashi, apparently puzzled by the question how this process insures a "truthful" verdict, suggests that the "truthfulness" of the verdict is rooted in two factors: the faith of the litigants in the court and the balance of opinions among the judges. These two factors correspond to the goals of settling the dispute and of justice. Rashi's comment stimulated discussions by Rosh (chap. 3, par. 1) and Ran (Talmud commentary, ad loc.) about the role of objectivity and subjective bias in ferreting out the truth.

minority view. The Mishnah thus suggests—contrary to the views held by the original disputants—that these two disputes are not only interrelated, but are dependent upon one another. At every turn the majority view accords authority to the court, once the litigants have appointed the first two judges; two separate minority opinions dissent from the consensus at different junctures: Meir expands the control of the litigants over the conduct of the trial, while Simeon b. Gamaliel expands the right of the litigants to overturn the verdict.

Ohalot Chapter 7

M. 7:1	A solid monument (*nefesh*)	M. 7:6	One may not set aside a living being (*nefesh*) for the sake of another living being (*nefesh*)

Ohalot Chapter 7 exemplifies the Mishnah's seeming disregard for order and structure. It opens by differentiating between the ways in which corpse defilement is transmitted by a solid monument, namely, a solid enclosure of the corpse, and by a sealed tomb, namely, a hollow enclosure. It continues with the following topics: how different parts of a tent, comprising several corners and angles, transmit corpse defilement; defilement of openings within a house due to the possibility that a corpse in the house might be carried out through them; defilement of a house in which part of a stillborn birth occurred, due to the assumption that the infant's head emerged while still in the house; and—until which stage of birth is it permitted to abort the infant in order to save the mother's life? It is difficult to find a connecting thread among these topics, and indeed the last topic doesn't seem to belong in Ohalot at all, because it doesn't deal with corpse defilement.

The last pericope would appear to be a classic instance of a Mishnaic passage whose connection to the others is not topical but an associative link through the opening line it shares with the previous passage: a woman who is having a difficult and dangerous birth. However the *inclusio* that links the first and last units of the chapter demonstrates that the chapter has been designed as a literary unit, not as an assemblage of disparate and loosely connected units. The rarity of the word "monument" (*nefesh*) in the Mishnah—it appears in one other place in Ohalot (at 1:6) and in two further places in the Mishnah corpus (M. Erub. 5:1, M. Sheq. 2:5)—underscores its literary significance within the chapter. The word possesses two opposite meanings in its two appearances: at the beginning of the chapter it means a tomb monument and at the end of the chapter it indicates a live human being (its usual meaning). The *inclusio* is thus also a wordplay (see: Paranomasia, *infra*), which links the two poles of the chapter by means of a word that simultaneously suggests death and life. Further on we will examine another paranomasia in this chapter, and we will analyze the conceptual ramifications of the *inclusio* in that context.

Anaphora and Epiphora

Anaphora: M. Hul. 5:1, 6:1, 7:1, 10:1, 11:1, 12:1

> ... is practiced (1) in the Land and outside the Land, (2) in the time of the Temple and not in the time of the Temple, (3) regarding unconsecrated [and] \ [but not] consecrated [beasts].

Six of the twelve chapters of Tractate Hullin open with one of the two versions (and \ but not) of this formula, which the Mishnah's redactor utilizes to characterize the six commandments discussed in these chapters: not slaughtering an animal and its offspring (chap. 5); covering the blood of a slaughtered beast (chap. 6); the prohibition of the sinew of the thigh nerve (chap. 7); the gift to the priests of the shoulder, the two cheeks, and the maw (chap. 10); the gift to the priest of the first shearings of wool (chap. 11); and the sending forth of the dam from nest (chap. 12).[57] The formula contains the following information: (a) all of these commandments apply to unconsecrated beasts—the subject discussed in Tractate Hullin—whereas only two of them (animal and offspring, sinew of the thigh nerve) also apply to consecrated beasts; (b) all of these commandments apply equally inside and outside the land, i.e. they are not restricted in terms of place; (c) all of these commandments apply equally during the time of the Temple and after its destruction, i.e., they are not restricted in terms of historical time.

The application of these commandments to all places and all times sharply distinguishes these laws of unconsecrated beasts from the laws of consecrated beasts, as detailed in the other tractates belonging to the Order of Holy Things. The tractates preceding Hullin, Zebahim and Menahot, both focus heavily on the places where and times when sacrifices may be offered, and Zebahim closes (M. 14:4–10) with a detailed discussion of the places sacrifices are allowed during different

---

[57] The anaphora connecting these chapters has been noted by Albeck, *Commentary*, Introduction to Hullin, pp. 112f., and Epstein, *ITM*, p. 671.

historical eras. By opening half the chapters of Hullin with this specific opening formula, the Mishnah's redactor sets the laws of unconsecrated beasts against the backdrop of the laws of sacrifices. Thus, while halakhically differentiating the laws treated in Hullin from the laws treated in the other tractates in the Order of Holy Things, the formula binding these chapters together serves as a literary link between this tractate and the rest of the Order.[58]

The conceptual purpose of this literary design may be understood by noting the division of these six chapters into two groups of three, chaps. 5–7 and chaps. 10–12, divided by chaps. 8 and 9, which do not open with the formula.[59] Examination of the laws treated in each section suggests that the laws of unconsecrated beasts bear a close relationship to the laws of sacrifices. The first chapter of the first section (chap. 5: an animal and its offspring) and the last chapter of the second section (chap. 12: sending forth the dam) both deal with the need for sensitivity to the maternal feelings of the victim's mother, and this idea is closely associated with a parallel concept from sacrificial laws: not to sacrifice an animal until it has been with its mother for seven days.[60] The law of covering the blood invites comparison with the sprinkling

---

[58] Compare Neusner, *Halakhah*, vol. IV, pp. 255ff., 260ff. Neusner's understandable desire to stress the connection of tractate Hullin to other laws related to the Israelite household leads him to discuss tractate Hullin in this volume. Unfortunately, this decision weakens the literary effect of Hullin's language and structure by divorcing the tractate from its original textual setting and thus weakens Neusner's own (largely correct) conceptual analysis of the tractate.

[59] The formula missing from the opening of chap. 8 in the Mishnah does appear at the beginning of the chapter in the Tosefta (see Albeck, *Commentary*, Introduction to Hullin, p. 113 and n. 8; Epstein, *ITM*, p. 671). The Tosefta also supplies a link between chaps. 8 and 9, as Epstein (ibid.) points out. The omission of this opening formula from these two chapters requires further study.

[60] The connection between these laws, especially those of chap. 5, and the prohibition of sacrificing an animal "whose time has not yet come" (the Mishnah's term for an animal less than eight days old—see M. Zeb. 14:2–3 and M. Bekh. 9:4) may be supported by the following points: (a) the laws of "an animal and its offspring" and of an animal "whose time has not yet come" are juxtaposed both in Scripture (Lev. 22:27–28) and in the Mishnah (M. Zeb. 14:2); (b) M. 5:3, in illustrating a case of slaughtering an animal and its offspring, discusses a cow (female) and its (male) calf, apparently adopting the majority opinion cited in a baraita (B. Hul. 78b, B. Bekh. 45b) that the law applies only to female parents. This solidifies the connection between this law both to "sending forth the dam" and to "an animal whose time has not yet come" (it should be pointed out, however, that another baraita cited in B. Hul. 78b derives the limitation to female parents from the former law, which applies only to unconsecrated birds, rather than from the law applying to sacrifices); (c) M. 5:5 stresses and justifies the definition of "day" applicable to "an animal and its offspring" as a night followed by a day. Simeon b. Azzai, in a baraita cited in B. Hul. 83a–b, roots the need for this definition in the fact that "the entire passage [of Scripture in which

of the blood of sacrifices.[61] The second group of chapters, which deals with gifts given to the priests from unconsecrated animals, teaches that the centrality of the priests in the sacrificial service in the Temple is echoed outside the Temple in the laws governing the benefits which an Israelite enjoys from his domestic animals. More specifically, M. Zeb. 10:1 indicates that the gift to the priest of the shoulder, the two cheeks, and the maw of unconsecrated animals serves as a parallel to the parts of the sacrificial meat that are given to the priest[62] and the gift of the first shearings of wool as parallel to the receipt by the officiating priest of the hides of Most Holy Things (M. Zeb. 12:1–3).

The only law discussed in these chapters that has no apparent connection to the laws of sacrifices is the prohibition of the sinew of the thigh nerve (chap. 7). This lone exception, of course, does not challenge the underlying connection we have demonstrated between the two groups of chapters and laws of sacrifices. Nonetheless it would appear that Chapter 7 does include certain terms and themes which relate this practice to the laws of sacrifices. M. Zeb. 7:4–5 teach that a mixture including the sinew is forbidden if the sinew gives flavor (*noten ta'am*) to the mixture, and this ruling is reminiscent of the law pertaining to sacrifices in M. Zeb. 11:8.[63] The application of the prohibition of the sinew to both right and left thighs (M. Zeb. 7:1) contrasts sharply with the stress in the laws of sacrifices on the right side, and in particular on the gift to the priests specifically of the right thigh of certain sacrifices.[64]

---

the law appears] discusses nothing but consecrated things, and with regard to consecrated things the night follows the day." These points, which contain elements of correspondence and coherence, support the idea that the law of "an animal and its offspring," while applying (even) to unconsecrated beasts, should be understood in relation to similar concepts applying to consecrated beasts.

[61] Here too we may note material in chap. 6 reminiscent of material in tractate Zebahim, and most saliently M. 6:5, which echoes M. Zeb. 8:6.

[62] The bulk of chap. 10 (M. 10:1–3) stresses that consecrated beasts are exempt from this gift to the priests.

[63] The words *noten ta'am* also appear in chap. 8—perhaps suggesting that this chapter too has a connection to sacrificial law (see above, n. 59). Other than these appearances, the term does not appear elsewhere in the Order of Holy Things. Besides the nine appearances of the term in tractates Hullin (eight appearances) and Zebahim, it appears an additional fifteen times in the entire Mishnah corpus, in the context of sanctified foods (M. She. 7:7; M. Ter. 10:1), of forbidden foods (M. Hal. 3:10; M. Or. 2:1, 2:7; M. A.Z. 5:2, 5:8), and of foods that a person has vowed not to eat (M. Ned. 6:6–6:7).

[64] Lev. 7:32–34; M. Zeb. 10:2, 12:1. The terms "right" and "left" appear in the Mishnah thirty-two times, twenty-three of which are in the Order of Holy Things. Chapter 7 also stresses the connection between the prohibition of the sinew and the sanctity of the Israelite nation (see M. 7:2, 7:6), which may perhaps be related to our theme.

Many terms and concepts that appear in the six chapters that contain our opening formula emphasize the theme that predominates in much of Tractate Hullin: in order for the Israelite to enjoy the benefits of the meat (and wool) of unconsecrated beasts, he must observe laws which, while differing in many respects from the laws of sacrifices, nonetheless bear a strong relationship with the latter. This serves to consecrate the benefits which the Israelite enjoys from these beasts.

Epiphora: Rosh Hashana Chapters 1–2, 3–4

M. Rosh Hashana 1:9	**M. Rosh Hashana 2:9**
These are the set times of the Lord	These are the set times of the Lord, holy convocations
which you shall proclaim at their set times	which you shall proclaim Whether at their proper time or not at their proper time
They take in their hands staves	Come to me with your staff... He took his staff... in his hand
One ... who can't walk (*lehalekh*) ... For a journey (mahalakh) of a night ...	R. Aqiba went (*halakh*) and found ... [R. Joshua] went (*halakh*) to Yabneh

M. Rosh Hashanah 3:8	**M. Rosh Hashana 4:9**
Whoever is not obligated in the matter can't fulfill the obligation of the many	The agent of the community fulfills the obligation of the many

The redaction of Tractate Rosh Hashanah presents several knotty problems, many of which center on the tractate's chapter endings. The discussion of when and how witnesses to the New Moon are required to violate the Sabbath by traveling to the court is the main topic of chap. 1 (M. R.H. 1:4–9)[65] and continues through M. R.H. 2:5.[66] Chapter 2 ends on a dramatic note with the controversy between Gamaliel and Joshua, but this leaves M. R.H. 3:1, which concludes the laws of Sanctifying the New Moon, isolated in a chapter that deals with the laws of sounding the Shofar. Chapter 3 appears to close on a dramatic note, complementing the halakhic requirement of intent (*kawwannat halev*—lit., directing the heart) to hear the Shofar (M. R.H. 3:7) with the aggadic demand to direct one's heart towards the Heavenly Father

---

[65] The connection between this collection and M. 1:1–3 has attracted a great deal of scholarly attention. I have discussed this issue at length in *The Literary Method*, chap. 1.
[66] Epstein, *ITM*, pp. 396–397; *ITL*, p. 365. Epstein supports this claim, which is clearly implied by M. 2:5, by citing T. 1:16 and Y. 2:1, 57d.

(M. R.H. 3:8). But for no apparent reason the Mishnah redactor tacks on to the end of the chapter a law that disqualifies deaf-mutes, idiots, minors, and others who are not required to hear the Shofar from sounding the Shofar on behalf of the community. Like chap. 3, chap. 4 would appear to conclude by describing the order of Shofar blasts, but then shifts abruptly to a controversy whether the prayer of the community's agent suffices or each individual must pray on his own behalf as well.[67] Philologically-oriented scholars have approached these problems from a higher-critical standpoint,[68] but the epiphoras linking the endings of chaps. 1 and 2 and those of chaps. 3 and 4 indicate that the endings of these chapters are carefully calculated and designed.[69]

The chapter endings are marked not only by the use of parallel language but by salient contrasts. The prooftext for witnesses violating the Sabbath, which concludes chap. 1, requires that the festivals (*mo'adim*—lit., set times) be proclaimed at their appointed times (*b'moadam*). Aqiba brings a prooftext at the end of chap. 2 to establish that the date of the festival proclaimed by the court is decisive, regardless of whether they were established at their appointed times or not. The contrast between these two ideas, highlighted by the epiphora, focuses attention on a central theme of the first two chapters (and M. R.H. 3:1) of the tractate: how much autonomy does the court possess in determining the dates of the festivals? The endings of chaps. 3 and 4 also contrast with one another: The negative statement in M. R.H. 3:8 focuses on

---

[67] Neusner, *Halakha*, vol. II, p. 456, reads the end of M. 4:9 as referring to the community's agent for sounding the shofar. This reading is not supported, as far as I know, by any other translator or commentator (Albeck, *Commentary*, p. 491 brings this as a ramification, implied by the redaction, not as the literal meaning), and it is clearly contradicted by T. 2:8 (translated by Neusner on p. 457; the question of the reliability of the Tosefta in reflecting the meaning of the Mishnah cannot be discussed here). Nowhere else in Rabbinic literature does *sh'liah zibbur* (agent of the community) mean anything other than one who prays on behalf of the community, and Neusner's reading of M. 4:9 would also set the majority opinion in opposition to the uncontroverted ruling at the end of M. 3:9. There is no indication anywhere else in Rabbinic literature that an individual is required to sound the shofar on his own, and the one reference to such a practice in B. R.H. 30a clearly refers to a custom, rather than an obligation; see further *The Literary Method*, p. 221. Despite my disagreement with Neusner's translation, I believe that the location of this discussion at the end of M. 4:9 does imply that the controversy between Gamaliel and sages has ramifications for understanding the sounding of the shofar; see *infra*.

[68] See sources cited in my *The Literary Method*, pp. 38–39.

[69] Neusner, *Halakha*, vol. II, pp. 440–457, divides the chapters into thematic units, which masks this literary feature. In some of his translations, he translates repeated words and phrases differently each time, which further obscures the literary intent of the Mishnah's redaction.

the identity of the person who is or is not capable of fulfilling the communal obligation of sounding the Shofar, whereas the positive statement of Gamaliel, M. R.H. 4:9, focuses on the communal nature of the community's obligation of prayer.

Space does not permit analysis of both epiphoras here, and we will focus on the first one, the interpretation of which is both more obvious and more dramatic.[70] The prooftexts at the end of each chapter do more than support a particular halakhic principle. They both sum up central ideas developed in their respective chapters. The prooftext in chap. 1 that justifies the violation of the Sabbath by the witnesses to the New Moon implies that the duty of the community is to see to it that the time of celebrating their festivals corresponds to the time determined by heaven. The human agency for sanctifying the holy days is subordinated to the heavenly authority, as manifested by the appearance of the New Moon. The prooftext at the end of chap. 2 presents a seemingly opposite idea. Focusing on the words "These are" and "you shall proclaim"—and seemingly ignoring the word *b'mo'adam* (at their appointed times)[71]—Aqiba argues that only the days proclaimed by a human agency are accorded divine sanction as holy days.[72] Thus God subordinates His sanctified times to the decisions taken by a human court.[73]

The apparent contradiction between the subordination of man to God in chap. 1 and of God to man in chap. 2 is easily resolved, on a practical level. Ultimately the authority to sanctify the festivals is accorded to the court, whose determination is binding, regardless of the objective correctness of their ruling. On the other hand, the court, as well as all the witnesses who enable the court to function, are enjoined to strive to coordinate their determination with the objective heavenly facts, even to the point of violating the Sabbath in order to do so. But this pragmatic resolution of the contradiction does not take full account of the tension indicated by the strong literary ties that bind the end of

---

[70] For an interpretation of the second epiphora, see *The Literary Method*, pp. 237–240.

[71] Presumably Aqiba holds that the word *b'mo'adam* serves as an ab initio desideratum (as in chap. 1), but not as an absolute requirement, as argued below.

[72] According to B. R.H. 25a, Aqiba's interpretation of the verse focuses on the word *'otam* (them), and Rashi, s.v. *'otam*, explains that he reads the word as though it were vocalized *'atem* (you). However the language of Sifra, Emor 10, indicates that the key word in the midrashic interpretation of this verse is *tiqr'u* (you shall proclaim). See *The Literary Method*, p. 95.

[73] This idea is stated clearly in T. 1:11, which serves an important function in clarifying the internal logic of the tractate. See my *The Literary Method*, pp. 47–49, 77ff.

the two chapters. Conceptually the two chapter endings appear to suggest that the authority of God and the authority of man stand in a tenuous balance with one another. On one level, the two authorities may conflict, as indeed they do in Aqiba's bold midrash; however, on another level the rabbis of the Mishnah see the two authorities standing in symbiotic relationship with one another. God exercises His authority through His human agency, the court, while the Court derives their authoritative standing vis-à-vis the community from their divine authorization.

This idea may be corroborated by examining the story at the end of chap. 2 and by noting the literary parallels linking this story with the end of chap. 1. The confrontation between Gamaliel and Joshua revolves about two questions. On one level, the issue at stake—first raised by Dosa b. Harkinus and later resolved by Aqiba—is whether the rabbis who disagree with Gamaliel's ruling may act in accordance with the human authority of the Patriarch, when they are firmly convinced that this contradicts the heavenly/divinely ordained holy times. However, as the story unfolds, a second issue proves central: how may it be determined which human being is authorized to act as divine agent in proclaiming the holy times? Gamaliel's decree upon Joshua, more than an affirmation of the date of the Day of Atonement, serves as an affirmation of Gamaliel's authority. Dosa's homily, which finally convinces Joshua to submit to the decree, deals directly with the issue of Gamaliel's authority.[74] Ultimately Joshua submits to Gamaliel's authority, thereby also confirming that he believes this authority to have divine sanction. At the same time, the story stresses that the acceptance of the Patriarch's authority is an autonomous decision taken by Joshua, thus revealing that human authority is a dialectical concept. Only free acceptance of patriarchal authority on the part of the other rabbis gives substance to that authority. This tense balance between the exercise and the acceptance of authority is well-expressed in Gamaliel's welcome to Joshua. Standing on his feet as a sign of respect, Gamaliel acknowledges Joshua to be "My master in wisdom and my disciple in accepting my rulings."[75]

---

[74] This approach differs from that of W. S. Green, *The Traditions of Joshua ben Hananiah* (Leiden, 1981), vol. I, p. 117, and see the discussion in my *The Literary Method*, p. 97, n. 47.

[75] This idea also underlies Dosa's homiletical prooftext. Dosa establishes that a court equivalent to that of Moses is "every group of three who stood over Israel," namely,

Above we have noted the literary echoes of M. R.H. 1:9 in the story of Gamaliel and Joshua. The journey (*halakh*) of the witnesses to the court, while violating the Sabbath by taking staves in hand, is echoed by the journey (*halakh*) of Joshua, who defiles the day he believes to be the Day of Atonement by taking his staff in hand. These represent two different stages of sanctifying the holy times as well as two manifestations of the authority of the court. The common man traveling to the court on the Sabbath expresses both the importance of the divinely ordained times and the exclusive authorization of the court to proclaim these holy days. Joshua's traveling to Gamaliel bears witness that the humanly authorized holy days must be accorded exclusive recognition on the part of the community in order to be fully sanctified. The dialectical interdependence of patriarchal authority and communal acceptance echoes the dialectical interdependence of divine authority and human agency. Both of these symbiotic relationships are fraught with tension, which is given clear expression in the dramatic narrative that closes this literary unit of Rosh Hashanah Chapters 1 and 2.

Paranomasia

M. Ohalot 7:1–7:4

M. 7:1 A sealed tomb (*qever satum*)	M. 7:4 the womb opens (*niftah haqever*)

M. Oh. 7:1 deals with a law that would appear to be central both to the chapter and to the tractate: the special laws of defilement that apply to a tomb and the way in which the laws pertaining to a "sealed tomb" differ from those of a "solid monument" (*nefesh atuma*). M. Oh. 7:4–5, on the other hand, seems to be somewhat out of place, since it does not deal with the ways in which different structures contract and transmit corpse defilement but rather with ways of resolving doubts regarding which house was exposed to the defiling corpse of a stillborn infant. However the surprising use by the Mishnah of the word *qever* in M. Oh. 7:4 to denote the womb creates a fascinating wordplay between

---

every group of three judges whose authority was recognized by the nation. Note as well the wordplay between "stood over Israel" and Gamaliel's standing up before Joshua, which expresses a balance between the community's respect for its authoritative court and the court's respect for those subject to its authority.

the open *qever* (womb) in M. 7:4 and the sealed *qever* (tomb) of M. 7:1. Both the phrases, *qever satum* and *qever sheniftah*, are hapax legomena in the Mishnah,[76] strongly suggesting that the Mishnaic redactor inserted the unit M. Oh. 7:4–5 in this chapter because of the wordplay between these two unique phrases.

Powerful support for this conclusion may be adduced from the placement of M. Oh. 7:6 in this chapter. We have discussed this chapter above, as an example of *inclusio*, noting that M. Oh. 7:6, ostensibly here because of an associative link between its opening phrase and that of M. Oh. 7:4, links up literarily with M. Oh. 7:1 by employing the word *nefesh*. The collection M. Oh. 7:4–6 thus possesses two powerful literary links with M. Oh. 7:1: *qever satum/sheniftah* (M. Oh. 7:1–4) and *nefesh* (M. Oh. 7:1–6).

These two linguistic associations are both wordplays, and these two wordplays are particularly fascinating because they both point to a common conceptual nexus: womb/tomb (*qever*) and life/death (*nefesh*). The conceptual link of womb/tomb passes the "coherence" test, since the idea is supported by both wordplays. It also passes the "correspondence" test, since the womb/tomb connection echoes throughout human cultural history from primitive religions through James Joyce and is found as well in biblical and talmudic passages.[77] A particularly interesting parallel to this idea in Jewish literature is found in the Temple Scroll, p. 50, which rules that a stillborn baby in the womb defiles like a corpse in a tomb. While the Mishnah certainly rejects the halakhic ruling of the Temple Scroll—the stillborn baby defiles only once the womb has opened—the literary structure of the chapter suggests that the Mishnah shares the conceptual underpinnings of the Temple Scroll's ruling: a relationship between womb and tomb.

The womb and the tomb represent the two poles of human existence, the pre-existence of the fetus before entering the world of the living and the post-existence of the corpse after departing from it. The Mishnah examines the relationship between these two poles by considering the cases of an open womb and a sealed tomb. So long as the womb is closed, the dead fetus does not defile and the live fetus is considered a sub-human being, whose life may be terminated to save

---

[76] *Petihat Qever* appears several times in Amoraic sources, such as B. Shab. 21a, B. Nid. 21a, etc.

[77] Among biblical sources, see Job 1:21, 10:19; Ps. 5:10. For a Rabbinic source, see the homily of Tebi in the name of Yoshiya in B. Ber. 15b and B. San. 92a. See further discussion in Walfish, *Literary Phenomena in Mishnah and their Redactorial and Conceptual Meaning*, M.A. Thesis, Hebrew University in Jerusalem, 1994, pp. 82f. (Hebrew).

the life of the mother. The opening of the womb brings the fetus into the world, so that the live fetus possesses a right to life equivalent to that of the mother, and the dead fetus contaminates a house like any other corpse. Unlike the closed womb, the sealed tomb does not remove corpse impurity from the world, but it does change its nature. A solid monument (*nefesh atumah*), lacking an open space of a cubic handbreadth, is not considered a proper abode for a corpse, and the corpse continues to defile upwards and downwards as though it were not enhoused in a structure—in the language of the Mishnah the uncleanness "breaks forth and ascends, breaks forth and descends" (M. Oh. 7:1). Any structure possessing an open space of a cubic handbreadth is regarded as a proper abode, and henceforth the corpse is cut off from the world and is unable in and of itself to contaminate. The tomb itself is now regarded as a source of uncleanness and thus "he that touches it in any place (i.e. even from the sides, not only above and below the corpse) is unclean."[78] Thus both the sealed womb and the sealed tomb cut the fetus/corpse off from the realm of terrestrial existence; the difference between them is that, while the tomb itself serves as a source of defilement for those who come in contact with it, the womb containing a fetal corpse is not thereby transformed into an independent source of uncleanness.

The literary and conceptual parallel between womb and tomb may have further ramifications for understanding Rabbinic views regarding the relationship between life and death and the nature of corpse impurity, but space doesn't permit amplifying on this point.[79]

M. Ta'anit 2:1–2

M. 2:1	M. 2:2
They take out the *ark*...	They bring down before the *ark*...
The *eldest* among them...	an experienced *elder*
Rend your heart...	so that his **heart** should be ***whole***

M. Ta. 2:1–5 describes a fast-day service, which takes place in two stages. The ceremony described in M. Ta. 2:1, removing the ark of the Law from the synagogue and bedecking it and the heads of the

---

[78] This analysis of the difference between a solid monument and a sealed tomb is, to my mind, the simplest explanation of the Mishnah's ruling and is further supported by the conceptual parallel between womb and tomb, as explained in the text. For discussion of this and other possible readings of the Mishnah, see Walfish, ibid., pp. 76–80, 85–87, especially nn. 74, 116, 124.

[79] See ibid., pp. 82–87.

community with ashes, serves as a prelude to a sermon rendered by the community elder, who exhorts the people in the language of the prophets to mend their ways and rend their hearts, rather than their clothes. Here the fast day is presented as a way of repairing the broken relationship with God by rending the heart in repentance. M. Ta. 2:2 continues with a prayer service in which a special prayer leader—also an elder—stands before the ash-bedecked ark of the Law to lead the community in an expanded service. Thus the fast day is also a day of special prayers.

The Mishnah weaves these stages together through several linguistic connections. The ark and the two different elders play important roles in both parts of the service, but the Mishnah draws a more interesting connection through a striking wordplay. Whereas the first elder exhorts the community to rend their hearts in repentance, the elder who leads the prayers is described as having an empty household so that his heart may be whole (namely: wholly concentrated) in prayer. In M. Ta. 2:1 the heart is described as being torn, but in M. Ta. 2:2 it is described as being whole and entire! There is no logical contradiction here, inasmuch as the two pericopae describe different ceremonial performances. Nonetheless, from a literary standpoint, it is unlikely that the stark contrast between the rent heart and the whole heart in two successive pericopae is accidental. It is characteristic of the Mishnah's redactor to create wordplays, and before us we have a particularly suggestive example. The Mishnah appears to suggest that the whole heart and the torn heart are not mutually exclusive but rather one and the same. According to the famous apothegm of the Kotzker Rebbe, "there is nothing whole in this world except for a broken heart." In response to a broken relationship between man and God, the appropriate response is to enhance prayer by means of fasting, to rend one's heart in repentance in order to render it whole in prayer.

The idea suggested by this wordplay at the beginning of chap. 2 coheres with ideas suggested by other aspects of the chapter. M. Oh. 2:1 associates the fast for rain with symbols of exile, such as ashes and removing the ark from its proper protected abode to an exposed public location. The special prayers listed in m. 4 open and close with benedictions related to Jerusalem and the Temple Mount. The service for fast days is thus closely associated with the theme of the broken relationship between God and Israel, symbolized by ashes and by the exile of the source and symbol of holiness from the "mini-Temple"—the synagogue.

This idea also meshes nicely with ideas suggested by the literary structure of chap. 1, as described above. The divorce between Israel and the divine Presence, suggested by the lack of rain and the lack of divine response to prayer, is expressed in M. Ta. 1:4–7 by means of practices of self-affliction and of mourning. M. Ta. 2:1–5 gives liturgical expression to these same ideas by means of symbols of exile, a call to repentance, and prayers focused on the role of the Temple in eliciting a positive divine response. The literary technique of the Mishnaic redactor reinforces this constellation of ideas and helps to crystallize them. Repentance (M. 2:1) and prayer (M. 2:2–5) might seem to be different avenues of coping with the spiritual problem of chap. 1: the "sign of curse" expressed by the divine indifference to the community's prayers. One response to this problem is to intensify the prayer, as described in M. Ta. 2:2–5, while another response is to change the pray-er, requiring him to rend his heart in penitential soul-searching. The wordplay between M. Ta. 2:1 and 2:2 teaches that the Mishnah, while presenting them as distinct stages of a fast-day service, does not perceive them as disjointed. Only after the pray-er has changed the basis of his relationship with God by repentance is he permitted to attempt to arouse a divine response by intensifying the nature of his prayer. The dynamic interaction between the wordplay of M. Ta. 2:1–2 and other ideas that emerge from chaps. 1–2 validate the line of interpretation we have suggested and exemplify the unity of form and content which characterize the Mishnah redactor's artistry.

Summary

While space did not permit examination of more than a few examples of the Mishnaic redactor's use of poetic techniques, this analysis of these examples provides ample evidence of the kind of literary artistry involved in the redactor's shaping of his materials. Whatever conclusions we may come to regarding the aim of the redactor to create an authoritative code and his mnemotechnical techniques, clearly the redactor was guided in his work by considerations both aesthetic and conceptual. The linguistic associations embedded in the Mishnah's redaction evoke aesthetic pleasure but also suggest conceptual connections and ramifications that provide a key for understanding the philosophical and spiritual underpinnings of Rabbinic halakhic thought.

WHY WE CANNOT ASSUME THE HISTORICAL RELIABILITY OF ATTRIBUTIONS: THE CASE OF THE HOUSES IN MISHNAH-TOSEFTA MAKHSHIRIN

Jacob Neusner
Bard College

> To insist on questioning the accuracy of "attributions" in Rabbinic literature... on the grounds that later rabbis and/or the editors of the documents had some motivation to falsify them, and may in any case simply have misremembered, is salutary. But to conclude that we must assume the falsity of attributions, that therefore (?) the documents are essentially pseudepigraphic and can be assumed to provide evidence only for the interests of their redactors, is in fact no longer a skeptical but a positivist position and is less plausible than the one it replaced.
>
> Seth Schwartz[1]

This uncomprehending reprise of a position based on detailed research that is apparently unfamiliar to the critic substitutes surmise for evidence. The critic has at best a hazy and general impression of what has been said and of what is at stake. No one has questioned attributions *only* on grounds of possible motivation to falsify. Far weightier considerations come into play.

The same saying is attributed to two different sages in the same words, calling into question the accuracy of at least one of the attributions. Some documents freely revise what is attributed to sages, on grounds that their rulings must be consistent to a single theory of matters, calling into question what is attributed. We have no tests of validation or verification, no first-hand evidence from reliable witnesses—no evidence at all that an attribution is reliable, other than the mere assertion thereof. These are not matters of motivation but of fact.

---

[1] *Imperialism and Jewish Society. 200 B.C.E. to 640 C.E.* (Princeton and Oxford, 2002), p. 8.

No one has said that the documents are "essentially pseudepigraphic...." What has been said is what we cannot show we do not know—and have no reason to assume absent a test of falsification or verification. No one has alleged that attributions "can be assumed to provide evidence only for the interests of their redactors;" would that matters were so simple! How much labor might we save!

The problem of attributions—did the person to whom a saying is assigned really make that statement—proves complex, since diverse documents give evidence of diverse intentions in alleging that named authorities made particular statements. Stated simply: attributions mean different things in different documents. Not only so but different contexts are shown to impose different standards of verification of traditions that assign sayings to particular named authorities. A single example suffices to show that one must assume nothing but needs to demonstrate every claim as to fact that he wishes to set forth in a work of historical narrative and analysis. Here I shall show that skepticism as to the validity of attributions is founded on the philosophy of attributions characteristic of a given document or set of documents. I refer to the Mishnah and to the Tosefta.

What we shall see is simple. First, positions assigned to the Houses as named authorities in the Mishnah are routinely revised by the Tosefta's framers of the same discussion.

Second, when we examine the matter, we see that the Tosefta's versions of what the Mishnah's named authorities are supposed to have said conform to theories of the matter held by the Tosefta's several authorities. These named authorities flourished in the middle of the second century. Their predecessors, authorities from 70 to 120, held positions logically prior to those at issue in the later generation and took no position on the subtle matters on which the Houses are alleged by the mid-second-century authorities to have ruled.

What emerges is that to the Houses are attributed positions on issues vivid only more than a century after the Houses flourished and not among intervening authorities at all. In this context, the House of Hillel, which sets the norm, will be made to affirm the principle important to the Ushan authority on an issue not debated in Yavnean contexts at all.

The upshot is, the Tosefta's versions of a dispute set forth in the Mishnah turn out to manipulate attributions to validate positions to begin with attributed to the Tosefta's later authorities, rather than to the Mishnah's earlier ones. This we shall now see in acute detail.

I

Here we deal, specifically, with the role of man in imparting uncleanness to foodstuffs. Man's intentionality is what renders food susceptible. That is because of sages' reading of the law of the written Torah that food that is dry is insusceptible to uncleanness, but food that is wet is susceptible. That notion cannot puzzle sages, who, after all, understand corpse-uncleanness as a viscous liquid that flows in the dimensions of a square handbreadth. If corpse-uncleanness is the model of other uncleanness, then sages will deem quite routine the notion that uncleanness of other classifications, e.g., that which exudes from the dead creeping thing will correspond; now, it is to what is wet that that same viscous liquid flows, so it would seem. But what has all this to do with man's intentionality?

Sages take as fact that if produce is wet down by man's deliberate action, that is, by an informed intentionality confirmed by a concrete deed, then it is susceptible to uncleanness. But if produce is wet down naturally, on the one side, or by some action not initiated by man, on the other, then the produce is not rendered susceptible to uncleanness—even though it is wet. Then the Halakhah of Makhshirin will find its problematics in the nature and meaning of intentionality, and problem after problem will explore the concrete implications of conflicting positions on one issue: is intentionality without action effective, or do we require a deed to confirm the attitude that we impute to a person?

Scripture contributes the facts, sages the problematics. That is to say, sages understand Lev. 11:34, 37, to hold that produce that is dry is unaffected by uncleanness from any source and falls outside of the system. Only when produce is wet down is it susceptible. They further take as a fact that produce that is wet down by the intent of the owner is affected, but that wet down inadvertently, under duress, or by third parties is not. We look in vain for the Written Torah's recognition of that fact. The pertinent verses are these:

> Lev. 11:29–34, pass.: "And these are unclean to you among the swarming things that swarm upon the earth.... These are unclean to you among all that swarm; whoever touches them when they are dead shall be unclean until the evening. And anything upon which any of them falls when they are dead shall be unclean.... And if any of them falls into any earthen vessel, all that is in it shall be unclean, and you shall break it. Any food in it that may be eaten, upon which water may come, shall be unclean; and all drink that may be drunk from every such vessel shall be unclean."

Lev. 11:37: "And if any part of their carcass falls upon any seed for sowing that is to be sown, it is clean; but if water be put on the seed and any part of their carcass falls on it, it is unclean to you."

The predicate that is yielded, for the formulation of the law, by the pertinent verses is, "If water be put . . .," meaning, if the farmer deliberately wets down seed or produce then the produce is susceptible to uncleanness and is made unclean by any source of uncleanness (not just a dead creeping thing.

The Halakhah of Makhshirin forms a sustained essay on the problematics inherent in the theme, human intentionality. The opening question is, what happens if I change my mind? If I want something but then decide I do not want it, does that change of attitude affect the outcome? No, the Halakhah maintains, it does not. That is expressed in a simple way: Any liquid that in the beginning is acceptable, even though at the end it is not acceptable, or that at the end is acceptable, even though at the beginning it is not acceptable—lo, this is under the law, "If water be put." Concomitantly, do I have the power by an act of will to overcome a physical actuality? If liquid is unclean, can the fact that I do not want the liquid to wet down my produce prevent contamination of my produce? Predictably, since uncleanness works *ex opere operato*, uncleanness takes effect at the very moment of contact with the produce, and my will that the produce stay draw is null: Unclean liquids impart uncleanness [whether they are] acceptable or not acceptable.

Neither rule presents any surprises. Intention is temporally indivisible. Liquid gains but never loses the capacity to impart susceptibility to uncleanness and to render that on which it falls susceptible. Then if I want the liquid to fall in a given place and some of it does and some does not, then the liquid that has fallen other than where I want it is not deemed capable of imparting susceptibility to uncleanness (the Hillelite view being normative as usual). The contrary position is that all of the liquid has been subject to intentionality, while the normative view is that only part of the liquid has conformed to my intention.

The really critical and generative question asks about the relationship of action to intentionality. Do we decide on the basis of what one has done the character of his prior intention, that is, of what he intended to do? If I take up water in order to pour it out, does my ultimate action in pouring out the water govern the interpretation of my original plan for the water? If it does, then even though for a time I might have wanted the water in its present location, by my final disposition of the water, I have defined that original intention and determined that the water never was wanted; therefore, retrospectively it does not impart susceptibility to uncleanness. We have a variety of positions.

The first is, [1] intention without action is null; [2] action is retrospectively determinative of the character of intention—we judge the intention by the result.

A further view is that prior intention plays a balancing role in the interpretation of the status of the water. We do not decide solely by what one has done, by the ultimate disposition of the water. So if one's action never was intended to bring down water, the water is not utilized intentionally and does not impart susceptibility to uncleanness.

Or, third, the deed dictates the character of the intent, and the result is paramount in interpreting the means.

Or, fourth, what one wanted has to be balanced against what has happened. If one wants the water to fall, that is not the end of the matter; he wants it to fall in a particular place, and it falls both there and elsewhere; then, what has served his purpose imparts susceptibility, and what does not serve his purpose does not. What is incidental to one's main purpose is not taken into account, and that is without regard to the ultimate consequence of one's deeds. And then there is the possibility of distinguishing immediate from ultimate result, primary from subordinate outcome, and so on.

In applying the principle that water drawn ("detached") and used with approval imparts susceptibility to uncleanness, the Halakhah raises these secondary issues: do various substances absorb liquid, does someone intend that the liquid be absorbed; and, of greatest interest, is intention signified solely by confirming action? Then the source of water forms a variable. If wheat absorbs water that was sprinkled, it is susceptible; but if it is moistened through the moisture of a rock-floor, then it is not.

Then again, we ask about primary and subsidiary intentionality. If one gathers grass in the morning, the dew on the grass does not impart susceptibility to uncleanness to wheat. The man's primary intent was to gather not dew but grass. If he wanted the dew to dampen the wheat, then the wheat has been rendered susceptible. Further, one sage takes the view that we assess one's attitude toward a situation solely in terms of what he actually does. If rain falls on grain, he is glad to have the grain wet down. But unless he does some deed that serves to wet the grain down, that attitude alone is of no effect. An action then retrospectively indicates one's original attitude. Secondary disputes underscore that primary position.

Finally, we take account of the status of sequences of "wetting down," so that water that is wanted and imparts susceptibility to uncleanness is washed away by water that is not wanted and removes susceptibility. This is expressed in the case of the two rivers: He who immersed in a river, and there was before him another river—the water of the second river renders insusceptible the water of the first. If his fellow in drunkenness pushed him in to the second river, and so his beast, the water of the second river renders insusceptible the water of the first. So too water that is incidental to the utilization of a utensil is not detached with approval and does not impart susceptibility to uncleanness.

II

Now we turn to the generative issues of the Halakhic tractate, the premises on the foundations of which the second century positions were constructed. In regard to imparting susceptibility to uncleanness, authorities who thrived from 70 to 120, hereinafter, Yavneans, know two fundamental principles. First, for Yavneh the principle is established in Joshua's name, wet produce is susceptible to uncleanness *only* if it is *deliberately* made wet. Then, second, for Joshua's disciple, Aqiba, and his colleague, Tarfon, we may or may not distinguish between water that one really wants, essential to his purpose or intention, which imparts susceptibility to uncleanness, and water one does not want, peripheral to his purpose or intention, which he does not want. Joshua announces the first position, Aqiba and Tarfon take contrary positions on the second, and in the next layer of authorities, those identified with the town of Usha, hence, Ushans, Meir, Judah, Yose, Simeon, and others, who thrived after the Bar Kokhba war, both come under significant development and receive substantial restatement.

What about the Houses of Shammai and Hillel and ask about the relationship between principles at issue between the Houses, and conceptions attributed to Yavnean authorities and the later group, Ushans. Via the Tosefta if not in the Mishnah itself, the Ushans invariably attest to, and participate in, all the Houses' disputes of Makhshirin. The question is, are the Houses merely made to express opinions on issues live only after the bar Kokhba War, when the Houses no longer existed? We shall find ample reason to think so.

The data for answering this question are located in the protases of the disputes, since the apodoses (the House of Shammai say...the House of Hillel say . . .) are fixed and stereotype, with the Shammaites' perpetually maintaining, "It is under the law, If water be put," and the Hillelites taking the opposite position. But all the Houses' disputes not only bear Ushan attestations but, as formulated, address themselves to issues that are vivid and moot at Usha. These are, moreover, secondary developments of conceptions assigned to Yavneans, particularly to Tarfon and Aqiba. It follows that, in regard to the affect of liquid on dry produce, the tractate contains no ideas both attributed to authorities before 70 and clearly prior in conception to, and generative of, positions assigned to authorities thereafter.

What is given in the names of the Houses serves literary-mnemonic purposes, the powerful force of the fixed apodosis being in play; that invites the use of the names of the Houses. The generative conception of the shank of the tractate is contained in the notion attributed by Joshua to Abba Yose: water does not induce susceptibility to uncleanness unless it is deliberately applied. Whether or not that notion goes back before 70 we do not know. But the tractate as a whole does not exhibit a trace of significant development of it before the dispute between Tarfon and Aqiba, M. Makh. 5:4–5. It is only at the dispute of Tarfon and Aqiba that serious attention to the nature and meaning of intention comes into evidence. The bulk of the Ushan materials relates to that single dispute. The dominant conception of Makhshirin may begin at Yavneh but the articulation is nearly wholly attributed to Ushans.

III

What they do in assigning their mid-second century positions to authorities of the early first century is comparable to what Harold Cherniss finds in the study of Plato and Aristotle. He states:[2]

> They adopt the hypothesis of an oral doctrine which was set up to explain how Aristotle can ascribe to Plato a theory which is not to be found in the latter's writings. . . .

---

[2] Harold Cherniss, *The Riddle of the Early Academy* (Berkeley and Los Angeles, 1945), p. 17.

Further he observes:[3]

> This oral doctrine, a hypothesis set up to save the phenomena of Aristotle's testimony, has come to be treated as if it were itself part of the phenomena to be saved.... The only healthy and reasonable course ... is to discard this hypothesis and try another: to accept that part of Aristotle's testimony which agrees with the Platonic writings, and since this testimony is at variance with the identification of ideas and numbers, to see whether that identification may not have its origin and explanation in Aristotle's own critical interpretation of Academy thought rather than in any suppositious oral exposition of Plato's own.

Accordingly, Cherniss takes seriously the possibility that "Aristotle was capable of setting down something other than the objective truth when he had occasion to write about his predecessors."[4] The reason is that

> Aristotle was so consumed with the ideology of Platonism and the new concepts he had himself discovered or developed that it was impossible for him to imagine a time when thinking men did not see the problems of philosophy in the same terms as did he.... We know that certain concepts and theories were introduced by Aristotle and others by Plato. If a Presocratic theory is presented in a way which involves such a notion, there is clearly something wrong with the statement.[5]

Aristotle uses theories "as interlocutors in the artificial debates which he sets up to lead 'inevitably' to his own solutions."

This is Cherniss's solution to the problem posed by Aristotle's ascription to Plato of "a form of the theory of ideas which does not appear in Plato's dialogues."[6] Cherniss's success is based upon taking into consideration all the evidence, not merely relying upon general impressions. It follows that he has found it necessary "to interpret Platonic and Aristotelian texts ... and to interpret them furthermore in their full philosophical intention; but there is no automatic canon in any case, and it is certainly unreasonable to disregard part of our evidence on the supposition that we are thus eliminating the danger of misinterpretation."[7] And with Cherniss, we too must confess: "This may seem to make a tedious business still more tedious; but there can be no approach to common agreement on more general issues until scholars

---

[3] Ibid., p. 29.
[4] Harold Cherniss, *Aristotle's Criticism of Presocratic Philosophy* (Baltimore, 1945), p. ix.
[5] Ibid., pp. ix–x.
[6] Harold Cherniss, *Aristotle's Criticism of Plato and the Academy* (Baltimore, 1944), p. xii.
[7] Ibid., p. xxii.

stop passing by in silence the discordant interpretations of specific passages on which any sound decision of these larger issues must depend."[8]

IV

The importance of Cherniss's work for ours is both substantive and methodological. As to the latter, we follow his example in our stress on treating the later authorities, the Ushans, as active participants in the process of the formation of tradition. Ideas attributed by Ushans to the Houses may or may not have been held by the Houses, but most certainly were held by the Ushans, When, as we shall now observe, the Houses are made to debate matters under discussion at Usha, we must ask whether Ushans invariably attribute the issue to the Houses or discuss it also in their own names. It will be clear that the latter is the case, even within the narrow limits of the present tractate, all the more so when we consider disputes on the same moot principle found in other tractates.

This approach, moreover, seems especially called for when we notice that the Yavneans know nothing about the fundamental principles allegedly debated by the Houses, do not address themselves either to those principles (e.g., the Hillelite position) and do not take up and develop them. On the contrary, the Yavnean stratum is remarkably uninformed about the conflicted roles of intention and action in the interpretation of the effects of a deed. a gap of nearly a century is curious, especially so when we recall close interrelationships characteristically discerned between Yavnean conceptions and Ushan ones, or between those assigned to authorities before 70 and Yavnean ones. Where we have disputes between the Houses on the most primitive and fundamental issues of a tractate, e.g., at Niddah and Miqvaot, we also have disputes, development, in one line, of thought inaugurated before 70; we further find among Ushans still tertiary developments of the same linear sequence of logical issues, problems and principles. But here that is not the case, and I think the reason is clear.

---

[8] Ibid., p. xxii.

V

Just as, Cherniss shows, Aristotle could not imagine a time at which thinking men did not see the problems of philosophy in the same terms as did he, so the second-century authorities, in the mode of ahistorical, logical thinking natural to philosophers, likewise could not imagine that the Houses did not define and debate problems of moral philosophy in the same terms as did they.

M. 1:1 A–C: Any liquid which is put on with approval, even though it ultimately is not wanted, or *vice versa*, is under the law, If water be put.	*1. The process is indivisible and inexorable. Once, at any point, a person has shown that he wants the water or approves its being detached, the water has the capacity to impart susceptibility to uncleanness.

All of the later authorities are clear that if liquid is ultimately not wanted—e.g., if it is extrinsic to the accomplishment of a person's primary purpose—then that liquid is *not* under the law, If water be put. We want the liquid in the bucket; we have to wet down the rope as well; but liquid on parts of the bucket not necessary for use in drawing the water is not wanted and therefore insusceptible. The instance of the wheat wet down on a floor which we have washed is even clearer. Here is a case in which the remaining water is not wanted. Yet we wet the wheat down. Is the water ultimately wanted? Of course it is. Yet because it originally was not pertinent to the principal reason for detaching and using the water—washing the floor—the water does not impart susceptibility to uncleanness to the wheat. Tarfon assuredly can agree with the position of the present rule, and, as we shall see, so too can the House of Shammai. But Aqiba and his successors and the House of Hillel will find it difficult to harmonize their rulings with this principle. Still, in a moment we shall see matters in a different light.

M. 1:2–4A–C: He who shakes the tree to bring down fruit and water falls—water is not under the law, If water be put. D–G (= T. 1:1): If he shakes tree to bring down water—Shammaites: Drops which fall and drops which remain in the tree are.

> The water is incidental to one's purpose and is insusceptible, as Aqiba would agree.
> The water that is shaken down has conformed to one's intention, that which remains has not. Yose is explicit on this matter.

Hillelites: Drops which remain in the tree are not under the law, If water be put, because the man intends that all the water should fall from the entire tree.

> He who shakes tree and water fell from one branch to another—as above. He who shakes a bunch of herbs and water fell from top to bottom of the bunch—as above.
> T. 1:3: T. augments the debate of M. 1:4S.
> T. 1:4: Yose: The law for one sack and for two sacks is the same. Judah: Eliezer says that the law is the same for one and for two sacks: It is under the law, If water be put. Joshua says the law is the same as above: It is not under the law, etc. Aqiba says the lower one is under the law, and the upper is not.

T. 1:2: Yose b. R. Judah: The Houses agree that if one shook the tree to bring down liquids, what fell on detached pieces of fruit in the tree and unplucked produce on the ground is under the law, If water be put. They agree that if one picked the fruit after it dried, it is not under the law, If water be put. They differ about shaking the tree to bring down fruit, and moisture fell from one part of the tree to another + the usual apodosis.	Yose b. R. Judah has the Houses differ on M. 1:2A–C, shaking the tree to bring down fruit, and is indifferent to the dispute of M. 1:2. In his view, the dispute is on the fundamental, not the secondary, issue of M. That is, moisture not shaken when the man shakes the tree to bring down fruit—without regard to the moisture at all. The Shammaites deem the water to be under the law, If water be put.

Let us begin with the last rule, Yose b. R. Judah's. In his conception the issues have been wrongly stated at M. Why? Because the disagreement between the Houses is on the fundamental matter of whether water that falls only incidentally to one's main purpose is subject to the law, If water be put. The Hillelites, like Aqiba and the major Ushans, are in entire agreement that water which falls when I want the fruit is *not* subject to the law, If water be put. Why not? Because the man shook the tree for fruit and never intended to shake the water out of the tree at all. It has never been subject to his intention. The disagreements alleged in M. are resolved differently in Yose's view. The Houses agree that if one shakes down water from the tree, whatever falls as a result has been subject to his intention. How do we know it? Because the man shook the tree, and without regard to where the water falls, it falls because he wants it to. Like his father Judah, Yose therefore maintains that what one *does* is decisive, and not only so, but retrospectively imparts meaning to what he originally *thought* of doing. Accordingly, the deed is ultimately and exhaustively determinative. The deed is to shake down the tree to get moisture from it. Wherever the water falls, the man's original action has made it fall. Why should the Houses differ on that point? The indeed do not, Yose b. Judah maintains. Parenthetically, they also do not dispute about detaching the fruit formerly attached to the ground. It is not susceptible to uncleanness. Why not? Because the water dried up before the fruit was susceptible to its affects. Self-evidently, had the fruit been detached while still wet, the Houses would have agreed that the fruit *is* susceptible to uncleanness. Accordingly, Yose b. Judah concedes nothing in this last matter, which is peripheral to his main point. In summary, in insisting that the Houses differ on the fundamental matter of shaking the tree to get the fruit, Yose, Judah's son, imposes the conceptual principle of Judah, that action, and action alone, retrospectively is determinative and definitive of intent.

Let us return to M.'s (= Yose's) conception of the dispute. All parties agree, M. alleges, that if one shakes the tree for the fruit and water falls, the water is not subject to the law, If water be put. Why not? Because one's action never was intended to bring down water. Judah's view that the deed is determinative of the intent, the result paramount in interpreting the means, is rejected. Aqiba's position clearly is behind the notion that all parties agree water which comes down along with the fruit is insusceptible. But what if one brings down the water, but only part of it? Here we come to Yose's view at M. 1:5, which is verbatim that of the House of Hillel. And why not—since Yose's consistent position, as given at M. 1:5 and M. 5:2, is that water which does not ultimately and wholly conform to my intention is not susceptible! Why not? Because Yose differs from Judah on the determinative role of action in defining prior intention. He wishes to preserve a balance between what one ultimately does and what he to begin with wants to do. These matters must be interpreted in a balanced way. If one wants the water to fall, that is not the end of the matter. He wants it to fall in a particular place. It falls both there and elsewhere. Just as Aqiba distinguishes between what serves one's purpose, which is susceptible, and what is extrinsic to his purpose, which is not, so Yose distinguishes between what *has* served one's purpose, which is susceptible, and what has ultimately *not* served his purpose, which is not.

VI

Is there a third position? Simeon assuredly agrees that water not subject to one's intention is not able to impart susceptibility to uncleanness. If one intends to wet wheat and there is water for that purpose, then the wheat is susceptible. How does Simeon stand in the (from his perspective) decidedly subordinate matter at issue between Yose and Judah? M. 5:3 places Simeon squarely on Judah's side. If one has wet fruit and spreads out the water to dry, so that the whole will evaporate more rapidly, Simeon declares the fruit susceptible to uncleanness. The action, wetting down formerly dry fruit, it determinative. Even though one's ultimate intention is that the whole dry off, that is of no consequence against the actual deed. One actually has wet down dry fruit. One may or may not allow the process of evaporation to proceed. M. 1:1A–C is not invoked, but could be. Simeon's underling conception accords with Judah's. Yet, it is obvious, even though both take up a position congruent to a principle agreeable to Tarfon, their basic reasoning is Aqiba's, and they stand in direct line after him, debating a secondary and subordinate matter with Yose. This is a striking result, since it places both Simeon and Judah behind the gloss, *If he shook it off*, e.g., at M. 5:7–8. The water originally was not wanted, but, by a deed, a person has imposed a definition even on his prior intention.

We now return, *via* this rather circuitous route, to T. 1:4. Yose maintains that the Houses equally dispute one sack and two sacks. Why? Because, in line with his principle, there is no basis for making any distinction between the case of one and that of two sacks. As at M. 5:6, if one beats the pelt in the water, it is to get fresh water to flow over the pelt. If he beats it outside of the water, it is to get rid of the water. In both cases, for different reasons, the disposition of the water conforms to one's intent. Yose has no basis for making a distinction between one sack and two sacks. The Shammaites in all instances— just as at M. 1:2—will maintain that, however the water flows, it has been subject to one's intention, because he did leave the sacks in juxtaposition with one another. The Hillelites have a different position, *but* for a different reason. In all instances one wants only that the liquid flow out and disperse. Therefore what flows from the upper sack to the lower is not wanted, even though it wets down the lower sack— contrary to Simeon's and Judah's view—and what flows out of the two is not wanted, self-evidently, since one has by his action indicated that the water is wholly unwanted.

VII

Judah's three positions, by contrast, develop a different line of thought. Eliezer sees both sacks as affected by the water. Why? Because the water *ultimately* conforms to one's intention that is to flow out. This is a purely Shammaite conception, shown at M. 4:4–5. If in any way one disposes of the water, then we invoke the principle of M. 1:1A–C. What is unwanted at the end but wanted at the beginning imparts susceptibility, and, for a time, one does want the water. The reason is, of course, transparent. Wetting down the fruit is to one's advantage, as M. 3:1–2 indicate. Judah's Joshua takes the purely Hillelite position. Since one's action results in the water's flowing out, he does not want the water. In both cases, therefore, the Yavneans conform to Judah's conception of the paramount and exclusive importance of one's action, which is determinative of the interpretation of one's prior and primary intention. The net difference is in how one assesses the role of the water. That is, Judah's Eliezer holds that in all cases the action is determinative, in that one wants to wet down the fruit, while Judah's Joshua holds that in all cases the action is determinative, in that one wants to get rid of the water. Does Aqiba differ? Yes, Judah states, he does, *but* for the same reason agreed upon by all three parties. The upper sack is left to drain off. The lower sack is left to receive the water. Accordingly, we make a distinction in the matter, but only because of the *action* which one has taken. Placing the upper sack above the lower, one indicates that he wants the water to leak out of the upper sack. Therefore it is not susceptible to uncleanness. Action is determinative. Placing the lower sack below the upper, he indicates that he wants to wet it down. Therefore, once more, action is determinative. All parties thus agree to interpret the case in terms of what one actually *does*, not in terms of what one supposedly intends to do. But while the interpretation of the determinative deed is diverse, for the reasons given, all parties agree on Judah's principle.

We know that M. differs from Yose b. Judah. But how will Yose and Judah see M.? Clearly, Yose will be happy with M. 1:4, which has the Hillelites accord with his conception. Self-evidently, Judah must reject M. Why? Because, as just noted, its attributions are all wrong. If Judah were to construct the cases of M., he would give them a tripartite apodosis. In his opinion, M. 1:2A–C should provoke a disagreement, as his son has told us, with the authoritative party—let us assume, the House of Hillel—in the view that water which falls is not under the law, If water be put, *because* of the priority of ultimate, practical result over primary and prior intention. The Shammaites should disagree, since they must take up the (false) position that water which happens to come down along with the fruit is subject to the law, If water be put. (Tarfon maintains exactly that, as we know.) But, to fill out Judah's picture, we should have a third position, one which maintains that water which falls has conformed to the person's action, if not his original intention, and water which does not fall has not been subject to his intention at all—that is, Aqiba's position in T., but no one's position at M. 1:2A–C. Judah in respect to M. 1:2D–G certainly cannot be happy. Yose of course has his way. How would Judah want to construct M. 1:2D: *If one shakes the tree to bring down from it liquids*—then what? In Judah's view, all the drops have been shaken. All have been subjected to the man's will. But some have fallen, some have not. Here is a fine dispute, Judah will say. All that he will want to omit is M. 1:2G. His reason is not the man's prior intention. The dispute is possible solely because of the ambiguity of the ultimate result which generates three possible positions, not two, and therefore for formal (as well as substantive) cannot be served by the Houses.

VIII

M. 4:4–5: Jug into which water leaking from the roof came down—House of Shammai: It should be broken. House of Hillel: It is emptied out. But man can put his hand in and take out fruit.

Trough into which rain dripping from roof flowed—water in trough and drops of water that splashed out and overflowed are not under the law, If water be put. If he took the trough to empty it, House of Shammai: It is under the law, If water be put. House of Hillel: It is not under the law.

If one intentionally left trough out to collect water—drops of water that splashed out and those that overflowed—House of Shammai: They are under the law, etc. House of Hillel: Drops are not under the law, If one took it to pour it out, they agree that the water is wholly under the law, If water be put.

T. 2:5–6: Meir *vs.* Yose: Clean *vs.* unclean trough

3. If I pour out the water, I indicate that, for a time, it was where I wanted it, and in line with M. 1:1A–C was subject to approval and then not subject to approval, so is susceptible.	Drops which splash out are not where I want them, so are insusceptible in the Hillelite view.

This unit deals with three cases and two sorts of water, water one has never wanted and only wants to get rid of, and water he has deliberately collected by now wants to get rid of, this last producing the third of the three cases. At the first two the issue, as I said, is how to get rid of unwanted water. The distinction is between breaking and merely emptying the jug. Certainly Judah will agree with the Hillelites: the ultimate result of one's deed determines the original intent. Therefore if he picks up the jug—thus he wanted it where it was—and pours it out, the ultimate disposition of the water is determinative. I do not say, as at M. 1:1A–C, that what was wanted for a time but then unwanted is deemed capable of imparting susceptibility to uncleanness. Judah will of course disagree with the Shammaites, but so what? M. 4:5F–J repeat this same viewpoint.

If one deliberately gathered the water, by contrast, then he produces a quite separate case. It is, as noted, exactly the problem of M. 1:2's water which is shaken out as against that which remains in the tree. Does Judah have a solution to this problem? No, it is not even relevant to his principle. The issue is not what the man has done at all. Yose, by contrast, will find M. 4:5KN highly congenial, since it conforms to his conception of what is at issue at M., and, once more, leaves the Hillelites in Yose's position: the man wanted all the water to flow into the trough, just as, at M. 1:5, he wanted all the water to flow off the leek. That which remains, or, in the present case, that which splashes out, has not conformed to his wishes. Accordingly, the ultimate result is tempered by the original intention.

T. 2:6 shows that M. 4:5F–I conform to Yose's conception, as we surmised, but for a quite different reason. Here Yose rejects Meir's distinction between the clean and unclean trough. Meir maintains that if the trough is clean, then the House of Hillel rule that, if the man took the trough in order to pour it out, the water is not subject to the law, If water be put. But the reason is that the trough is *clean*. The water has not hand an opportunity to become unclean. What if the water falls into an unclean trough? Then, Meir maintains, the water is under the law, If water be put, if the man takes the trough to pour the water out. Why? Because, as soon as the man moves the trough, the water becomes susceptible to uncleanness—and unclean!

IX

Accordingly, does Meir agree with Judah? Hardly. Judah will regard the water as insusceptible to uncleanness because of the man's ultimate disposition of the water. The deed is finally determinative. Meir cannot take that position. Yose disagrees with Meir, T. maintains, but not because of the matter of the clean or unclean trough. No, Yose's reason is his own and does not meet Meir's head-on. The reason that the water in the trough that the man took and poured out is not under the law, If water be put, so far as the Hillelites are concerned, has nothing to do with the status of the trough, but solely with the interplay of intention and action. This brings us back to where we started, leaving only Meir.

So far as Meir is concerned, water in the unclean trough *is* under the law, If water be put. The view of all parties is that the water has been deliberately collected and therefore is outside of the purview of our tractate. The water to begin with *is* susceptible to uncleanness. This brings to the peculiar reading of T. 2:6A–B, *A trough into which water dripping from the roof has fallen—the drops of water which splash out and those which overflow* are *subject to the law, If water be put.* If one took it to pour it out, Meir continues, the water (of course) is subject to the law, If water be put, so far as the Shammaites are concerned. The Hillelites differ only in the case of a clean trough. Water dripping from the roof into a trough indeed has been collected with approval, which accounts for the view that drops in the trough and those which splash out *are* subject to the law, If water be put. To be sure, if the trough is clean, the water has not been made unclean, and on that account the Hillelites rule, T. 2:6E/H, that the water is *clean.* That must be Meir's intent, since B's reading does not permit Mir to maintain that the water in the trough cannot be subject to the law, If water be put. He has already maintained that it *is* under the law, If water be put.

Accordingly, Meir claims the Hillelites agree in the case of a clean trough that, if one takes the trough to pour the water out, the water is *clean*—and why should they not maintain the water is clean? For what is there to make the water unclean? In the case of an unclean trough, however, Meir maintains that the Hillelites rule the water indeed is unclean, just as do the Shammaites. T.'s reading at B therefore is sound, and we have to read the remainder of the pericope in accord with Meir's distinction between *unclean* and *clean*, not between *If water be put* and *not*. Meir's ruling, therefore, really is about a quite separate matter, to which neither Judah nor Yose attend: the status of the water which has dripped into the trough. Meir maintains all parties agree the water is subject to the law, If water be put. What is the basis for his ruling? We have to turn to M. Miq. 4:1 to find the answer.

At M. Miq. 4:1 Meir maintains that the Houses ultimately agree that water collected in utensils under a waterspout is deemed gathered in a utensil and useless for an immersion-pool, which requires water gathered naturally upon the ground. Passage through the utensil spoils the water. The issue is whether leaving utensils under a waterspout is equivalent to forgetting them. At the outset the Shammaites declare that that is the case, and the Hillelites hold that if one forgets the utensils, water is not spoiled for use in the immersion-pool. Meir maintains that the Houses took a vote and the Shammaites prevailed. Accordingly, as in the present case, *all parties agree that water which merely happens to drip from the roof into a utensil*—there, the jug, here, the trough—*has been deliberately collected*. It will follow, for Makhshirin, that the water *is* subject to the law, If water be put. Therefore, as I said, the only moot point is whether the water is contaminated, and all parties must agree that if the trough is unclean, the water is made unclean thereby! Let us go over the details of the *locus classicus*, M. Miq. 4:1:

M. Miq. 4:1: He who leaves utensils under the water spout [to collect rainwater in them] spoils the pool. All the same is one who leaves and one who forgets, so the House of Shammai. House of Hillel declare clean in the case of one who forgets. Meir: Took a vote and House of Shammai won. Yose: No vote, no decision.	The houses are in agreement that mere passage of the water through the utensils spoils it. But the reason is intent. Since the person left the utensils under the spout, what could he expect, except that the utensils would fill up? And so his action testifies to his intent, which was to gather rain-water in utensils. The water is invalid. The secondary issue is whether forgetting the utensils is of the same character as leaving them with intent. The Shammaites hold that it is. Action testifies to prior intent. The Hillelites hold that is not so. Forgetfulness is not the same as intent, and the subsequent result does not prove the original fact.

As we see, it follows that Meir's version of M. 4:4–5 requires the Houses to agree that the water dripping from the roof into the trough *is* subject to the law, If water be put. Only Yose can maintain M.'s conception of the matter, and T.'s testimony on that point is unambivalent, since it assigns M. verbatim to Yose.

X

It remains to examine M. Miq. 2:7–9, because the apodosis of the Houses' dispute at M. Makh. 4:4 is reminiscent of that of the dispute of Eliezer and Joshua at the former pericope and its point is relevant to M. Miq. 4:1. The issue is the status of rain-water collected in jars on the roof. If it is deliberately collected, then it cannot be used for the immersion-pool. If not, then it can. In that case, how do we get at the water? We may not raise up the jugs, for that is tantamount to drawing the water. We break them, which allows the water naturally to flow into the pool. Eliezer holds that if one left the jars during the rainy season, then he expected water to collect; he has deliberately gathered it by his action; the water is unfit for the pool. Joshua says that, whether or not it is the rainy season, the water is not deemed deliberately gathered, and therefore the jugs may be broken and the water used for a pool. The details of the item are as follows:

M. Miq. 2:7–9: He who leaves wine-jars on top of roof and they filled with water—Eliezer: rainy season/if there is in it as little water as is in cistern—breaks them.
Joshua: One way or the other, he breaks.
Plasterer who forgot lime-pot in cistern, etc.

This pericope is to be interpreted in its original version, not as it is developed in line with M. Miq. 2:4's Eliezer. And then the issue is the affect upon the rain-water of passage through the jars. Eliezer's position is that if the jars are left on the roof and are filled with rain, it is deemed drawn water. Why? Because mere passage through the jars suffices to turn rain-water into drawn-water. The man's action, as in Judah's view, is determinative, and he has left jars on the roof in the rainy season. Since it has rained, the intent of the action is defined by its result.

(continued on next page)

Joshua's position is that since the man did not intend to gather the water in the jars, his purpose having been to dry them, the fact that the rain-water collected in the jars does not change matters. He rejects Judah's principle. The rain-water remains rain-water. Accordingly, as to Yose, so to Joshua, the issue of prior intention is paramount. So long as the man did not intend to collect the water in the jars, what happens in the natural course of events does not change the picture. Self-evidently, the man is not to lift up the jars. Joshua will agree that if he removes the water by pouring it out, emptying it into the cistern, he indeed turns the rain-water into drawn-water. Accordingly, Joshua will not reject the view that one's deed in connection with the water is paramount. Yose, T. Miq. 3+2B, explains Joshua's opinion in exactly these terms: one must not pick up the jar and turn it over. Accordingly, to Joshua the water is fit, and the only concern is that by our *action* we render it drawn-water.

Certainly Joshua and Aqiba will concur: what is incidental to one's main purpose is not taken into account, and this, Joshua must add, is without regard to the ultimate consequence of one's deeds. Aqiba proposes to distinguish between what one intended and what actually happened, thus between water on the rope or the outer part of the jug essential in dipping the jug into the cistern, and water on parts of the rope not essential in dipping the jug into the cistern. Equivalently, Joshua maintains that one's intention was to dry the jugs. If rain-water falls in, that is not within one's original plan. The water is valid for a pool. One line of thought therefore goes from Joshua through Aqiba to all the Ushans who distinguish primary from secondary aspects of the wetting down. The other flows from Eliezer through Tarfon to those Ushans who make no such distinction, on the one side, and to Judah and Simeon, who, for quite separate reasons, maintain that the deed is determinative of the prior intention, on the other. Just as Eliezer maintains that, having left the jars on the roof in the rainy season, one cannot disclaim responsibility for the rain which falls into them, so Tarfon rules that we cannot distinguish among the drops of water on diverse parts of the jug and rope. He has, after all, let the whole down into the cistern. And Judah, though in appropriate instances in agreement with Aqiba's conception, nonetheless stands with Eliezer in maintaining the ultimately determinative force of deed. It goes without saying that the Hillelite apodosis at M. Makh. 4:4 has to be interpreted in its own terms, and not in relationship to M. Miq. 2:7–9, to which it is not pertinent. The breaking of M. Miq. 2:7 is necessitated by the facts of the law of Miqvaot; the pouring out of M. Makh. 4:4 is permitted because of the givens of Makhshirin.

XI

If we now summarize the central and generative theme of Tractate Makhshirin, we may state matters as follows.

First, liquids are capable of imparting susceptibility to uncleanness only if they are useful to men, e.g., drawn with approval, or otherwise subject to human deliberation and intention. The contrary view is that all liquids without distinction impart susceptibility to uncleanness.

Second, liquids capable of imparting susceptibility to uncleanness do so only if they serve a person's purpose, are deliberately applied to produce, or otherwise irrigate something through human deliberation and intention. The contrary view is that however something is wet down, once it is wet, it falls within the rule of Lev. 11:34, 38 and is subject to uncleanness.

If the opposition to Abba Yose-Joshua had had its way, there is no doubt that we would have no tractate of Makhshirin at all. For what law is needed to develop the simple proposition that what is wet, whatever the source of wetness may be, and however the wetness may happen to come upon produce, is susceptible to uncleanness? Accordingly, our tractate's first principle, its distinction between liquids which do and do not impart susceptibility to uncleanness, derives from circles including Aqiba, and its second principle, the distinction between intentional and unintentional wetting down, assuredly comes to us from Aqiba, in a direct line from Abba Yose-Joshua. The tractate as a whole begins its major conceptual development with Aqiba. What forms its center and unifies its diverse pericopae into a single, remarkably coherent document is the thought of Aqiba on the principal role of human intention in activating the super-natural forces of uncleanness.

The upshot of our inquiry is to locate the primary conceptual development of the first five chapters of Makhshirin—the dominant theme of the interplay of intention and the capacity of liquids to impart susceptibility to uncleanness—among Ushan followers of Aqiba. The Yavnean stratum, however, is so remarkably slight—a single saying attributed by Joshua to Abba Yose, and one dispute of Tarfon and Aqiba—as to render rather uncertain the theory that the Ushans inherit and carry forward Yavnean conceptions. On the contrary, what we find at Usha in the main is the repetition of the two contrary conceptions on an essentially secondary matter, attributed to Yavneans, Aqiba, and, alongside, Tarfon.

It may be even that that single stray item is of the same pseudepigraphic sort as the pericopae attributed to the Houses by Ushans. That is, it may in fact also be the creation of Ushans. Of this we cannot be sure. The net result is that the conceptual shank of the tractate Makhshirin begins its history, at the earliest, at the turn of the second century, formed of five layers of conception, in sequence:

1. Dry produce is insusceptible, a notion that begins in the plain meaning of Lev. 11:34, 38.
2. Wet produce is susceptible only when intentionally wet down, a view expressed in gross terms by Abba Yose as cited by Joshua.
3. Then follow the refinements of the meaning and effects of intention, beginning in Aqiba's and Tarfon's dispute, in which the secondary matter of what is tangential to one's primary motive is investigated.
4. This yields the contrary views, assuredly belonging to Ushans, that what is essential imparts susceptibility and what is peripheral to one's primary purpose does not; and that both what is essential and what is peripheral impart susceptibility to uncleanness. (A corollary to this matter is the refinement that what is wet down under constraint is not deemed wet down by deliberation.)
5. The Ushan dispute on the interpretation of intention—is it solely defined by what one actually does or modified also by what one has wanted to do as well as by what one has done?—belongs to Yose and Judah and his son Yose and is attributed by them to the Houses.

In point of fact, of course, the difference of opinion begins in the gross principle assigned to Aqiba. We do not vastly exaggerate, therefore, in declaring that Makhshirin is a second century tractate, with roots in the later strata of Yavnean thought, and is, in the main, the work of Aqiba and his Ushan successors and continuators.

XII

In conclusion, we observe that a tractate devoted to the issues predominant in Makhshirin therefore is possible only within the suppositions of Aqiba. Significant development, not merely restatement, of those suppositions, moreover, is conceivable only within the subtle conceptions of Judah, Judah's son Yose, Simeon, and Yose. Had the problematic of the tractate been subjected to the development of Eliezer, for the one part, of the opposition to Abba Yose, and possibly even of Tarfon, for the other, there would have been no Makhshirin at all. The Houses attributions of positions to the Houses are all fabrications of second century authorities seeking validation in the House of Hillel.

SUBJECT INDEX

Abodah Zarah, 93, 96
Acts, and sectarinism, 4n9
Ages, for marriage, 63–67
"Agnon's Writing: An Additional Tier in the Talmuic-Aggadic Literature" (Hoshen), 36n1
Agriculture (Zera'im), religious system of, 88–89
Albeck, Hanokh, 36n2, 38, 117, 156
Amos, 117
Antioch, Council of, 31
Antiquities (Josephus), 3
Appointed Times (Mo'ed), religious system of, 89–91
Aqiba, 6n14, 195
Arakhin, 97, 98
Archaeology
  as direct evidence, 21
  partitioned ritual baths, and Mishnaic tradition, 144–48
  partitioned ritual baths, and "priestly" purity, 148–49
  and Rabbinic culture, 136–37
  ritual baths with "treasury," 149–51
  stone vessels and red heifer ritual, 137–42
  stone vessels attesting to Hullin purity, 142–43
Arianism, 32
Aristotle, 196–98
Athanasius, 32
Attributions to Houses
  accuracy, in general, 190–91
  by later authorities, 195–96
  in Makhshirin, 192–95, 199–212

Baba Batra, 93, 96
Baba Mesia, 93, 96
Baba Qamma, 93, 96
Bailments, 95
Bar Kokhba revolt, 81, 84
Bar-Efrat, Shimon, 161n24
Bekhorot, 97
Benê bayit, 57–58, 69
Berakhot, 165–68
Besah, 90
Betar, Fall of, 10

Bird, F., 126
Birkath hamminim, 27–32
Bloch, Marc, 8–9, 20–21
Bruns, Gerald, 6
Burgass, Catherine, 164n33

Cherniss, Harold, 196–98
Christians/Christianity, and Yavneh, 1–2, 25, 27–32
Civil law, 93–97
Cohen, Shaye, 1–2, 5–6, 7, 25
Coherence and correspondence, 164–65
Commerce and trade, 93–97
Constantine, 1–2
Contra Apionem (Josephus), 3
Corpse uncleanness, 131–34, 137–42
Courtyards, status of, 58–59
Creation, 104
Credibility of texts, 8–9
Cultic practices, 97–98
"Curse of the Christians," 27–32
Cyrus, 83

Damages (civil law), religious system of, 93–97
Daughters, and marriage, 62, 66–69
Daum, Robert, 5n11
Davies, William David, 27n67, 32
Day laborers, 57
Death, in households, 70–71
Divorce, 65–66, 77, 92, 154–55
Dowry, 76–77

Eilberg-Schwartz, Howard, 123–24
Eliezer, 6n14
Emotions, in household, 70
Epstein, Jacob N., 156, 169n46
Erubin, 90, 158
Essenes, 4n7
Exilarchate, 84
Exum, J. Cheryl, 162n26

Faur, Jose, 163n29
Festivals, 90–91
Flusser, David, 28
Food and drink, 99
Foundation myths, 26

SUBJECT INDEX

Fraenkel, Jonah, 166n40
Frankel, Zacharias, 156, 169n46
Friedman, Shamma, 16n40

Galilee, 148
Gamaliel, 84, 86
Gezer, 147
Gittin, 91, 92, 154–55
Gnosticism, 103–6
Goldberg, Abraham, 156
Goldberg, Arnold Maria, 23n60
Goodblatt, David, 18n47
Goodman, Martin, 2, 4–5, 7, 25
Goshen-Gottstein, Alon, 17n42
Gospels, 25
Government, in the Mishnah, 96–97

Hagigah, 90
Hair, 127–29
"Haireseis," 3, 4n9
Hall, Jonathan, 7, 21–22
Havelock, Ellis, 160n22
Hebrew Scriptures, canon, 2
Hebron, 147
Heinemann, Isaac, 54, 162
Herod, 83–84
Herodion, 146
High priests, 66n35
Hillel, House of, 192–93, 202, 203–12
Hirsch, E.D., Jr., 162n26
The Historian's Craft (Bloch), 20–21
Holy Things (Qodoshim), religious system of, 97–98
Horayot, 94
Households, in the Mishnah
  and actual practice, 75–80
  death and inheritance, 69–72
  formation of, and patriarchy, 62–69
  kinship in, 72–75
  members and roles in, 56–61
Hullin, 97, 98, 142–43, 178–79

Icon of Council of Yavneh, 1–2
Intentionality, 85, 88–89, 192–96
Intentionality of texts, 8–9
Iotapata (Iodphat), 142–43
Israel, after 70, 85, 87–88

Jaffee, Martin, 162n25
Jakobson, Roman, 159
Jericho, 145, 147, 148
Jerusalem, 147
Jesus, 7n16, 25
Jewish Antiquities (Josephus), 3

Josephus, 3–4, 117
Joshua, 195
Judah, 199–201, 203–10
Judaism
  religious identity, 4n7
  sectarianism of, 2–6
Judaism, Rabbinic. *see* Rabbinic Judaism

Kadushin, Max, 162
Kallal vessels, 140
Kelim, 99, 156
Kellner, Hans, 12
Keritot, 97
Ketûbâ, 61, 63n30, 76, 78
Ketubot, 91, 92, 112
Kimelman, Reuven, 27, 31n81
Kinship, in households, 72–75

Labor contracts, 57
LaCapra, Dominick, 17n44
Law, civil, 93–97
Licht, J., 117
Lieberman, Saul, 30
Liquids/fluids, 99
Literature, the Mishnah as, 159–60

Maccabees, 83
Maimonides, 112, 153n2, 155n7
Majority, age of, 59n16
Makhshirin, 99, 192–93, 199–212
Makkot, 94, 96
Marcus Aurelius, 4n9
Marriage
  ages for, 63–67
  dowry, 76–77
  household formation and patriarchy, 62–69
  in the Mishnah, 91–93
  wives, in household, 60–61
Martyn, J. Louis, 31–32
Masada, 146
Mazar, B., 139
"Measuring cup" vessels, 140
Meeks, Wayne, 27, 28n69
Megillah, 90, 156
Meilah, 97, 98
Meir, 204, 205, 206–8
Menahot, 97
Middot, 97
Midrash, 38
Minim/minut, 5
Miqvaot, 99, 144–46, 208–10
Mishnah
  critical focus on ordinary daily life, 106

SUBJECT INDEX

households, 55–80
human preeminence as central, 109
Israel's social order delineated in, 88–101
as literature, 159–60
nature and purpose of text, 101
opening of, 42–54
as Oral Law, 36–41, 53
Pharisaic characteristics of, 85–88
redaction of, 153–57
resolved crisis of 135, 101–9
textual qualities of, 42–43, 46–54
urbanization's influence, 79
Mishnah—poetic phenomena in
alliteration and rhyme, 157
anaphora, 158, 178–81
appropriateness of literary interpretation, 161–63
defining and identifying, 159–61
epiphora, 181–85
inclusio, 157–58, 165–78
paranomasia, 157, 185–89
types, 157–59
validity in interpreting, 163–65
Moed Qatan, 90
Mythologization, 139

Nagy, Gregory, 29n74
Narratives of origin, 9
Nazir, 91, 92, 93
and corpse uncleanness, 131–34
exit/reentry ritual, 127–31
placement in Division of Women, 112–19
prohibition of drinking wine, 131–34
Scriptural foundations, 119–25
and Temple destruction, 110–11
three prohibitions, 125–27
Nedarim, 91, 92, 112
Negaim, 99
Neusner, Jacob, 7n16, 8n20, 10n28, 11n29, 14n35, 17n42, 18n47, 55n1, 111, 112–13, 118, 121, 139, 141, 155n7, 163n29, 179n58, 182n67
New Criticism, 164
"New Historicism," 17–19
New Moon, 155
Nicea, council of, 1–2, 26, 31
Niddah, 99

Offerings, 97–98
Ohalot, 99, 177–78, 185–87
Oral Law, 36–41, 53
Oral traditions, 23n58

Parah, 99
Parthians, 84
Patriarch, 83
Paul, 4n9
Paul of Samosata, 31
Paulinus of Nola, 16n41
Pearson, Birger, 28n71
Persians, 83
Pesahim, 90
Pharisees/Pharisaism, 2, 4n7, 30–31, 84, 85–88, 149–51
Philo, 4n7, 117
Pisgat Ze'ev, 147, 149
Plato, 196–198
Positivist historiography, 21–24
Priesthood, 82–84
Priestly purity, 148–49
Priests, and Nazir, 117–18
Property, and women, 92–93
Property inheritance, 57, 71
and wives, in household, 60–61
Purities (Tohorot), religious system of, 98–101

Qiddushin, 91, 92
Qinnim, 97
Qumran, 147, 150–51

Rabbinic Judaism
foundations of, 83–88, 102–3
origins, 9–10
Pharisees and, 86–87
Rabbinic literature
authorship, 13–14
dating of traditions in, 15–19
historical narrative in, 11–13
incompleteness of, 41–42
positivist historiography of, 19–24
Rabbis, origins of, 86, 117, 118
Rashi, 40, 43
Real estate transactions, 95–96, 97
Red heifer ritual, 137–42
Repetitive learning, 37–40
Ritual, 126–27
Ritual baths
and Hullin purity, 142–43
partitioned, and Mishnaic tradition, 144–48
partitioned, and "priestly" purity, 148–49
with "treasury," 149–51
Roman imperial policy, 83–84
Rosenthal, E.S., 169n45
Rosh Hashanah, 90, 155, 181–85

SUBJECT INDEX

Sabbath, in households, 58–59
Sacrificial system, 97–98
Sadducees, 4n7, 5, 150
Samaritans, 4n7
Sanctification, 88–89, 100
Sanctuary, rules for the, 97–98
Sanhedrin, 94, 96, 171–77
Sarason, Richard S., 88–89
Sasanians, 84
Schäfer, Peter, 24n60, 27
Schechter, Solomon, 156
Schwartz, Seth, 4, 190
Scribes, 83, 84
Sectarianism, Jewish, 2–5
Segal, Alan, 15
Sermon on the Mount, 32
Shabbat, 90, 153–54, 158
Shame, 70
Shammai, House of, 195, 202, 203–12
Shebuot, 94, 96
Shema, 168
Sheqalim, 90, 147
Shinun, 40–41, 43–44
Simeon b. Gamaliel, 84, 174, 202
Skarsaune, Oskar, 28n73
Slaves, 62, 69
Sotah, 92
Stemberger, Günther, 27
Stone vessels
  attesting to Hullin purity, 142–43
  and red heifer ritual, 137–42
Sukkah, 90

Taanit, 90, 169–71, 187–89
Talmud, and Mishnah, 43–52
Tamid, 97, 98
Tannaim, 141
Tarfon, 195
Taylor, Joan E., 6n14
Tebul Yom, 99
Temple, 4n7
  destruction as central question of the Mishnah, 81–82, 102–3
  historical context pre-70, 82–84
  response to destruction, 86
Temurah, 97
Texts
  intentionality and credibility of, 8–9
  Rabbinic textuality, 11
Tithes/tithing. *see* offerings
Tohorot, 99
Torah, 40n14, 40n16, 104

Torah study, 86
Tosefta, 195–96
Transactions, 95–96
Trout, Dennis, 16n41
True value, 97

Uncleanness, 98–101, 192–96
Uqsin, 99
Ushan period, and attribution, 195–96, 199–212
Usury, 97
Utensils, 99

Van der Horst, P. W., 30

Warren, Austin, 159
Wellek, Rene, 159
White, Hayden, 12–13
Widows, 65n33, 71–72
Wilson, Stephen G., 28, 28n71, 29
Wine, 131–33
Wives, in household, 60–61
Women
  anomalous nature of, 114
  dowry, 76–77
  and kinship, 74–75
  marriage and household formation, 62–69
  in Nashim, 91–93
  and uncleanness, 99
  wives, in household, 60–61
Women (Nashim)
  Nazir's place in, 110–19
  religious system of, 91–93
Written Law, 53

Yadayim, 99
Yavnean period, and attribution, 195–96, 199–212
Yavneh, council of, 1–11
  and "curse of the Christians," 27–32
  narrative conceptions of, 24–27
Yebamot, 91, 92
Yoma, 90
Yose b. Judah, 199–201, 203–10

Zab, 99
Zabim, 99
Zahavy, Tzvee, 166n39
Zebahim, 97, 178–80
Zekhut, 116–17

www.ingramcontent.com/pod-product-compliance
Lightning Source LLC
Chambersburg PA
CBHW031709230426
43668CB00006B/166